THE GOOD SHEPHERD CALLS

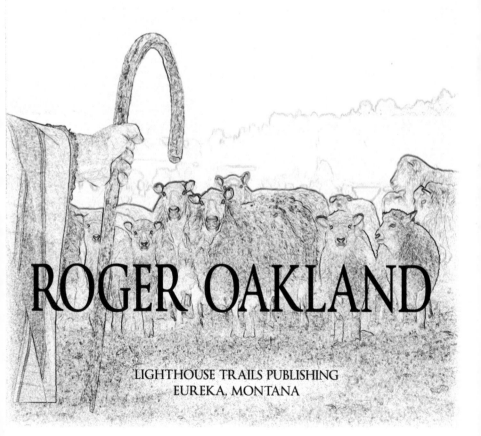

AN URGENT MESSAGE
TO THE LAST-DAYS CHURCH

THE
GOOD SHEPHERD
CALLS

ROGER OAKLAND

LIGHTHOUSE TRAILS PUBLISHING
EUREKA, MONTANA

Library of Congress Cataloging-in-Publication Data

Names: Oakland, Roger, 1947- author.
Title: The good shepherd calls : an urgent message to the last-days church /
   Roger Oakland.
Description: Eureka : Lighthouse Trails Publishing, 2017. | Includes
   bibliographical references and index.
Identifiers: LCCN 2016056987 | ISBN 9781942423126 (softbound :
alk. paper)
Subjects: LCSH: Christianity. | Church history. | Christianity--21st
century.
Classification: LCC BR121.3 .O24 2017 | DDC 270.8/3--dc23 LC
record available at https://lccn.loc.gov/2016056987

DEDICATED TO ALL THE SHEPHERDS

WHO ARE FAITHFULLY FOLLOWING

THE GOOD SHEPHERD

Also by ROGER OAKLAND

BOOKS

Another Jesus: The Eucharistic Christ and the New Evangelization

Faith Undone: The Emerging Church—A New Reformation or an End-Time Deception

Let There Be Light (Roger Oakland's biography)

The Evolution Conspiracy: The Impact of Darwinism on the World and the Church (with Caryl Matrisciana)

DVDs

Queen of Rome, Queen of Islam, Queen of All (with Jim Tetlow and Brad Meyers)

The Emerging Church Lecture series: Man's Spiritual Journey, the Road to Rome, the Road to Babylon, Proclaiming the Gospel

Searching for the Truth on Origins Lecture Series

The Wiles of the Devil Lecture: End Times Deception in the World and the Church

BOOKLETS

A Christian Perspective on the Environment

The New Missiology: Doing Missions Without the Gospel

The Catholic Mary and the Eucharistic Christ

The Jesuit Agenda

The New Evangelization From Rome or Finding the True Jesus Christ

Contents

PREFACE

This book is for shepherds and for the sheep who follow them. The title for this book, *The Good Shepherd Calls: An Urgent Warning for the End-Times Church*, flooded into my mind like a lightning bolt flashing in the darkness. In all honesty, I had no desire or motivation to write another book. Whenever I was asked about doing so, I told people I was in retirement.

For the last five years, my ministry had shifted away from focusing on discerning the times to our Bryce Homes International program, assisting poor and underprivileged children around the world. I was satisfied to live out the rest of my life without facing the pressures and the hostility so common in a ministry that deals with contending for the faith.

For almost four decades of my life, I have been on the front lines directing an apologetics ministry called Understand The Times. As the result of a serious illness that nearly ended my life in 2009 when I was in my early 60s, I reasoned the time had come to let others take my place in the battle. However, that suddenly changed after reading an article and watching a video that showed Jesuit Pope Francis proclaiming that all religions including "Christianity" worship the same God. Something in me snapped. How could I not send out a warning?

Immediately, I wrote and published a commentary on our website showing that Bible prophecy is in the process of being fulfilled, indicating that the return of Jesus Christ is drawing near. I could no longer remain silent. Something had to be done to wake up the pastors and the church. We are living in the crucial last days the Bible foretells will unfold, and the time is short.

Yet there is a huge problem. The closer we get to the return of Christ, fewer and fewer recognize what is happening. Satan's deceptive plan to set up a one-world global religion in the name of Christ for the cause of peace is being fulfilled to set up the religion for the Antichrist. Why are the pastors not warning the sheep? Worse yet, why are so many pastors promoting global ecumenism and praising the pope?

Then I asked myself another question: how did the church of Jesus Christ get into this situation in the first place? I have been a Christian long enough to know that this delusion did not happen overnight. From what I have observed, the apostasy has come upon the church in a gradual process but now can best be compared to a devastating avalanche. What is going on? Obviously, the sheep have been led astray by shepherds who have neglected what they have been called to do—protect the sheep. This deception has impacted every evangelical and Protestant denomination, and it is worldwide.

Thus, the reason for this book. The objective is to help the reader understand why this delusion is happening, what it looks like, where it is heading, and what can still be done to warn believers and unbelievers that time is short.

While I know there will be those who will negatively react to what this book has to say, my love and concern for people cannot be exhibited by remaining silent. The truth must always be told in love. It is not my goal to attack or ridicule pastors but to encourage them. I pray pastors will read this book and examine how they are leading their flocks and realize the consequences of what happens when the blind lead the blind.

This book is about following Jesus Christ, the "Good Shepherd." I pray the book will help connect the dots and reveal the truth in a way that will be easily understood and will bring honor to our Lord and God Jesus Christ.

1

THE MELTDOWN OF CHRISTIANITY

Since the turn of the millennium, in particular since September 11, 2001 when America was attacked by terrorists triggering a global-wide spiritual paradigm shift, Christianity as we have known it has experienced a major meltdown. While many are saying Christianity is on the brink of a great revival and even a "new reformation," in reality, we are witnessing the greatest apostasy in modern-day history.

In one word, Christianity is being redefined. Scores of pastors have chosen to abandon the Bible in favor of postmodernism (that is, what they view as progressive and culturally relevant). Light has turned into darkness. What was once believed to be true is now proclaimed to be a lie. Those who once claimed to be followers of Jesus and the Bible are now following men and their philosophies, and all without question.

Rather than reaching out to the world with the Gospel of Jesus Christ, pastors, professors, and Bible teachers are abandoning the Bible and embracing the world. They look for ways to market what they *call* Christianity by incorporating sensual gimmicks that are supposed to attract the masses. Hymn books are tossed out of churches from the pews. Pews have been replaced by soft theater seats and in some cases, even include credit card terminals. Being comfortable while attending church has become the standard. Don't mention sin or that Jesus shed His blood on the Cross to pay for our sins because that would be offensive.

The God of the Bible, who created all things according to the Book of Genesis, has been rendered to be nothing more than an ancient religious myth. The theory of evolution has become the science that proves that an explosion plus time and chance is the formula for the origin of all life.

The New Age movement has infiltrated the evangelical churches; they have been Hinduized as growing numbers of Christians think Yoga is a Christian exercise. To hear God's voice, Christians are humming mantras, "getting centered," or practicing the "presence of God" (i.e., eastern mystical contemplative prayers that will put your mind into a "sacred space").

Have multitudes of Christians had their minds snatched by seducing demons as worldwide delusion becomes the norm?

Countless Christians are overtaken with extra-biblical experiences such as getting drunk in the "Spirit" or barking like a dog because of the "transferrable anointing." Where is that kind of behavior found in Scripture? Are Christians being prepared for a great revival, or are they being seduced by another spirit?

Then there are those who are embracing the ecumenical agenda that plans to unite the Protestant church to the Roman Catholic Church and eventually unite all religions into one common body. They say the term Protestant is a word that should be retired to the past and has no significance in the church today. Charismatic leaders claim there is no difference between the Pentecostal Jesus and the Catholic Eucharistic Christ worshiped and adored in a Roman Catholic monstrance.* They have forgotten that in the past many Christians underwent torture and death over this very issue because they understood that inherent to the Eucharist is a works-based gospel offered to "another Jesus." Or perhaps they believe these martyrs simply died for no reason at all!

---

*The container used when a priest consecrates a wafer.

And an alarming number of proclaiming Christians believe Jesus is nothing more than a cosmic "Christ" that sees all is one, and one is all. This "Jesus" is the universal Jesus of the New Age. Those who don't believe in this "Cosmic Christ" are deemed as outdated, paranoid, intolerant, and not willing to unite with the rest of humanity to bring it into a harmonic convergence.

Then there is the charismatic bridge located on the road to ecumenical unity. It provides a connection for the gap that once existed between Roman Catholics and the separated brethren. But many of those on both sides realize that "ecumenism" to the Catholic clergy does not mean mingling but absorption; it means finding a way to get those on the Protestant side to cross over the bridge that is headed to Rome. Even Catholic Charismatics who have tasted of the grace and victory of knowing Jesus Christ as their Savior will one day awaken or succumb to the heretical doctrines they will be required to embrace on the road ahead.

Some are calling for the Second Pentecost claiming that the world will turn to Christ and establish the kingdom of God here on Earth without the presence of the King. Many are on this path already, and it's a path lined with apostles and prophets who are more than willing to point the way to go.

Further, Israel no longer has a significant place in Scripture. Jews and Israel are a problem to the new emerging progressive church. Adherents of replacement theology (where the church replaces Israel) have ignored the Israel of the Bible and replaced God's chosen people with a church that is about to establish the kingdom of God here on Earth. In other words, Christianity has been reformed, and those who refuse to accept this are standing in the way of world peace.

Bible prophecy and the warnings about apostasy are totally relegated to a museum. A one-world religion for peace is in the making, and the pope and the environment is the man to do it. The postmodern mindset has hijacked true biblical Christianity and made God into a god of their own imagination. The Word of God has been degraded into a myth.

The church-growth emphasis has swept the world with pur-pose-driven, seeker-friendly megachurches that deemphasize what they consider restrictive old-fashioned Christianity in exchange for market-driven, self-gratifying, self-realizing, and entertainment-focused churches. The churches that stress the Bible and salvation through Jesus Christ alone are being pushed to the sidelines, and the shepherds of these smaller churches are being pressured by anxious elder boards and congregations who want to see "success" and get with the flow. The big get bigger and the small are getting smaller. It appears that Bible-believing Christianity is on the verge of becoming next to extinct.

Scattered, Shattered, Battered, and Gathered

Nearly everyone has thought about death at some point or another. Eternity is a long time to spend in the afterlife. The Bible teaches that the wages of sin is death (Romans 6:23), and without salvation, Hell is our destiny. A person dies when the heart no longer beats and life signs such as pulse, respiration, and brain activity have ceased.

Now another significant issue is at hand. Where will you or I spend eternity? The answer to this question is very simple, but we need to make a decision regarding Jesus the Savior, the Good Shepherd. When someone accepts the free gift of eternal life, that person will live with Him forever. When you reject who He is and what He did for you at Calvary and choose some other belief system, your works are of no value. Jesus is the One whose life was sacrificed for sin. His blood was shed as the perfect sacrifice. All that is required is a willful choice to accept Him and ask for forgiveness. "He is faithful and just to forgive us our sins and to cleanse us from all unrighteousness" (1 John 1:9). His Spirit then dwells within us.

Now here is the rub! Life is brief and like the passing wind. It comes and goes sometimes before we know it. In some cases, friends and relatives perish without warning. We should always be prepared for the final bell as there are no second chances.

Further, there are many complications. Sometimes people believe they have believed but instead are deceived. Jesus mentioned this on more than one occasion. It is actually possible to believe in the Savior intellectually in name only without knowing Him personally and trusting in Him as Lord and Savior. This would mean that although people believe they believe, they are actually on their way to Hell.

Therefore, everyone should examine their personal lives carefully. Even people of spiritual stature can be deceived. This includes pastors, teachers, elders, and members of church boards. A Christian is not voted into position but is repentant and obedient. The Bible says many, not a few will end up in Hell. And there will be those who think they are going to stand before Jesus as their Savior when instead He will turn out to be their judge, not because He is unmerciful but because they refused to hear the call of the Good Shepherd.

Following Men Instead of the Good Shepherd

History has revealed many common patterns over time. Often men and women are easily influenced. This is why the Bible equates humans with sheep and preachers with shepherds. For some unknown reason, humans are easily misled. Men and women who desire power often gather weak sheep into their folds and take advantage of them.

While the Bible makes it clear that strong leaders must be biblical, Satan knows the weakness of humans and provides apostate deceivers. Often, pastors, teachers, and evangelists are clever manipulators and use the Scriptures to trick the sheep into thinking they are sound when they are actually dangerous.

As the old adage by the poet Robert Burns states: "The best laid schemes of Mice and Men oft go awry and leave us nothing but grief and pain." Simply speaking, following men will nearly always lead to a catastrophic end. Knowing this in advance and knowing the Bible is true, it would be best to ignore following men and be led instead by the Holy Spirit rather than driven by deceived men. A true shepherd will continually guide his flock with the Word of God and point them to the only Good Shepherd who is able to seek and to save. Like John the Baptist, he is willing to decrease that the Lord may increase. But too many shepherds want ownership of the flock, not realizing the awesome responsibility of the sacred trust they have been given.

Perhaps few have counted the cost of the disastrous results of following false shepherds. These are men who are really wolves in sheep's clothing. Many have done untold damage as they have ravaged flocks of sheep that were once in folds. They are now scattered and forlorn. Comparatively speaking, they are like ships without a rudder and sailboats without a sail. They bob up and down on the waves of the ocean, wandering souls seeking help and counsel.

The Gathering

Many sheep have been scattered, shattered, and battered. Sheep without a shepherd are in the balance, and there are those who are willing to battle for the truth. The truth is the Word of God (John 17:17) states the Bible. Thy Word!

In these last days of time as we know it, is it possible that God will raise up a standard? Will the stones from the rubble and the burned gates be reconstructed so that the Gospel will go forward? Or is all hopeless, and the remnant will be snuffed out?

The biblical answer to these questions is simple. God has not forgotten His people! He never has. He is the Creator of the universe, the God who knows all things and who is omnipresent. He will raise up the standard, and He will continue to warn until the Day of Judgment.

He is the God of Salvation. He is the God who loves us. As you read through the pages of this book, you will encounter some hard facts, so keep these things always in the back of your mind. Yes, apostasy is on the rise, just as the Bible predicts; but as the darkness gets darker, the light will shine brighter. While this book will present a picture of the darkness so that you will recognize it when it's in your midst, it will also paint a picture of the opposite—who the Good Shepherd is, what He is like, and what He has planned for His sheep. Now He is calling: "Arise, let us go hence" (John 14:31).

2

THE GOOD SHEPHERD

I am the good shepherd: the good shepherd
giveth his life for the sheep. (John 10:11)

This verse reveals the very heart and core of the Christian faith. Christianity is all about Jesus. It is about recognizing who He is and what He has done, accepting Him as our Savior and Lord, and following Him. Jesus referred to Himself as a simple shepherd who has the responsibility of leading and caring for "the sheep of His pasture." This is something that every human being can understand, even a child. It is also something that every Christian should pay attention to. Consider how Jesus sees us as sheep, lost and wandering and in need of a shepherd:

But when he saw the multitudes, he was moved
with compassion on them, because they fainted, and
were scattered abroad, as sheep having no shepherd.
(Matthew 9:36)

According to Isaiah 53:6, we all are like sheep who are prone to wander if not for the careful diligent leading and protection of the shepherd:

All we like sheep have gone astray; we have turned every one to his own way; and the LORD hath laid on him the iniquity of us all.

According to the Bible, the Good Shepherd we need is Jesus Christ.

The Job Description of a Good Shepherd

Both the Old and New Testaments consist of numerous references that provide the guidelines required for a leader to be classified as a good shepherd. It makes sense that we would look to the Scriptures for guidance because the Bible is the inspired Word of God (2 Timothy 3:16) and should be our ultimate authority when it comes to discussing this topic.

First, the Psalmist describes the Good Shepherd as the one who goes ahead of the flock to lead the sheep. He is a true leader always on the lookout for their safety.

Thou leddest thy people like a flock by the hand of Moses and Aaron. (Psalms 77:20)

But made his own people to go forth like sheep, and guided them in the wilderness like a flock. And he led them on safely, so that they feared not: but the sea overwhelmed their enemies. (Psalms 78:52-53)

Give ear, O Shepherd of Israel, thou that leadest Joseph like a flock; thou that dwellest between the cherubims, shine forth. Before Ephraim and Benjamin and Manasseh stir up thy strength, and come and save us. (Psalms 80:1-2)

Second, a good shepherd is constantly aware of where his sheep are in relationship to himself and concerned about their well-being. He is always searching them out when they are lost or remaining behind and does all he can to bring them back to the flock.

For thus saith the Lord GOD; Behold, I, even I, will both search my sheep, and seek them out. As a shepherd seeketh out his flock in the day that he is among his sheep that are scattered; so will I seek out my sheep, and will deliver them out of all places where they have been scattered in the cloudy and dark day. (Ezekiel 34:11-12)

What man of you, having an hundred sheep, if he lose one of them, doth not leave the ninety and nine in the wilderness, and go after that which is lost, until he find it? And when he hath found it, he layeth it on his shoulders, rejoicing. And when he cometh home, he calleth together his friends and neighbours, saying unto them, Rejoice with me; for I have found my sheep which was lost. (Luke 15: 4-6)

Third, a good shepherd shows tenderness for the weak, the ewes, and the young lambs. He attends those who are sick and in need of special care.

I will seek that which was lost, and bring again that which was driven away, and will bind up that which was broken, and will strengthen that which was sick. (Ezekiel 34:16)

And he said unto him, My lord knoweth that the children are tender, and the flocks and herds with young are with me: and if men should overdrive them one day, all the flock will die. Let my lord, I pray thee, pass over before his servant: and I will lead on softly, according as the cattle that goeth before me and the children be able to endure, until I come unto my lord unto Seir. (Genesis 33: 13-14)

So he [David] fed them according to the integrity of his heart; and guided them by the skilfulness of his hands. (Psalms 78:72)

While many other characteristics of a good shepherd are found in the Bible, there is one more in particular I want to include. A good shepherd watches out for and protects his sheep from wild beasts or predators such as wolves that feed upon the sheep. The good shepherd will lay down his life to protect them with a strong dedication and commitment as we see here:

> And David said unto Saul, Thy servant kept his father's sheep, and there came a lion, and a bear, and took a lamb out of the flock . . . Thy servant slew both the lion and the bear: and this uncircumcised Philistine shall be as one of them, seeing he hath defied the armies of the living God. (1 Samuel 17:34, 36)

> I am the good shepherd: the good shepherd giveth his life for the sheep. But he that is an hireling, and not the shepherd, whose own the sheep are not, seeth the wolf coming, and leaveth the sheep, and fleeth: and the wolf catcheth them, and scattereth the sheep. The hireling fleeth, because he is an hireling, and careth not for the sheep. I am the good shepherd, and know my sheep, and am known of mine. As the Father knoweth me, even so know I the Father: and I lay down my life for the sheep. (John 10:11-15)

In the next chapter, we will draw the connection between the term good shepherd and the well-known term pastor. While Christians have made this connection and given this title to leaders who stand behind pulpits, oftentimes these leaders are not being true to the biblical qualifications. Walking in the flesh (human nature) rather than the Spirit, these men are driven by man's fallen nature which seeks power and attention thereby corrupting what it means to be a pastor. This, of course, has impacted Christianity throughout the ages, but over the past several decades the problem has accelerated to the point where we are now witnessing this present apostasy ravaging churches throughout the nations.

Addressing this topic is not easy nor will it be welcomed by many. Efforts to be helpful will be met by an avalanche of opposition. So many of today's Christian leaders believe they are above reproach and should not be challenged. In fact, they find biblical correction useless and unnecessary, especially when headed down Apostasy Road. However, the Bible is clear that God has serious concerns about those who pervert the Word of God and lead the sheep astray. For such, serious consequences lie ahead.

Jeremiah's warning to the spiritual leaders of his day is a good reminder for us today. Consider the similarities to what is happening at present:

> Thus saith the LORD of hosts, Hearken not unto the words of the prophets that prophesy unto you: they make you vain: they speak a vision of their own heart, and not out of the mouth of the LORD. They say still unto them that despise me, The LORD hath said, Ye shall have peace; and they say unto every one that walketh after the imagination of his own heart, No evil shall come upon you. (Jeremiah 23: 16-17)

As in Jeremiah's day, our modern-day prophets speak of peace and prosperity. But if they were truly speaking for the Lord, they would be preaching of repentance from sin and faith toward God as becomes apparent below:

> For who hath stood in the counsel of the LORD, and hath perceived and heard his word? who hath marked his word, and heard it? Behold, a whirlwind of the LORD is gone forth in fury, even a grievous whirlwind: it shall fall grievously upon the head of the wicked. The anger of the LORD shall not return, until he have executed, and till he have performed the thoughts of his heart: in the latter days ye shall consider it perfectly. I have not sent these prophets, yet they ran: I have not spoken to them, yet they prophesied. But if they had stood in my counsel,

and had caused my people to hear my words, then they should have turned them from their evil way, and from the evil of their doings. Am I a God at hand, saith the LORD, and not a God afar off? Can any hide himself in secret places that I shall not see him? saith the LORD. Do not I fill heaven and earth? saith the LORD. I have heard what the prophets said, that prophesy lies in my name, saying, I have dreamed, I have dreamed. . . . Which think to cause my people to forget my name by their dreams which they tell every man to his neighbour, as their fathers have forgotten my name for Baal. (Jeremiah 23:18-25, 27)

The prophet Jeremiah concludes this passage with an urgent appeal to the shepherds of the land not to speak falsely but to proclaim the Word of the Lord. We have a powerful Gospel that needs to be proclaimed to an increasingly godless world, but the words of peace and prosperity we hear are only vanity, while God's Word shall never return void:

The prophet that hath a dream, let him tell a dream; and he that hath my word, let him speak my word faithfully. What is the chaff to the wheat? saith the LORD. Is not my word like as a fire? saith the LORD; and like a hammer that breaketh the rock in pieces? Therefore, behold, I am against the prophets, saith the LORD, that steal my words every one from his neighbour. (Jeremiah 23: 28-30)

While we have the Good Shepherd to follow—a Shepherd who is faithful and true—our own earthly shepherds and leaders should remember with soberness that leaders will be judged more strictly than others (James 3:1). It is a calling that should never be taken lightly.

3

FOLLOWING MEN INSTEAD OF FOLLOWING GOD

J ust as there are good and bad shepherds, there are also good and bad sheep. Sheep that stray away from the flock do so because they make their own choices. Unfortunately, some sheep place their total trust in their shepherds and don't have the ability or take the time to reason for themselves when danger lurks.

As the Bible draws the comparison between humans and sheep, it is insightful to examine some of the characteristics of sheep in order to understand human nature. This will even provide insight as to why professing Christians behave the way they often do.

According to a brochure titled *Sheep 201: A Beginners Guide to Raising Sheep*, four characteristics of sheep are listed:

> **FOLLOW THE LEADER:** When one sheep moves, the rest will follow, even if it is not a good idea. The flocking and following instinct of sheep is so strong that it caused the death of 400 sheep in 2006 in eastern Turkey. The sheep plunged to their deaths after one of the sheep tried to cross a 15-meter deep ravine, and the rest of the flock followed.

SHEEP SENSES: Senses are the tools that animals use to interact with their environment. Sheep and other animals share five basic senses: sight, sound, smell, taste, and touch. As a prey animal, sheep must have excellent senses to ensure their survival.

NORMAL SHEEP BEHAVIOR: Changes in normal behavior can be an early sign of illness in sheep. The most obvious example of this relates to the sheep's most natural behavioral instinct, their flocking instinct. A sheep or lamb that is isolated from the rest of the flock is likely showing early signs of illness (unless it is lost). Even the last sheep through the gate should be suspected of not feeling well, especially if it is usually one of the first.

SOCIAL: Sheep are a very social animal. In a grazing situation, they need to see other sheep. In fact, ensuring that sheep always have visual contact with other sheep will prevent excess stress when moving or handling them. According to animal behaviorists, a group of five sheep is usually necessary for sheep to display their normal flocking behavior. A sheep will become highly agitated if it is separated from the rest of the flock.[1]

Examining these four characteristics found in the *Sheep 201* brochure provides a glimpse to understanding sheep behavior and therefore a comparison to human behavior in light of the Bible. Sheep have a mind of their own and can often be stubborn and difficult to lead. Sheep follow leaders, sometimes dangerous leaders to their own demise. While they have senses to help them discern when danger lurks, they do not always heed or use these God-given senses, thus jeopardizing their survival. Sheep that isolate themselves from the flock may show signs of weakness and may even influence others to follow them. Because sheep are sheep, they depend on a trustworthy shepherd to oversee them to provide care, security, and guidance.

Abide in Him

While Jesus identified himself as the "good shepherd" in John 10, He strongly encouraged those who acknowledged Him to follow Him closely and remain safely in His fold by being familiar with His Word. Consider His words to the Jewish believers in the eighth chapter of John:

> Then said Jesus to those Jews which believed on him, If ye continue in my word, then are ye my disciples indeed; and ye shall know the truth, and the truth shall make you free. (John 8:31-32)

In the fifteenth chapter of John, Jesus added:

> Abide in me, and I in you. As the branch cannot bear fruit of itself, except it abide in the vine; no more can ye, except ye abide in me. . . . If a man abide not in me, he is cast forth as a branch, and is withered; and men gather them, and cast them into the fire, and they are burned. (John 15:4, 6)

Following Jesus, the Good Shepherd, is directly related to knowing and believing His Word. While a large percentage of the world's population may consider themselves members of Christianity, they do not comprehend what it means to abide in His Word, believe in Him as Lord and Savior, and follow Him in obedience. In reality, they are like sheep without a shepherd. They wander aimlessly and dangerously without any discernment, following men and their ideas, dogmas, and traditions and are thus led astray.

So they presume they have biblical faith while, in reality, they are deceived. The result is devastating and a sober reminder of the consequences. If only they had placed their trust in Christ alone, who paid the penalty for our sins fully and completely, and allowed Him to be Lord over their lives as the Good Shepherd!

Knowing More About the Identity
of the Good Shepherd

The Scriptures have already identified Jesus Christ as the Good Shepherd, but further study of the Bible helps us to appreciate that placing our hand in His and following Him is a very wise decision. Paul, writing to the Colossians, explained clearly some of the credentials of the Good Shepherd. He stated:

> . . . who hath delivered us from the power of darkness, and hath translated us into the kingdom of his dear Son: In whom we have redemption through his blood, even the forgiveness of sins: Who is the image of the invisible God, the firstborn of every creature: For by him were all things created, that are in heaven, and that are in earth, visible and invisible, whether they be thrones, or dominions, or principalities, or powers: all things were created by him, and for him: And he is before all things, and by him all things consist. And he is the head of the body, the church: who is the beginning, the firstborn from the dead; that in all things he might have the preeminence. (Colossians 1:13-18)

Think of the significance! The One who made everything that exists in the universe is our Good Shepherd. He is omniscient, omnipresent, and omnipotent. He is God almighty! More so, He is the one who has provided our only way to salvation. To follow anyone or anything else is blasphemous when we are faced with this fact. Following Jesus Christ alone is of utmost significance. Christians, to qualify to be one of His followers, we must follow Him and Him alone.

4

THE WILES OF THE DEVIL

Put on the whole armour of God, that ye may be able to
stand against the wiles of the devil. (Ephesians 6:11)

We know God has an adversary who hates Jesus
Christ and the Gospel. Satan has a plan to deceive
the world (Revelation 12:9). A vital part of understanding Christianity is being aware of Satan's
devices and how he deceives the world *and* the church.

It is impossible to properly understand the Bible and Christianity
without understanding Satan's plan to deceive and destroy. Once a
mighty angel created by God, he decided he wanted to become like
God because of his great pride and ambition (Isaiah 14:12-15). According to the Bible, one-third of the created angelic beings rebelled
and followed him. The plan was to destroy everything God had
made, focusing on the crown of God's creation, which is mankind.

Satan appeared in the Garden of Eden shortly after creation and
immediately put his plan in place. He convinced Eve that choosing
to be obedient to God was a mistake and that godhood was available
to her on her own. Adam also disobeyed by taking of the forbidden
fruit, and the rest is history. Man was no longer in harmony with his

Creator, physical death was introduced, and the curse has impacted planet Earth to this day.

However, we know because of the grace and mercy of God, a way of salvation was provided allowing humans to have a restored relationship with God. Of course, this is the Gospel message found in the Bible explaining how the Creator Himself came to this fallen planet and lived a perfect sinless life. The son of God, Jesus Christ, was sacrificed on the Cross at Calvary. His blood was shed as a sacrifice for the sins of mankind. After three days in the grave, Jesus rose, and He lives today. He offers eternal life *freely* to all who turn from their sins, ask for forgiveness, and put their trust in Him. Once more, the relationship with the Creator could be established and eternal life with Him could be a reality. The Spirit of God also now dwells in the hearts of those who have accepted Him. The Good Shepherd dwells in us.

> Behold, I stand at the door, and knock: if any man hear my voice, and open the door, I will come in to him, and will sup with him, and he with me. (Revelation 3:20)

Satan's agenda behind the scenes is to deceive the whole world. He also deceives those who have believed and have followed the Good Shepherd. His objective is to get humans to either deny the message of the Gospel or to pervert it in some way. The Bible says Satan is like a "roaring lion . . . seeking whom he may devour" (1 Peter 5:8), but much of his work is done by appearing innocent while transforming himself "into an angel of light" for the specific purpose of deceiving unbelievers and Christians alike (see 2 Corinthians 11:13-15).

One of the main objectives of this book is to help the reader understand Satan's plan to deceive man, especially in these last days. While it has *always* been important to follow Jesus Christ, things are intensifying more than ever before. In these days of end-times apostasy, Satan's agenda accelerates knowing his time is short. In the four decades that I have been following Christ, my experience has convinced me that fewer shepherds and sheep who profess to be following Jesus are taking heed to the warnings found in Scripture. Instead, so many are comfortable with the status quo; and so many shepherds seek ways to be comfortable while adding to their numbers without warning the sheep of the reality of where we are headed in light of Bible prophecy.

In this book, we will be examining the most important trends showing how Satan is working in the world (and the church) today. Rather than following the Good Shepherd and His Word, the sheep are following men and women, their methods, and their movements. So often these "shepherds" are wolves in sheep's clothing seeking to elevate themselves to the position of the Good Shepherd, but clearly they are leading the sheep down the road to destruction. Rather than shepherds who protect and nurture, these wolves in sheep's clothing are devouring the flock. Unfortunately, because of the lack of discernment, the sheep are headed toward a steep precipice that has the potential to drop them into the pit of Hell, and they are paying shepherds whom they trust for doing them this service.

In the past, when God's people were led astray to follow false teachers and false prophets and then worship other gods, God raised up watchmen to warn the people of the coming consequences. But also as in the past, today's watchmen on the walls are not always received.

5

THE WATCHMAN: WATCHING AND WARNING

The Jeremiah Calling

The Bible provides a vast list of characters God has used to fulfill His plan on planet Earth. Few are more dynamic in the way they fulfilled their calling than Jeremiah, one of the prophets we read about in the Old Testament. Jeremiah's ministry covered approximately forty years until a few years after Judah ceased to be a state in 586 BC.

As with other prophets that God raised up to speak and warn about the terrible apostasy that impacted Israel, Jeremiah was not popular. In fact, the task of a prophet of God is often characterized by loneliness and despair. No one wants to hear the bad news of the mandate that the prophet has been given to proclaim.

Jeremiah had no choice but to tell the truth, as this was his call. He knew it was the truth that would set sinners free. He was also aware that hiding the truth would bring further destruction. Jeremiah had compassion for those who were deceived but also had passion to let the deceived know there were consequences for turning away from God and serving other gods.

He also understood that history has a pattern of repeating itself. He knew what had happened in the past and what would occur when the children of Israel refused to hear God and His Word. He could see his colleagues and friends falling into the same trap. On one occasion, his passion is obvious from the words he spoke:

> And the LORD said unto me, A conspiracy is found among the men of Judah, and among the inhabitants of Jerusalem. They are turned back to the iniquities of their forefathers, which refused to hear my words; and they went after other gods to serve them: the house of Israel and the house of Judah have broken my covenant which I made with their fathers. Therefore thus saith the LORD, Behold, I will bring evil upon them, which they shall not be able to escape; and though they shall cry unto me, I will not hearken unto them. Then shall the cities of Judah and inhabitants of Jerusalem go, and cry unto the gods unto whom they offer incense: but they shall not save them at all in the time of their trouble. (Jeremiah 11: 9-12)

The children of Israel were disobedient mostly because they did not trust God to keep His Word, and their unbelief led them to rebellion against God (Hebrews 3:17-19). God had already warned them. They knew what to expect if they chose other gods; but they went after those gods anyway. Further, they had placed their trust in man rather than in God. The writing was on the wall. Judgment was just around the corner. Jeremiah pleaded with his people. The leaders of Israel scoffed at him and attacked him personally. However, the Word of God explains that the gods the people worshiped did not prevent the Lord from judging them. The people were taken captive into Babylon just as God warned.

Jeremiah was a true prophet. He could not keep quiet. He had to speak. He was called by God and appointed to be a prophet to the nations (Jeremiah 1:5). While he was not always enthusiastic about what God had called him to do, his calling commanded him to speak with boldness and not to be afraid of those whom he was directed to warn (Jeremiah 1: 7-8).

Further, Jeremiah did not have to lay awake at night to think up what he was going to tell the leaders of Israel (Jeremiah 1:9). His message was not candy-coated. It was harsh. It was a message of warning. He was a watchman in a spiritual battle (chapters 1-45). He warned that sin would be judged and that leaders and their followers who were sinning would be exposed.

They and their sin *were* exposed. Sin will be judged whether it is covered up or not. The same is true of the past, the present, and the future.

Jeremiah's message was not all negative. There was a positive side as well. He was called to build and to plant. When one plants, one has enlisted in the field of agriculture. This means that seeds are put in the soil with the faith there will be a crop and therefore a harvest. While most Bible expositors are good at pointing out that Jeremiah was good at exposing sin and error, not many actually see him as an evangelist. Jeremiah proclaimed the truth of the Gospel; he was a witness to the nations as well (Jeremiah chapters 46 – 52).

Warrior, Watchman, and Witness

The Jeremiah calling is still in place today. In other words, God still raises up watchmen to warn of impending judgment when God's people are willfully disobedient. God is speaking to his people to be warriors for the truth. This does not mean to attack unbelievers and apostate deceivers with a sword. No. What this means is that we should be the kind of warriors who use the Word as the sword.

> For the word of God is quick, and powerful, and sharper than any two edged sword, piercing even to the dividing asunder of soul and spirit, and of the joints and marrow, and is a discerner of the thoughts and intents of the heart. (Hebrews 4:12)

While there are those who claim they *do* use the Word as they teach the Word, it is obvious this is not always true. Sometimes they use the Word of God in a way that advances their own false beliefs in order to gain power and control.

A warrior is one who is willing to lay down his or her life for the truth. This is what Jesus did. Few are willing to lay down their lives today and risk their lives to take a stand, whatever the cost. Few are willing to pick up their cross and follow Him. But Jesus told His disciples:

> If any man will come after me, let him deny himself, and take up his cross, and follow me. (Mathew 16:24)

Certainly, this does not mean that a person who chooses to follow Christ at all costs is perfect. As the Bible says, "all have sinned, and come short of the glory of God" (Romans 3:23). Only One gave His life so we can have eternal life. Only One is worthy. We must always be looking to Him and Him alone.

A watchman is someone always prepared to be on the wall looking toward the horizon to see if danger is coming. Sometimes those who are supposed to be watching have instead grown weary or aged and have fallen asleep. Others have been sidetracked by the cares of the world or the attraction of money, power, and possessions. They no longer see spiritual danger. This is very tragic indeed. Often when this happens, God will simply raise up other watchmen.

A witness is someone who will share the Gospel of Jesus Christ. Jeremiah laid the foundation for the Gospel by pointing the people of his day to God's Word, which is the truth. The Gospel of Jesus Christ is based on the truth, which is the Word of God; therefore, Jeremiah was a true witness for the Lord.

THE WATCHMAN
By Scottish pastor, Horatius Bonar (1808-1889)

Thy way, not mine, O Lord, however dark it be;
Lead me by Thine own hand, choose out the path for me.

Some one, then, must undertake the ungracious task of probing and laying bare the evils of the age; for men must not be allowed to congratulate themselves that all is well. If others will not, he will.

If others shrink from the obloquy of such a work, he will not. He loves his fellow-men too well. They may upbraid him; they may call him a misanthropist, or a prophet of evil; they may ascribe his warnings to the worst of motives, such as pride, or arrogance, or self-esteem, or malice, or envy; but he will give no heed to these unjust insinuations.

He will prefer being thus misunderstood and maligned, to allowing men to precipitate themselves upon a ruin which they see not. Rather than that they should perish, he will allow his own good name to be spoken against. He will risk every thing, even the hatred of brethren, rather than withhold the warning. If they give no heed to it, he has, at least, saved his own soul. If they do, he has saved both his own soul and theirs.

He would rather take up the glad tidings of peace, and tell men of Him who came the first time for shame and death, and who is coming the second time for glory and dominion; but he feels as one who has a special and personal message to deliver, which cannot be postponed.

He must remember that he is a watchman; and, having seen danger pressing on, he must not hesitate to make it known. He must speak his message of forewarning and rebuke, sparing no arrows, and neither smoothing down nor hiding any form of sin, but laying his finger upon every sore, and beseeching men to turn from their ungodliness. The evils around him press upon him sadly; the coming evils are foreshadowed upon his spirit, and, therefore, he lifts up his voice like a trumpet.

The Watchman: A Messenger
With an Unwanted Message

The term watchman describes a person called into duty to perform the specific task of providing security for others. From an Old Testament viewpoint, the watchman was a person who stood on the wall surrounding the city. The wall functioned as a barrier of protection to keep enemies out of the city. From this higher vantage point, the watchman could see an approaching enemy from far off, sound the trumpet, instruct that the gates of the city be closed, and warn the people in the city that they were soon to be under attack.

Also from a biblical context, the watchman was called by God to identify spiritual danger by warning the people what was coming if they continued to disobey the Lord. This was necessary when the spiritual leaders were not doing their job as shepherds. Instead, they had compromised with the enemy and even embraced their heretical pagan beliefs. They no longer were following God and the warnings they had been given in His Word.

We see this pattern repeats throughout Scripture. For example, the children of Israel were promised God's blessing if they would follow Him, but they were also warned of the serious consequences if they did not. We read in Deuteronomy:

> See, I have set before thee this day life and good, and death and evil; In that I command thee this day to love the LORD thy God, to walk in his ways, and to keep his commandments and his statutes and his judgments, that thou mayest live and multiply: and the LORD thy God shall bless thee in the land whither thou goest to possess it. But if thine heart turn away, so that thou wilt not hear, but shalt be drawn away, and worship other gods, and serve them; I denounce unto you this day, that ye shall surely perish, and that ye shall not prolong your days upon the land, whither thou passest over Jordan to go to possess it. (Deuteronomy 30: 15-18)

Further, Scripture explains exactly what happened. Rebelling and defying God, they chose to go their own way and ended up following other gods. We read in the Book of Judges:

> And the children of Israel did evil in the sight of the LORD, and served Baalim: And they forsook the LORD God of their fathers, which brought them out of the land of Egypt, and followed other gods, of the gods of the people that were round about them, and bowed themselves unto them. (Judges 2: 11-12)

God used the prophets who were the watchmen to convey His messages audibly so the people could hear. These messengers, inspired by God, spoke with clarity, sincerity, and urgency. While their messages were for all the Jews to hear, the prophets singled out the spiritual leaders who should have been leading the flocks and protecting them from heresy. In this next section, we will continue to examine some of the message that was proclaimed and the response these watchmen received for simply being obedient to God's call.

Calling Out the Shepherds

While we have already described Jeremiah's role as a watchman, we have not mentioned other portions of Scripture that define even more precisely the message proclaimed. In the fifth chapter of Jeremiah, we read the words God had instructed Jeremiah to proclaim against the leaders:

> Go ye up upon her walls, and destroy; but make not a full end: take away her battlements; for they are not the LORD'S. For the house of Israel and the house of Judah have dealt very treacherously against me, saith the LORD. They have belied the LORD, and said, It is not he; neither shall evil come upon us; neither shall we see sword nor famine: And the prophets shall become wind,

and the word is not in them: thus shall it be done unto them. (Jeremiah 5: 10-13)

Continuing in the fifth chapter, we can see a further exposé on the problems Jeremiah was confronting with God's people. With God's Words coming out of his mouth like fire, Jeremiah declared:

> But this people hath a revolting and a rebellious heart; they are revolted and gone. Neither say they in their heart, Let us now fear the LORD our God, that giveth rain, both the former and the latter, in his season: he reserveth unto us the appointed weeks of the harvest. (vss. 23-24)

As Jeremiah has just indicated, it is God's normal pattern to bless His people when they follow Him, just as He sends the rain needed for crops to grow and then "reserves" it at the time of harvest. It is our iniquities that "withhold good things":

> Your iniquities have turned away these things, and your sins have withholden good things from you. For among my people are found wicked men: they lay wait, as he that setteth snares; they set a trap, they catch men. (vss. 25-26)

Though the wicked may enjoy vast wealth and prosperity now, it is a very sobering thought to know that in reality this prosperity will only be short lived . . . and then judgment will come:

> As a cage is full of birds, so are their houses full of deceit: therefore they are become great, and waxen rich. They are waxen fat, they shine: yea, they overpass the deeds of the wicked: they judge not the cause, the cause of the fatherless, yet they prosper; and the right of the needy do they not judge. Shall I not visit for these things? saith the LORD: shall not my soul be avenged on such a nation as this? (vss. 27-29)

Then, in chapter six, comes an additional plea from the mouth of Jeremiah from the heart of God:

> Thus saith the LORD, Stand ye in the ways, and see, and ask for the old paths, where is the good way, and walk therein, and ye shall find rest for your souls. But they said, We will not walk therein. Also I set watchmen over you, saying, Hearken to the sound of the trumpet. But they said, We will not hearken. Therefore hear, ye nations, and know, O congregation, what is among them. Hear, O earth: behold, I will bring evil upon this people, even the fruit of their thoughts, because they have not hearkened unto my words, nor to my law, but rejected it. (Jeremiah 6: 16-19)

It is a beautiful thought to know that God wants to bless His people as they return to walking the old paths of faith and obedience to Him—to walk in sweet fellowship with the Lord. But man, in his fallen condition, will dash God's pleadings to the ground.

While we could spend much more time writing about Old Testament watchmen and their unwanted messages, one more example will suffice. Ezekiel was also a man with a message from God designed to wake up God's people who had drifted away from Him because of ungodly leadership or just through their own outright stubbornness and pride. Ezekiel received his call as recorded in the third chapter of Ezekiel. We read:

> When I say unto the wicked, Thou shalt surely die; and thou givest him not warning, nor speakest to warn the wicked from his wicked way, to save his life; the same wicked man shall die in his iniquity; but his blood will I require at thine hand. (Ezekiel 3:18)

While fulfilling the role of a watchman in our present day will not bring popularity, according to the Bible, there is no other choice. While more and more pressure is put on pastors to conform to a reinvented form of Christianity that no longer uses God's infallible Word as the foundation of faith, from God's perspective, nothing has changed.

Throughout the world mainstream and evangelical Christianity is headed down the road toward welcoming a global unified spirituality for the cause of peace. The warnings found in the Old and New Testaments have been set aside, and the sheep are following blindly. If the majority of pastors are not willing to stop what they are doing and stand up for the truth, God will raise up others to sound the alarm. While the last-days global delusion cannot be prevented (because Scripture says it is going to happen), God will raise up a remnant of pastors and believers who will be willing to sound the alarm no matter the cost.

6

NEW TESTAMENT
WARNINGS

The overview I have presented thus far in this book, where we have examined Old Testament prophets and watchmen, shows a common pattern. God's people who refuse to follow God's Word and rather follow men and their ideas inevitably end up following Satan and the fallen spiritual realm, often without recognizing what has happened. They are driven by Satan and end up serving the kingdom of darkness. Jesus made it evident that this is true when He pointed out that we cannot serve two masters. He said, "No man can serve two masters: for either he will hate the one, and love the other; or else he will hold to the one, and despise the other" (Matthew 6:24). But the fact remains that while we cannot serve both, we *will* end up serving one or the other. If it won't be God, it will surely be Satan.

God is merciful and patient, and He always gives spiritual leaders and the sheep a final warning before He sends judgment. In most cases, the pastors and the sheep ignore this critical message and attack the messenger instead. Apostasy continues, and judgment is the consequence.

If this has not already been established clearly enough in the introductory portion of this book, then the following Scriptures taken from the Book of Jeremiah will document this pattern once more:

> Woe be unto the pastors that destroy and scatter the sheep of my pasture! saith the LORD. Therefore thus saith the LORD God of Israel against the pastors that feed my people; Ye have scattered my flock, and driven them away, and have not visited them: behold, I will visit upon you the evil of your doings, saith the LORD. (Jeremiah 23: 1-2)

Repeating the warning in the same chapter:

> Thus saith the LORD of hosts, Hearken not unto the words of the prophets that prophesy unto you: they make you vain: they speak a vision of their own heart, and not out of the mouth of the LORD. They say still unto them that despise me, The LORD hath said, Ye shall have peace; and they say unto every one that walketh after the imagination of his own heart, No evil shall come upon you. For who hath stood in the counsel of the LORD, and hath perceived and heard his word? who hath marked his word, and heard it? Behold, a whirlwind of the LORD is gone forth in fury, even a grievous whirlwind: it shall fall grievously upon the head of the wicked. The anger of the LORD shall not return, until he have executed, and till he have performed the thoughts of his heart: in the latter days ye shall consider it perfectly. (Jeremiah 23: 16-20)

The message sent to correct the shepherds so that they would redirect the sheep and lead them back to the truth was not only rejected, it was ridiculed and the messenger was insulted and attacked. Jeremiah gives the following account from an earlier chapter of the turmoil he was already going through:

Then said they, Come, and let us devise devices against
Jeremiah; for the law shall not perish from the priest, nor
counsel from the wise, nor the word from the prophet.
Come, and let us smite him with the tongue, and let
us not give heed to any of his words. (Jeremiah 18:18)

———◆———

HUMAN BEHAVIOR EXHIBITED TODAY IS NO DIFFERENT THAN HUMAN BEHAVIOR OF THE PAST. PERHAPS MAN'S SINFUL PRIDE IS ONE OF THE MOST EFFECTIVE BARRIERS THAT PREVENTS HUMANS FROM ACCEPTING GOD'S WARNINGS.

———◆———

Many today refuse to study the messages given by the Old
Testament prophets by reasoning their words have little relevance
for today. Not so. The entire Bible is profitable for doctrine,
correction, and righteousness (2 Timothy 3:16). Human behavior
exhibited today is no different than human behavior of the past.
Perhaps man's sinful pride is one of the most effective barriers that
prevents humans from accepting God's warnings. Isn't it curious
that the opposition Jeremiah encountered is the same kind as what
is targeted at God's watchmen today? Most assume that all the
mirth associated with our apostate church will continue endlessly

unchecked. Not so, for "judgment must begin at the house of God" (1 Peter 4:17).

The New Testament Reveals Same Warnings

The New Testament also has ample warnings from watchmen who were inspired by the Good Shepherd and God's Spirit; thus, even for Christians who stick only to the New Testament for instruction and guidance, there is no excuse to remain in darkness regarding our times and the times that lie ahead. The problem is that once again leaders professing to be shepherds are not doing their job in reminding the sheep to follow the Good Shepherd.

At the very least, it would not be unreasonable to expect every Christian shepherd to direct every member of his flock to read and pay close attention to the words recorded in the New Testament showing that Jesus himself warned about Satan's deceptive plan for man in the days before His return. When asked by his disciples what signs to look for that would indicate His second coming, Jesus responded emphatically:

> Take heed that no man deceive you. For many shall come in my name, saying, I am Christ; and shall deceive many. (Matthew 24:4-5)

The fact that the very first sign Jesus mentioned dealt with warning about deception should speak for itself. Second, He said "many" would be deceived by "many." Third, the deception would be in His name, the name of Jesus Christ. What more do those who say they are shepherds following the Good Shepherd need to know to diligently watch over their flocks and warn them? The other signs Jesus gave in Matthew 24 further confirm the days Jesus was talking about are the very days we are living in right now.

Finally, the fact Jesus used the phrase "take heed" indicates urgency and danger. A study of the word "heed" from the

International Standard Bible Encyclopedia indicates Jesus intended that His answer to the disciples' question would be taken very seriously. According to this source, the word "heed" means:

> This word, in the sense of giving careful attention ("take heed," "give heed," etc.), represents several Hebrew and Greek words; chief among them shamar, "to watch"; blepo, "to look," horao, "to see." As opposed to thoughtlessness, disregard of God's words, of the counsels of wisdom, of care for one's ways, it is constantly inculcated as a duty of supreme importance in the moral and spiritual life.[1]

Every person who claims to be called to the position of pastor in these crucial days of history has an obligation to take heed to the message the Good Shepherd proclaimed to His own disciples. There are those who argue that because Jesus was speaking to Jews, his message was for Jews only. The other signs Jesus mentioned shed light on the fact that the end-time scenario will be from a global perspective. Further study of statements made by the apostle Paul will confirm that Jesus' comments should be taken literally by those who are supposed to be representing Him as leaders in the Christian church today.

Watchman Paul

It is impossible to read through the writings of the apostle Paul that make up the majority of the New Testament epistles and not be aware that he warned about deception in the church, particularly in the last days. While Paul's writings primarily define the Gospel of Jesus Christ and the sound biblical doctrine which forms the basis of Christianity, nearly every book he wrote helps reveal Satan's agenda to deceive the church in the last days. Paul also, under the inspiration of the Holy Spirit, commands that leaders stand strong and sound the alarm when they see the danger.

Perhaps the best-known portion of Scripture summarizing the end-times deception taking place in the name of Christ is found in 1 Timothy chapter four. These are also words written by Paul, inspired by the Holy Spirit:

> Now the Spirit speaketh expressly, that in the latter times some shall depart from the faith, giving heed to seducing spirits, and doctrines of devils; Speaking lies in hypocrisy; having their conscience seared with a hot iron . . . If thou put the brethren in remembrance of these things, thou shalt be a good minister of Jesus Christ, nourished up in the words of faith and of good doctrine, whereunto thou hast attained. (1 Timothy 4: 1-2, 6)

In this portion of Scripture, Paul speaks about the last-days departure from believing in God's Word, why and how the seduction occurs, and the counterfeit form of Christianity that will develop. He describes the professing leaders who fall away as hypocrites without a conscience. Further, he explains that a good shepherd who represents Jesus Christ is grounded in the Word of God with sound doctrine and will stand up against this hypocrisy, not remaining silent.

Later in Second Timothy, Paul describes the antidote to counter this time of delusion when Christianity becomes an apostate faith as those who once had biblical faith turn away from the truth. Christians need to preach the Word with conviction, doing everything possible to proclaim the true Gospel while there is still time to do so. This pure unadulterated Gospel is what should motivate every sincere Bible-believing person, especially those in leadership who are responsible for others.

> I charge thee therefore before God, and the Lord Jesus Christ, who shall judge the quick and the dead at his appearing and his kingdom; Preach the word; be instant in season, out of season; reprove, rebuke, exhort with

all longsuffering and doctrine. For the time will come when they will not endure sound doctrine; but after their own lusts shall they heap to themselves teachers, having itching ears; And they shall turn away their ears from the truth, and shall be turned unto fables. But watch thou in all things, endure afflictions, do the work of an evangelist, make full proof of thy ministry. (2 Timothy 4:1-5)

Peter's Perspective of the Last Days Deception

There are many who claim that biblical statements made in the past about future events have little value or are worthless. Peter disagrees. He states:

> We have also a more sure word of prophecy; whereunto ye do well that ye take heed, as unto a light that shineth in a dark place, until the day dawn, and the day star arise in your hearts. (2 Peter 1:19)

Bible prophecy, for those who will pay attention to what God has revealed in His Word, is like a light shining into a dark place. It is one hundred percent accurate. No other book can make that claim. All statements in the Bible that are prophetic in nature have either already been fulfilled, are in the process of being fulfilled, or will be fulfilled.

Regarding the deception that Christianity will encounter in the last days, the apostle Peter prophesies:

> But there were false prophets also among the people, even as there shall be false teachers among you, who privily shall bring in damnable heresies, even denying the Lord that bought them, and bring upon themselves swift destruction. And many shall follow their pernicious

ways; by reason of whom the way of truth shall be evil spoken of. And through covetousness shall they with feigned words make merchandise of you: whose judgment now of a long time lingereth not, and their damnation slumbereth not. (2 Peter 2:1-3)

The warnings from Scripture show that spiritual deception is the most significant sign of the last days, and every pastor should be warning and protecting the sheep. However, as we are going to document later in this book, the trends of our day show the very opposite. Biblical illiteracy is rampant. Christianity is being reinvented, and doctrines of demons are being accepted without any resistance whatsoever.

The most common question I am asked when I speak at conferences all over the world is "where can I go to find a church in my area that still teaches the Bible?"

Peter's message to the church and pastors in the past remains the message for the hour today. He pleads:

The elders which are among you I exhort, who am also an elder, and a witness of the sufferings of Christ, and also a partaker of the glory that shall be revealed: Feed the flock of God which is among you, taking the oversight thereof, not by constraint, but willingly; not for filthy lucre, but of a ready mind; Neither as being lords over God's heritage, but being ensamples to the flock. And when the chief Shepherd shall appear, ye shall receive a crown of glory that fadeth not away. (1 Peter 5: 1-4)

7

MORE NEW TESTAMENT WARNINGS

The history of Christianity is riddled with the pattern showing that sheep are constantly led away from the Good Shepherd to follow human beings who lead them astray. This is one of Satan's most effective ploys. If the sheep can still believe they are following when instead they are being driven to market to bring about their demise, Satan's goal has been accomplished.

It is quite apparent the early church was warned about this very fact by Paul—sheep stealing was already underway. The only way we can be certain we know the biblical Jesus and understand we are following the Good Shepherd is to know the Word of God. Paul, when writing the Corinthians, explained to them how Satan had infiltrated their midst with false teachers and false doctrine. He wrote:

> But I fear, lest by any means, as the serpent beguiled Eve through his subtilty, so your minds should be corrupted from the simplicity that is in Christ. For if he that cometh preacheth another Jesus, whom we have not preached, or if ye receive another spirit, which ye have not received, or another gospel, which ye have not accepted, ye might well bear with him. (2 Corinthians 11: 3-4)

Just as Eve had been deceived by the serpent, the church had also been deceived. It had been led away by false teachers to another Jesus because of "another Jesus," "another spirit," and "another gospel" (2 Corinthians 11:4).

Despite these clear warnings, we know the Scriptures tell us many will be deceived into believing in "another Jesus." These people were convinced they knew the biblical Jesus but instead had been seduced by Satan. In Jesus' own words:

> Not every one that saith unto me, Lord, Lord, shall enter into the kingdom of heaven; but he that doeth the will of my Father which is in heaven. Many will say to me in that day, Lord, Lord, have we not prophesied in thy name? and in thy name have cast out devils? and in thy name done many wonderful works? And then will I profess unto them, I never knew you. (Matthew 7: 21-23)

The very fact that Jesus never knew *them* means they never knew *Him*. This clearly suggests that people can be deceived and spend eternity in Hell because they made the wrong choice and believed in "another Jesus."

Consider why Paul warned the Galatians and the Corinthians about this very danger. They had embraced the biblical Jesus, but with a twist. They had accepted the biblical Jesus but added an additional requirement for salvation. Instead of Jesus alone it was Jesus plus works.

Paul did not hesitate to speak the truth with boldness. His rebuke was harsh:

> O foolish Galatians, who hath bewitched you, that ye should not obey the truth, before whose eyes Jesus Christ hath been evidently set forth, crucified among you? (Galatians 3:1)

It is important, therefore, that we be armed with a scriptural arsenal to help us identify how to discern impostors who masquerade in Jesus' name. In Second Corinthians, chapter eleven, Paul gives us the only answer we need to detect a counterfeit. He said: "For if he who comes preaches another Jesus whom we have not preached . . ." (vs. 4). Any Jesus who is not the Jesus *according to* Scripture is not the Jesus *of* Scripture.

Is it possible to believe in the biblical traditional Jesus who died on the Cross and shed His blood for our sins, but then add an additional twist or requirement that nullifies the true Gospel? Based on Scripture, it is very possible!

Certain Men Crept in

Jude was called by God to send a message to the church. It is clear he was warning the church because the simple Gospel of Jesus Christ was being compromised. Apparently "certain men had crept in" and were the cause of great concern. He began by making an emphatic statement:

> Beloved, when I gave all diligence to write unto you of the common salvation, it was needful for me to write unto you, and exhort you that *ye should earnestly contend for the faith* which was once delivered unto the saints. (Jude 1:3; emphasis added)

Why earnestly? He explains:

> For there are certain men crept in unawares, who were before of old ordained to this condemnation, ungodly men, turning the grace of our God into lasciviousness, and denying the only Lord God, and our Lord Jesus Christ. (Jude 1: 4)

The word *earnest* means "Ardent in the pursuit of an object; eager to obtain; having a longing desire; warmly engaged or incited."[1] We must ask ourselves, are we eager to obtain, and do we have a longing desire to contend for the faith?

Now, imagine if you were a member of a church that had received a letter from Jude. He was the half-brother of Jesus Christ. His message certainly must have carried some weight. His letter opened by stating that although he had intended to write and share about the wonderful salvation accomplished through the finished work of the Cross, his mind was somehow changed. Instead, he felt it imperative to deal with a major problem that had developed.

Apparently "certain men" had "crept in unawares" and had become enemies of the simple Gospel. Rather than being messengers of the Gospel, these impostors had become stealth deceivers who needed to be exposed before more innocent followers of Jesus were led astray. What had happened was the very thing Paul had previously warned the church at Corinth about when he had written to them and stated his concern for them in receiving "another Jesus," "another spirit," and "another gospel" (2 Corinthians 11:3-4).

Paul had already warned the church at Corinth about one of Satan's most effective plans to deceive the brethren. Further, in the Book of Acts, Paul prophetically warned what would occur after his departure from the scene. He wrote:

> For I know this, that after my departing shall grievous wolves enter in among you, not sparing the flock. Also of your own selves shall men arise, speaking perverse things, to draw away disciples after them. (Acts 20:29-30)

Paul saw Satan's plan clearly and warned what was coming. Jude saw it happening in *his* day. Further, these warnings which are included in the inspired Word of God are timeless and are for the church right now.

What would Paul and Jude write to the church if they were here today? Would their message have changed in any way? Based on current trends that dilute the Gospel of Jesus and make it into a social-humanistic-psychological-what's-in-it-for-me gospel, definitely not!

Let these same warnings be a wakeup call for us today!

8

THE REFORMATION
AND THE COUNTER
REFORMATION

A study of church history reveals that the plan by the serpent to infiltrate Christianity has been relentless through the ages. This plan continues today and is accelerating as the apostasy foretold in the Bible unfolds. Later in this book, we will document how the counterfeit bride (what the Bible calls the harlot) is assembling an amalgamation of apostate "Christianity" with the world's religions for establishing a peace plan. This peace plan will in turn set up a one-world religion in the name of Christ to further the cause of peace. What is happening right now in the political, economic, and religious sectors is a gradual unfolding of this plan that will build up speed and momentum as we approach the coming of the Antichrist.

While it is impossible to accomplish a complete study of church history in one chapter, I have chosen one period of time that will help us to comprehend a number of principles we are trying to clarify. While Christianity can become distorted and separated from the foundation of the Bible so it is no longer recognizable as biblical Christianity, God always calls out those who hear His voice. As Jesus said: "My sheep hear my voice, and I know them, and they follow me" (John 10: 27).

Throughout church history, those who are called out form a remnant. Hearing the voice of the Good Shepherd in the midst of a Christianity that has gone astray and then speaking out against this deception is always met with opposition, hostility, and even death. Of course, this would be expected according to the battle described in the Bible between good and evil, God and Satan.

The area of church history we will be discussing in this chapter is a time known as the Reformation when the reformers split from the Roman Catholic Church in an attempt to re-establish what they believed was a Bible-based Christianity. The reformers, and those who followed their lead, then faced what was called the Counter Reformation (by Rome) and were persecuted. In many cases, they were tortured or killed because of their refusal to submit to papal teachings such as those that said Jesus could be found in a wafer (the Eucharist), and they would not pledge their allegiance to Rome or the pope. The reason it is necessary to include this portion of church history in this book is that many Christians today have either forgotten about the Reformation and the Counter Reformation, do not understand the implications of what took place, or have never even heard about this period of time.

It is also important to point out that those who led the Reformation were not infallible individuals. They were grieved by the way Christianity had departed from Scripture and had a desire to make corrections. But some of their corrections were not biblically based. How tragic it is today that many sheep follow these men (even naming themselves after them) and their ideas more than they follow the Lord Jesus Christ and His Word. Even though a correction to the course of Christianity was made, the corrections often did not go far enough, or in some cases veered away from biblical truth altogether. In other cases, some reformers did not want to leave the Catholic Church but rather desired to change *some* things but leave other beliefs that were just as detrimental intact. Nevertheless, many of these men and women suffered greatly for their efforts to stand for truth.

It is essential that we examine and understand the past because many proclaiming Christians today are being led down the same path as the past, as if they are trying to rediscover the wheel, and they don't understand that the Bible was written so we don't have to thrash about aimlessly in the tides of life.

As the reformers discovered, contending for the faith is not an easy road to walk. My prayer is that those believers today who are indeed contending for the faith and trying to warn the deceived can do so in love. Contending is not being contentious. Instead, contending should be sharing the truth in love with the deceived.

Brief Overview of the Reformation

One source describes the Reformation in the following way:

> The Protestant Reformation was the 16th-century religious, political, intellectual and cultural upheaval that splintered Catholic Europe, setting in place the structures and beliefs that would define the continent in the modern era. In northern and central Europe, reformers like Martin Luther, John Calvin and Henry VIII challenged papal authority and questioned the Catholic Church's ability to define Christian practice. They argued for a religious and political redistribution of power into the hands of Bible- and pamphlet-reading pastors and princes. The disruption triggered wars, persecutions and the so-called Counter Reformation, the Catholic Church's delayed but forceful response to the Protestants.[1]

More information from the same document suggests the goal of the reformers was to guide people away from a man-made system of power and control (purported to represent Christ) back to following Christ and His Word alone. We read:

> Historians usually date the start of the Protestant Reformation to the 1517 publication of Martin Luther's "95 Theses." Its ending can be placed anywhere from the 1555 Peace of Augsburg, which allowed for the coexistence of Catholicism and Lutheranism in Germany, to the 1648 Treaty of Westphalia, which ended the Thirty Years' War.

The key ideas of the Reformation—a call to purify the church and a belief that the Bible, not tradition, should be the sole source of spiritual authority—were not themselves novel. However, Luther and the other reformers became the first to skillfully use the power of the printing press to give their ideas a wide audience.[2]

The most significant contribution of the Reformation is its illumination and recognition of the true Gospel of justification (salvation) by grace alone through faith in Christ alone apart from earning salvation through works; this fundamental truth exploded as the Word of God (the Bible) became available to the common people. We can even thank the more obscure events, such as the invention of the printing press around 1440 by Johannes Gutenberg and the efforts of Bible translators for making this possible. Meanwhile, many other extra-biblical dogmas and traditions that had reinvented biblical Christianity with outright non-Christian beliefs had been implemented to control the sheep as well. Some of these were:

- Selling of indulgences
- Purgatory
- Praying to dead "saints"
- A focus on Mary as the mother of God
- The rosary and repetitive prayers to "Mary"
- The "Holy doors" opened on Roman Catholic Jubilee for forgiveness
- Transubstantiation
- The Eucharistic Jesus
- Eucharistic adoration
- Popery and the infallibility of the pope

While there were many different Reformation leaders in various countries, we will reference only a few.

Germany and Lutherism

Martin Luther (1483-1546) was an Augustinian monk and university lecturer in Wittenberg when he composed his "95 Theses," which protested the pope's sale of indulgences in lieu of doing penance.

After Luther read and came to understand Romans 1:17 that says, "For therein is the righteousness of God revealed from faith to faith: as it is written, The just shall live by faith," Luther's spiritual life was radically changed as he came to realize he was not under this continuous weight of condemnation but through Christ had found justification through faith alone. This understanding helped spark the Reformation.

Although he had hoped to spur renewal from within the Catholic Church, in 1521 he was summoned before the Diet of Worms and excommunicated. Sheltered by Friedrich, elector of Saxony, Luther translated the Bible into German and continued his production of vernacular pamphlets. When German peasants, inspired in part by Luther's empowering "priesthood of all believers," revolted in 1524, Luther sided with Germany's princes. By the Reformation's end, Lutheranism had become the state religion throughout much of Germany, Scandinavia, and the Baltics.[3]

Sadly, Luther later turned against the Jews after becoming discouraged because they wouldn't convert. Tragically, Adolph Hitler utilized Luther's anti-Jewish sentiments to help convince the German people to turn against the Jews.[4]

As far as Luther's contribution of his discovery of the essence of the Gospel, that justification is through faith and not works, it cannot be understated, and he did suffer persecution for his reform efforts.

Switzerland and Calvinism

The Swiss Reformation began in 1519 with the sermons of Ulrich Zwingli, whose teachings largely paralleled Luther's. In 1541, John Calvin, a French Protestant who had spent the previous decade in exile writing his *Institutes of the Christian Religion*, was invited to settle in Geneva and put his Reformed doctrine into practice—which stressed an extreme view of God's sovereignty and humanity's predestined fate where man has no control over his fate nor the free will to choose or reject Christ, as these things are predetermined. These teachings have brought much confusion to Christians over the centuries in that Calvin's doctrine contradicts the message of the Gospel that "whosoever believeth in him should not perish, but have everlasting life" (John 3:16) and this verse from the Book of Revelation:

> And the Spirit and the bride say, Come. And let him
> that heareth say, Come. And let him that is athirst come.
> And whosoever will, let him take the water of life freely.
> (Revelation 22:17)

The result of Calvin's work was a theocratic regime of enforced, austere morality. Calvin's Geneva became a hotbed for Protestant exiles, and his doctrines quickly spread to Scotland, France, Transylvania and the Low Countries, where Dutch Calvinism became a religious and economic force for the next 400 years.[5]

Like Luther, Calvin was fallible, and in addition, he was the cause of much human suffering. This can be documented in the writings of Bernard Cottret, a university professor who greatly admired Calvin, and whose book (published by Eerdman's) was intended to be a favorable portrait of Calvin, yet it describes more than 38 executions attributed to Calvin.

> He [Cottret] documents the dates of each of John Calvin's
> despicable acts and shows that Calvin's methods included
> imprisonment, torture, and execution by beheading and
> by burning at the stake.[6]

Michael Servetus was a scientist and a theologian who was born in 1511. Calvin had given Servetus a copy of his writings hoping for admiration and a favorable review. When Servetus returned Calvin's writings to him with review and critique comments in the margins, Calvin was infuriated. On October 27, 1553, at the age of 42, Servetus was burned alive at the stake. To add to his agony, Calvin had Servetus' own theological book tied to his chest, the flames of which rose against his face. While Michael Servetus' doctrines may not have all been biblically sound, Calvin's torture and execution of this man is inexcusable.[7]

Another problem with Calvinism is that it offers no assurance of salvation. The reason for this is that while the Bible declares "whosoever" may come, Calvin's grasp and understanding of "predestination" was so all consuming as to become "another gospel" where one gets saved if and only if God has already chosen to save someone; hence, receiving the Gospel according to Scripture is both impossible and of no avail to someone predestined to Hell. It is worth noting that in his will, Calvin wrote a plea to God to save him if He can find it in His will to do so.[8] This is completely contrary to Scripture that promises us assurance of salvation:

> He that believeth on the Son hath everlasting life: and he that believeth not the Son shall not see life; but the wrath of God abideth on him. (John 3:36)

> These things have I written unto you that believe on the name of the Son of God; that ye may know that ye have eternal life, and that ye may believe on the name of the Son of God. (1 John 5:13)

England and the "Middle Way"

The history of Christianity in England is marked by some extreme highs and lows, often happening simultaneously, where good and evil were always present, clashing with but never eradicating the other. King Henry VIII had a highly questionable personal life, but through the course of related events, broke away from Rome, instituted an English church, and made the Bible available to the people. Below is a brief historical synopsis of this turbulent period of English history:

> In England, the Reformation began with Henry VIII's quest for a male heir. When Pope Clement VII refused to annul Henry's marriage to Catherine of Aragon so he could remarry, the English king declared in 1534 that he alone should be the final authority in matters relating to the English church. Henry dissolved England's monasteries

to confiscate their wealth and worked to place the Bible in the hands of the people. Beginning in 1536, every parish was required to have a copy.

After Henry's death, England tilted toward Calvinist-infused Protestantism during Edward VI's six-year reign and then endured five years of reactionary Catholicism under Mary I. In 1559, Elizabeth I took the throne and, during her 44-year reign, cast the Church of England as a "middle way" between Calvinism and Catholicism, with vernacular worship and a revised Book of Common Prayer.[9]

Without a doubt, a reformation was needed. And the reformers paid a high price, some with their lives, to help pave a road away from the heresies of the Roman Catholic Church and toward biblical purity. But even though their roles in this were substantial, nevertheless, they were still just fallible men and women who were used of God and in some cases of our adversary. They should not have been put on spiritual pedestals to be esteemed so highly that centuries later, when a Christian challenges their writings, he is sorely ostracized by much of today's Christian academia.

The Counter Reformation

Understanding some of the history behind Ignatius Loyola, the founder of the Jesuits, and the Jesuit agenda to bring back the "separated brethren" to the "Mother of All Churches" reveals one of the darkest periods of church history. Untold numbers (some estimates are in the tens of thousands, others in the tens of millions) of Christians, Jews, and other non-Catholics were tortured and killed if they refused submission to the pope, refused to accept that Jesus Christ was present in the Eucharist, or simply refused to be Catholic.

In fact, at this point, I would suggest our readers either read or re-read a copy of *Foxe's Book of Martyrs*. This will give an excellent overview of the suffering and torture imposed on Bible believers during the Reformation and Counter Reformation Period by the Roman Catholic hierarchy. For those who are unable to read the book, we will provide an example, quoting a source that explains who the Huguenots were and the persecution they endured because they desired to follow the Good Shepherd:

> The Huguenots were French Protestants. The tide of the Reformation reached France early in the sixteenth century and was part of the religious and political fomentation of the times. It was quickly embraced by members of the nobility, by the intellectual elite, and by professionals in trades, medicine, and crafts. It was a respectable movement involving the most responsible and accomplished people of France. It signified their desire for greater freedom religiously and politically.
>
> However, ninety percent of France was Roman Catholic, and the Catholic Church was determined to remain the controlling power. The Huguenots alternated between high favor and outrageous persecution. Inevitably, there were clashes between Roman Catholics and Huguenots, many erupting into the shedding of blood.
>
> Thousands of Huguenots were in Paris . . . on August 24, 1572. On that day, soldiers and organized mobs fell upon the Huguenots, and thousands of them were slaughtered. . . .
>
> On April 13, 1598 . . . the newly crowned Henry IV [who favored the Huguenots] . . . issued the Edict of Nantes, which granted to the Huguenots toleration and liberty to worship in their own way. For a time, at least, there was more freedom for the Huguenots. However, about one hundred years later, on October 18, 1685, Louis XIV revoked the Edict of Nantes. Practice of the "heretical" religion was forbidden. Huguenots were ordered to renounce their faith and join the Catholic Church. They were denied exit from France under pain of death. And, Louis XIV hired 300,000 troops to hunt the heretics down and confiscate their property.[10]

Nothing New Under the Sun

This brief study of the Reformation and the Counter Reformation opens a window to the past that has either been forgotten or ignored. We know that most Catholics today would be totally against people being tortured and burned at the stake, and while it is not our objective to open old wounds or to be called "Catholic bashers," it is important to understand what happened in the past from a biblical perspective with the hope it won't happen again.

Unfortunately, something is happening in the Protestant church today that would shock and horrify those believers who have gone before us suffering torturous deaths because they would not bow the knee to the Catholic Church. Many of today's Protestants, who at one time agreed that the Reformation needed to take place, have now proclaimed that the Reformation has no relevance anymore and that Protestantism and Catholicism need to see themselves as one church. While the same unbiblical dogmas, traditions, and ideas are being taught by the Catholic Church (and being labeled as harmless by many Protestant leaders), the martyrs of the Reformation are now considered anti-ecumenical crackpots who endured tremendous suffering and death for what is now seen as trivial and unnecessary.

The church that once relied on the Word of God now follows men who have compromised the truth or ignored the truth entirely. Church history is being repeated, perhaps for the last time, and many have fallen asleep or are willingly ignorant.

History repeats itself. The last-days delusion is upon us. Many Christians who are attempting to maintain biblical integrity, and not "go with the flow" of megachurch madness, cannot even find a church to attend that has not compromised the faith. Denominations and associations of fellowships that were once on track have been derailed.

If we have heeded the warnings and instruction of Scripture, we must expect this attack on biblical faith. Like those who were willing to speak the truth in the past and suffer the consequences, the Good Shepherd is calling those who are willing to take a similar stand today.

WHEN CHRISTIANITY BECOMES A CULT

The time has come to deal with some of the major attacks against biblical doctrine masquerading today in the name of Christianity. Rather than trusting God's Word, people are trusting in men's ideas inspired by Satan. Pastors playing the role of shepherd are leading the sheep astray down the wide road to Hell rather than the narrow road that leads to eternity with Jesus.

> [F]or wide is the gate, and broad is the way, that leadeth to destruction, and many there be which go in thereat: Because strait is the gate, and narrow is the way, which leadeth unto life, and few there be that find it. (Matthew 7:13-14)

If Jesus said He is the Good Shepherd and that we are to follow Him, why are so many seeking after men and their false teachings? Has Satan cleverly distorted the true meaning of the Christian faith?

Cult mentality is formed when humans follow human leadership. Often proclaiming to be divinely inspired, cult leaders mix biblical truth with lies as a tool for deceiving. What makes a false teacher effective is the fact that followers are unable to discern truth from error. Effective false teachers work on the principle that people are gullible and attracted to appealing promises. When examined in the light of the Scriptures, their teachings can be exposed. In many of these cases, the Bible is even forbidden, or the people are told that only the chosen or those ordained by the cult leader are capable of interpreting truth.

Characteristics of a Cult

Researcher and author Mike Oppenheimer, from Let Us Reason Ministries, provides some important insights to help recognize if someone is involved in a cult. These are questions that can help us identify as to whether we are in such a situation. While not all cults necessarily exhibit these characteristics, these questions are useful for helping us to understand deviant movements that embrace unbiblical, abusive ideas and beliefs dangerous to the Christian faith as well as personal lives. Here are some of the questions that Oppenheimer presents; the more questions you can answer "yes" to, the more likely it is that you or a loved one may be involved in a cult or a cult-like group:

- Are you told not to question what is being taught because the leaders say they are honest and want the best for you so you must trust them?

- Has someone replaced your own choices in life?

- Are you told not to ask questions why anyone left? You're to accept the answers the leaders give you such as: they fell into sin; they didn't receive correction; they weren't open; or they had a bad heart and didn't want to be disciples.

- Are you told that you must belong to that particular church or group to be saved and go to Heaven?

- If you want to leave, are you being told no other church practices truth, and if you leave, you will go to Hell?

- Are you made to feel like a failure, that your performance is not up to par to the group's standards?

- Do they put down others to make themselves look better, calling themselves righteous and others unrighteous?

- Do they stop you from reading anything negative about themselves or recommend that you don't read it for your own spiritual protection?

- Do they recommend for you to be around *their* people, expecting you to be at all the group activities? If not, your spirituality and dedication are questioned.

- Do they defend all that they do even when it can be harmful or morally wrong?

- Do they operate in false humility, or are they arrogant and demand you to obey if you are considering otherwise? Or is it done subtly by manipulating you into obeying by statements such as, "real Christians obey their leaders," or "if you were following Jesus, you would see what I'm saying is right." "True disciples do not question Jesus," cult leaders often say. [1]

Things of Which to Be Aware

- People telling you how talented you are and saying you can really go places (flattery goes a long way in cults).

- When you ask questions about their own history or the group's history, they are vague in their answers or avoid answering them (not answering or postponing it makes it go away).

- Are they emphasizing their church and who *they* are more than Christ? They teach that one can only be a Christian by joining them (exclusive spirituality appeals to our pride and works well today).

- Cults will always divide the family unit instead of bringing it together. Scriptures are used such as Jesus came not to bring peace, but a sword (Matthew 10:34), or one must give up brothers, sisters, wife, and house for the kingdom (Matthew 19:29) to be a true follower. In cults, children often become the most hurt because of strict rules enforced on them. They are deeply affected, being unable to adjust later in life. Religious systems that are not balanced can be socially and psychologically disastrous for innocent children.[2]

If you think you might be in a cult or cult-like group, I would highly recommend you read a booklet by researcher and author Chris Lawson titled *How to Know if You Are Being Spiritually Abused or Deceived—A Spiritual Abuse Questionnaire* for further insights.[3]

Some Sobering Thoughts

Now that you have had a few moments to ponder these questions, I am going to ask you to consider several more questions. What about a group of professing Christians that believes their leader is infallible and that he can make proclamations or proclaim dogmas that contradict Scripture? What about the well-being of those who leave the group and who are shunned by their pastors and their families? What about those who refuse to follow the rules made up by this group which has determined the basis of salvation is good works rather than putting one's trust in Jesus Christ and receiving salvation freely by His grace?

I have purposely not mentioned why I have asked these questions. Readers will be able to read between the lines. Nor will I focus on one particular group. Entire denominations overseen by individual pastors have very large fellowships and exhibit many of the characteristics presented in this chapter. Millions of sheep are reading books written by popular leaders rather than reading their Bibles. What if the methods and the models presented by these authors are riddled with arsenic leading people away from the Bible and the Bible's warnings to be aware of apostasy?

Or what about a fellowship of pastors that starts out by teaching the Bible verse by verse from Genesis to Revelation but ends up with several pastors in that fellowship who look for new and exciting ways to incorporate church-growth methods so they can reach the postmodern generation?

The postmodern generation has been taught to believe there is no such thing as right or wrong and that all religions have truth. Can churches be high-jacked by men who are misleading their flocks in their search for success? It is a fact that proclaiming the truth these days may come at the expense of losing attendees and therefore affecting how the budget will be covered. It is also a fact that when pillars of the church try to warn their pastors of the dangers being entertained, they are asked to leave that church or remain silent and go along with the new form of Christianity being invented.

Clearly, countless proclaiming Christians filling the churches each week are following what has become the cult of Christianity—not biblical Christianity but rather another "Christianity" that leads followers toward "another" shepherd. Rather than following the Good Shepherd, they are following the voice of a false shepherd.

Consider the cost of being misled.

Buried in Unmarked Graves

Vast are the burial grounds resulting from man-centered Christianity. When men follow men rather than the Good Shepherd, they seek after wealth, kingdoms, power, and illicit sexual relationships—anything to feed the flesh, which we know is never satisfied. When this happens, it is no longer Christianity but rather another "Christianity," a dead and harmful religion (which is man's invention) promoting another Jesus. Religion robs the innocent from true freedom in Jesus. The temples, the cathedrals, the shrines, and the modern day megachurches often testify to the accomplishments of man more than they speak of the wonders of God, who sent His Son to redeem us from our sins.

Further, study the hierarchies that humans construct—the popes, the cardinals, the bishops, and the priests. Or replace the "Holy Catholic Church" with the "Protestant" counterparts, and you find the same thing. While there may be a different configuration, the end results are the same. Followers are abused and misused by the power brokers that control them.

Many are those who have been beaten and hurt. They are buried in unmarked graves without tombstones covered over by time. Those responsible for their demise continue from generation to generation. They are abusive powerful despots who boldly proclaim "how dare you touch God's anointed" as they bury more and more. They believe their threats have a scriptural basis.

Such is the case for many in a fellowship of pastors I was once involved with. For this reason, two Norwegian brothers (myself being one of them) felt led to warn these men, many of whom got their focus off the Good Shepherd. Sadly, they started out right but ended up wrong. As the Bible states, it is not how you start but how you finish that counts.

This group lost their moorings. Many of them were so encapsulated by power, success, and church growth, they did not realize they had become lukewarm and then cold. While the Good Shepherd warns them in His Word, they chose to ignore the warnings. Just like the Bible proclaims, Ichabod (meaning God's glory departed) became a reality and an era of struggle that should have been laden with victories for Christ ended with the death of this group's heart-broken founder.[4] Isn't it interesting how history repeats itself? Whatever has happened before can and does happen again.

The Word of God is light. The Word of God shines into the darkness, and the darkness hates the light. Often those in darkness think they are in light and do not see the light when the light shines.

Nevertheless, the God of the Bible always wins. Sometimes the scenario plays out with a very unhappy ending. God is a God of justice, and justice always prevails. The good news for the deceivers is that God is also a God of mercy, and He gives man the opportunity to repent until the day he takes his last breath. God does not desire that any should perish but wants all to come to repentance.

THE GOOD SHEPHERD— OUR CREATOR

According to the letter Paul wrote to the Colossians, the Creator is Jesus Christ our Redeemer, and He expects us to give Him first place in our lives:

> . . . [Jesus] In whom we have redemption through his blood, even the forgiveness of sins . . . For by him were all things created, that are in heaven, and that are in earth, visible and invisible, whether they be thrones, or dominions, or principalities, or powers: all things were created by him, and for him: And he is before all things, and by him all things consist. And he is the head of the body, the church: who is the beginning, the firstborn from the dead; that in all things he might have the preeminence. (Colossians 1: 14, 16-18)

Therefore, believing in the Genesis account of creation is a prerequisite for His followers. Jesus, the Creator, while on Earth, told His disciples about the fact of creation. Echoing what had already been proclaimed by Moses in Genesis 1: 27 and Genesis 5:2, relating to the creation of Adam and Eve, Jesus reminded His disciples with the following words in the Book of Mark:

> And Jesus answered and said unto them, For the hardness
> of your heart he wrote you this precept. But from the
> beginning of the creation God made them male and
> female. (Mark 10: 5-6)

The debate regarding how life originated for those who believe
and follow Jesus is over. Jesus, the Creator, believed in creation.
Therefore, the Genesis record found in the Bible inspired by the
Creator provides us with the revelation of creation. Men who refuse
to believe in this revelation have explained away this supernatural
event by substituting a concept called evolution which is based on
speculation. They say that matter, chance, and time have brought
all things into existence including themselves.

In essence, this is the bottom line. We have two alternatives. We
can believe what God has said in His Word, or we can rely on the
speculation of fallen men looking for a way to distance themselves from
God. The latter idea, encouraged by God's adversary, the devil, has
been very effective in blinding the minds of billions of people on this
planet from understanding and believing the Gospel of Jesus Christ.

It is impossible to understand the Gospel if we do not understand
that God is the Creator; and when He created everything, He "saw that
it was good" (Genesis 1). The perfect relationship between God and
man was shattered by the fall of man when man sinned. Death was
introduced, and man, by his own choice and rebellion, was destined to
Hell. The Creator, who became the Savior, came to Earth and provided
a way where we once more can know Him. Creation is the foundation
of the Christian faith. Without this pillar of faith, Christianity fails.

Creation or Evolution?

For many years of my life, I was an unbeliever who taught the
basics of biology at a university level from a Darwinian evolutionary perspective and was completely committed to the evolutionary
worldview. Then one day, I saw, by God's grace, the fallacy of evolution, and changed my point of view to creation. My new-found

grasp of creation helped revolutionize my life in that several months later, I became a Christian.[1] Now that I *am* a Christian, I can see no alternative to the biblical view. I also have a special appreciation for the Bible beginning with the words, "In the beginning God created the heaven and the earth" (Genesis 1:1) in that my knowledge of a creator was foundational in later receiving John's Gospel message—"For God so loved the world, that he gave his only begotten Son . . ." (John 3:16).

How credible are the foundational principles of evolution? Is evolution based on the facts? Despite what you may have been told, the founding fathers of evolutionary thinking were not overwhelmed by evidence that caused them to reject the creation view. They had far less respectable motives. They were looking for a way to explain away the existence of God. Evolution was an idea that served their agenda. A brief overview of the foundational principles of evolution will show there is nothing scientific to substantiate the idea. It is a theory without substance, and it should be declared bankrupt by all those who know there is a God.

Besides the lack of physical evidence to support evolution, the concept is absolutely opposed to the very character of God. According to the Bible, God originally made all things perfect. Evolution claims that complexity arises out of disorder without any plan or design. Many other irreconcilable differences exist between evolution and creation. To begin with, evolution states that millions of generations suffered and died as the fittest struggled to climb to the top of the pile. The Bible says that all things were created perfectly by a plan and for a purpose, then began to degenerate and die because of a curse that resulted from man's sin.

It is also a tragedy to the field of science that an established law of science should be overthrown by a speculative and unsubstantiated theory. The second law of thermodynamics declares that everything in the physical universe is moving toward a random state—from order to disorder. But evolution declares the opposite, contrary to observable evidence.

Creation claims that the design and complexity of all living things is the handiwork of a Designer, not an accumulation of mistakes over time. Yet, despite the overwhelming evidence that supports the creation view, it is becoming increasingly difficult to answer the critics of creation who are convinced the God of the Bible is nothing more than legend and myth. Tragically, many so-called Christian college professors have turned their backs on the Genesis record so that this present generation of Christian leaders is being indoctrinated.

For the past several decades, opposition to a biblical creation worldview by members of the scientific community has become more outspoken and hostile. A quick survey of several anti-creation books reveals that those who believe in God as the Creator are categorized as "narrow-minded" and "zealous bigots" who are "pseudo-scientific" and "pea-brained."

Today, especially in North America, the agenda to advance the idea of evolution is the number one priority for those who believe in the humanist cause.

To be effective witnesses to our generation, it is very important that we are able to confront the fallacy of evolution with some basic undeniable facts about the subject of life's origins.

Theistic Evolution

When it comes to origins, there are three basic views—evolution, creation, and the idea that God used evolution to create. So what about this view that the biblical creator used the Darwinian process of chance and time to bring all life into existence? Why do so many Christians accept this view? Is it biblically acceptable, or is it a compromise of faith?

I have given thousands of lectures in universities, schools, churches, and conferences around the world on the topic of origins. These lectures usually contrast the differences between the evolution and creation worldviews. While it is not possible to prove either view scientifically because we cannot observe what occurred in the distant unobservable past, it is possible to examine the facts we see in the present.

In my introduction to these lectures, I always tell the people only two basic models for origins exist—evolution or creation. Then we examine the claims of evolution and the claims of creation, demonstrating that evolution is based on false assumptions (e.g., explosions do not create order, life does not originate from non-life spontaneously, nor is there a mechanism to show life has evolved from simple to complex).

THE DARWINIAN VIEW PROPOSES THAT LIFE HAS ARISEN FROM LOWER TO HIGHER, FROM SIMPLE TO COMPLEX, BY PROCESSES OVER MILLIONS OF YEARS OF TIME, AS LIFE LIVED AND DIED WHILE COMPETING. HOW DO YOU RECONCILE THIS WITH THE GENESIS RECORD?

Following these meetings, it is almost guaranteed I will be confronted by people who insist they believe in God. However, they believe God used millions of years of evolutionary processes to create. They say there is no problem, whatsoever, accommodating Darwinism into the Bible. God, they say, and evolution are compatible.

So what about this view? Is it credible? Is it compatible with what the Bible teaches? What about from the Darwinian perspective? Does evolution have a supernatural directing force?

Speaking of Darwinism, Charles Darwin was asked during his lifetime if he thought God could have used evolution to create? His answer was abrupt. Evolution is purely a natural process he said. That was the basis and the reason for his theory. No supernatural directing force was necessary—only matter, time, and chance.

For me, I have a personal reason for rejecting "Christian evolution." When I taught biology as an unbeliever, I was an evolutionist. Evolution was my reason or excuse for explaining away the Creator. My conversion to Christianity was from evolution to creation to Christ. Now as a Christian, I question why other Christians seem so confident that God could have used evolution to create. Why would you use a process that has been used to explain away God, to explain God? It just doesn't make sense.

Further, there is another major problem with trying to accommodate evolution into the Bible. The Darwinian view proposes that life has arisen from lower to higher, from simple to complex, by processes over millions of years of time, as life lived and died while competing. How do you reconcile this with the Genesis record? The Bible states that death in this world became a reality when Adam sinned. In order to believe in theistic evolution, one has to believe billions of years of death and survival of the fittest took place before Adam ever came on the scene.

It should be obvious that evolution and creation are two separate explanations for origins. To combine the two is what is called an oxymoron. It is like saying that I saw a flaming snow flake.

The Rejection of the Creator by the Church

While speaking at a conference in Rome in 2007 to a small group of evangelicals who wanted to hear about the evidence for biblical creation, the former pope, Benedict, made an announcement on the news that caught the group's attention. MSNBC reported Pope Benedict's thoughts on the validity of the Genesis record. An article titled "Pope: Creation vs. Evolution Clash an 'Absurdity,'" stated:

> Pope Benedict XVI said the debate raging in some countries— particularly the United States and his native

Germany— between creationism and evolution was an "absurdity," saying that evolution can coexist with faith. The pontiff, speaking as he was concluding his holiday in northern Italy, also said that while there is much scientific proof to support evolution, the theory could not exclude a role by God. "They are presented as alternatives that exclude each other," the pope said. "This clash is an absurdity because on one hand there is much scientific proof in favor of evolution, which appears as a reality that we must see and which enriches our understanding of life and being as such."[2]

This same article expressed additional thoughts Benedict had expressed to reporters while on vacation in northern Italy. He expressed the need now in Earth's history to "reverence the creation" now at a time when the Earth faces many ecological problems and the planet and its occupants face a dilemma. The article continues:

The pope, leader of some 1.1 billion Roman Catholics worldwide, said: "We must respect the interior laws of creation, of this Earth, to learn these laws and obey them if we want to survive. This obedience to the voice of the Earth is more important for our future happiness . . . than the desires of the moment. Our Earth is talking to us and we must listen to it and decipher its message if we want to survive," he said.[3]

Pope Francis has taken Pope Benedict's idea of speaking to the Earth one step further. He has taken on himself the responsibility of lobbying scientists, politicians, and religious leaders to join in a global effort to reverence the Earth because of climate change. He too, in an article posted by *Newsweek*, presents his view saying "evolutionary teaching does not contradict biblical teaching." The article states:

Pope Francis told an audience from the Pontifical Academy of Sciences in Vatican City on Monday that theories of evolution and the Big Bang are not inconsistent with creationism and biblical teaching. "The evolution in nature is not opposed to the notion of Creation, because evolution presupposes the creation of beings that evolve," Pope Francis said, according to a Vatican newswire transcript of the event.[4]

As "Vicars" of Christ, according to the Catholic Church, both Pope Benedict and Pope Francis have taken it upon themselves to speak on behalf of the Creator, Jesus Christ, and put their approval on the theory of evolution embraced by billions of people all over the world who reject the God of the Bible. Worse yet, as we will examine later in this book, when humans reverence the Earth and speak to the creation, they are opening themselves to the ancient pagan religion of Babylonianism and the fallen spiritual realm.

Pastors For Evolution

While I have pointed out the dangerous direction the leadership of the Roman Catholic Church is taking, I would be remiss if I did not point out that many, many evangelical and Protestant pastors and educators are holding to the view that evolution and God are not in conflict with each other.

While evolutionists understand the importance of creation to Christianity, many Christians do not realize that creation is vital to belief in God. The first verse of the Bible begins with creation and serves as a foundation for the Gospel, for without a creator, mankind would be responsible to no one; consequently, there would be no need for a Savior. Indoctrination occurs when a student is presented with limited evidence. Everyone knows this happened in former communist countries. The minds of children were manipulated. They were told God was a myth. Darwinism replaced creation as a fact of science and supported atheism.

Over the past several years several school districts in the United States have recognized students should be taught to think critically.

When it comes to evolution theory, some school boards have *encouraged* policy to allow students to examine the claims of evolution critically. However, such efforts have been met with much opposition.

Ironically, among such opposition, one group of pastors signed a letter requesting that evolution be presented to children in their district *without challenge*. They insisted the Bible and evolution can co-exist. Here is how one journalist reported the controversy in an article titled "Pastor's Protest District Policy: Letter Says Evolution, Bible Can Coexist":

> Nearly 200 Wisconsin clergy want school officials in Grantsburg, Wisconsin to ensure evolution remains at the center of scientific teaching in the schools. . . . The pastors want evolution to be treated "the same as all scientific theories" and not singled out for special scrutiny.[5]

The letter of protest came about because of a controversy that occurred in the Grantsburg district. First, there had been a policy introduced that allowed for scientific theories other than evolution to be taught. This policy was overturned by a protest from the "scientific" establishment. Following this, a revised policy was proposed that contained an expectation that students would be permitted to examine "the scientific strengths and weaknesses of evolution theory."

It was this revised policy that triggered the letter signed by 188 pastors—from Baptist, Catholic, Episcopal, Lutheran, Methodist, and other denominations. The letter said the revised policy was nothing more than "a standard creationist tactic" and that evolution should be treated "the same as all scientific theories" and not "singled out for special scrutiny." Criticism of the evolution theory should be left to professional scientists who have proper credentials, the pastors suggested.[6]

However, these pastors seem to have a serious lack of understanding of what it means for a theory to be treated "the same as all scientific theories," for a theory can never become a law of science nor should it be treated as such until or if it has been proven—and this requires scrutiny, scientific testing, and confirmation. As things are, evolution is being treated as if it were a law.

Quoting further from the actual letter the pastors signed:

> While virtually all Christians take the Bible seriously, and hold to it to be authoritative in matters of faith and practice, the overwhelming majority do not read the Bible literally, as they would a science textbook. Many of the beloved stories found in the Bible—the Creation, Adam and Eve, Noah and the ark—convey timeless truths about God, human beings, and the proper relationship between Creator and creation expressed in the only form capable of transmitting these truths from generation to generation. Religious truth is of a different order from scientific truth. Its purpose is not to convey information but to transform hearts.[7]

Finally, one additional statement from the letter signed by the pastors:

> We urge school board members to preserve the integrity of the science curriculum by affirming the teaching of the theory of evolution as a core component of human knowledge. We ask that science remain science and that religion remain religion, two very different, but complementary, forms of truth.[8]

My experience as a lecturer for over 35 years on the topic of creation in a variety of church denominations confirms the direction these pastors are promoting. It is a sign of the times, proving further that the Bible is both true and literal (except in cases where the text itself makes it clear that a figure of speech is being used). When Christian leaders choose to reject the evidence that God is the Creator, this puts them on a slippery pathway downwards which eventually results in complete apostasy. When man chooses to reject the overwhelming evidence for creation, the consequences are shattering.

EVOLUTION: BRINGING AN IDOL INTO THE SANCTUARY

P aul, writing to the Romans, made it very evident that serious consequences occur when the overwhelming evidence for creation which points directly to a Creator God is ignored. He wrote:

> For the wrath of God is revealed from heaven against all ungodliness and unrighteousness of men, who hold the truth in unrighteousness; Because that which may be known of God is manifest in them; for God hath shewed it unto them. For the invisible things of him from the creation of the world are clearly seen, being understood by the things that are made, even his eternal power and Godhead; so that they are without excuse. (Romans 1: 18-20)

According to Paul, creation proves God's "eternal power and Godhead," but countless pastors today have been willingly duped into believing a lie, then feeding it to their congregations. Paul said they "changed the truth of God into a lie, and worshipped and served the creature more than the Creator" (Romans 1:25). So the real question is, where lies the eternal power and Godhead of the vast complexity and intricacy of creation—is it God or evolution, for it cannot be both at the same time? The word "worship" in the Hebrew means to bow down or fall down and do reverence; in the Greek, it means to revere or adore, often by falling or bowing down* (see *Strong's Concordance*); in English, the word comes from the Old English *weorthscipe,* which means literally to acknowledge or ascribe the worth of someone or something, hence doing reverence, devotion, homage, or veneration in an acknowledgment of worthiness.[1]

But, how can we properly ascribe to God His worth if we are too proud to believe He could have created the universe in six days and rested on the seventh? With theistic evolution, we see God as impotent rather than omnipotent, as ignorant rather than omniscient, and therefore having to sit back for billions of years and watch the mighty forces of evolution do their task—and all without a brain or any intellect.

We have therefore replaced worship with blasphemy, all in the name of truth and science—falsely so-called.

Creation itself proves and gives credence to the fact there is a Creator. When man chooses to ignore that evidence, he is without excuse. Paul goes on to explain the consequences that will impact any individual or an entire society that refuses to accept the evidence for creation. They make a choice to be willingly ignorant. Paul explained:

> Because that, when they knew God, they glorified him not as God, neither were thankful; but became vain in their imaginations, and their foolish heart was darkened. Professing themselves to be wise, they became fools, And changed the glory of the uncorruptible God into an image made like to corruptible man, and to birds, and fourfooted beasts, and creeping things. Wherefore God also gave them up to uncleanness through the lusts of their own hearts, to dishonour their own bodies between

---

*This is talking about falling forward or bowing down on knees. It is not the same as what is commonly known in the charismatic movement as "being slain in the Spirit." For an explanation of that practice, read *Slain in the Spirit: Is it a Biblical Practice?* by Kevin Reeves.

themselves: Who changed the truth of God into a lie, and worshipped and served the creature more than the Creator, who is blessed for ever. Amen. (Romans 1: 21-25)

Not only will man worship the creation rather than the Creator who made everything, the immorality and depravity of man takes over. Paul's words reveal what happens when man rebels and chooses to remove God and make up his own rules.

While we have already demonstrated that Roman Catholic popes and Protestant pastors have chosen to trust in man and what they have been told as the "facts" of evolution by those who have credentials attained through their scientific research, Paul warned Timothy of this very danger. He wrote:

O Timothy, keep that which is committed to thy trust, avoiding profane and vain babblings, and oppositions of science falsely so called: Which some professing have erred concerning the faith. Grace be with thee. Amen. (1 Timothy 6: 20-21)

Nothing New Under the Sun

As I previously pointed out, disregarding God and trusting in human reasoning will eventually and inevitably lead to the worship of the fallen spiritual realm. It was during the early 1980s when I started to see how the indoctrination of Darwinian evolution on a global scale was setting up the world for an invasion of eastern metaphysical thought. As Paul explained, when man turns away from God by refusing to accept the overwhelming evidence for creation, he will eventually worship everything that God has made, including himself.

Pantheism (i.e., all things are God or divine), the fallen spirituality that permeated the Babylonian civilization, was reappearing in the '80s in the form of the New Age movement. It was clear this was not a new thing. The same metaphysical methods and practices promoted by the religions of Buddhism and Hinduism were being promoted based on the idea of evolution as a potential pathway to higher levels of consciousness.

In order to warn the church, Caryl Matrisciana and I co-authored a book called *The Evolution Conspiracy.* Based on Caryl's experience as a young girl growing up in India and the observations I was making as I traveled throughout the world, it was apparent to us that a revival of Babylonianism was underway, fulfilling Bible prophecy.

Later, in the 1990s, I realized I was no longer welcome at some of the churches I had once spoken at in the past. For example, a day after speaking at a large church in southern California, I received a phone call from the pastor saying I would not be invited back. Apparently, his wife was the head of the women's fellowship at their church. She herself was leading the ladies' Yoga-practice fellowship!

Christian Yoga?

I have been following the New Age movement even before the term New Age movement was made popular. In the early '80s, I became very aware that eastern religion was being widely promoted in the west as something new. While New Agers were enthusiastically advocating Yoga, meditation, crystals, spirit guides, and humming mantras as the ways and means to achieve global consciousness and enlightenment, professing Christians I knew could see Satan's strategy. In fact, then, no Bible-believing Christian would ever fall for such deception!

That was 25 years ago. Time has a way of changing things. Today, it is not uncommon to hear about churches promoting "Christian Yoga"[2] for exercise or "Christian" leaders suggesting the best way to get in contact with God and hear His voice is to enhance one's prayer life by chanting mantra-like words or phrases or practicing *breath prayers.*[3] What was once described as New Age and the occult is now spiritually acceptable. What has happened? Has God changed His Word, or has Yoga become Christian? Is it possible that Christians have been duped by Satan and lulled to sleep? Worse yet, have they been seduced by seducing spirits (demons) that the Bible warns will deceive many and cause a great falling away?

Anyone who cares to do the research will find that Yoga and its connection to eastern religion remains the same.[4] Linking oneself with the universal energy is still the goal. A Christian can believe that Yoga is for health and well-being if he or she wants, but the facts have not changed. But many Christians have. Listen to what Professor Subhas R. Tiwari of the Hindu University of America says about "Christian" Yoga:

> In the past few months I have received several calls from journalists around the country seeking my views on the question of whether the newly minted "Christian Yoga" is really yoga.
>
> My response is, "The simple, immutable fact is that yoga originated from the Vedic or Hindu culture. Its techniques were not adopted by Hinduism, but originated from it." . . . The effort to separate yoga from Hinduism must be challenged because it runs counter to the fundamental principles upon which yoga itself is premised. . . . Efforts to separate yoga from its spiritual center reveal ignorance of the goal of yoga. . . .
>
> [Yoga] was intended by the Vedic seers as an instrument which can lead one to apprehend the Absolute, Ultimate Reality, called the Brahman Reality, or God. If this attempt to co-opt yoga into their own tradition continues, in several decades of incessantly spinning the untruth as truth through re-labelings such as "Christian yoga," who will know that yoga is—or was—part of Hindu culture?[5]

And yet, more and more evangelical and Protestant Christians are practicing Yoga, and an increasing number of churches are bringing Yoga classes into their churches, often through the pastor's wife or the women's ministry leader. Yoga has been practiced largely by women, but that is changing. Recent studies show that the number of men who are practicing Yoga is climbing steadily. One 2016 study found that over 36 million people in America practice Yoga, up from 20.4 million in 2012.[6] As for the Christian population, they have jumped on the Yoga bandwagon. A thirty-year-old Christian woman told my publisher that she only knows one Christian woman her age who is *not* practicing Yoga. And these are women who attend evangelical churches!

It is simply amazing how quickly Christianity has changed in such a short period. Why has this happened? Does it have something to do with the Word of God being undermined? While countless Christians have joined hands with the New Age (not calling it that, of course), we now have a New Age "Christianity" of which the Bible warns us.

I am reminded of the heavy statements we find in the Old Testament when the children of Israel rebelled against God. For example, this is what we read in Deuteronomy:

> When thou art come into the land which the LORD thy God giveth thee, thou shalt not learn to do after the abominations of those nations. There shall not be found among you any one that maketh his son or his daughter to pass through the fire, or that useth divination, or an observer of times, or an enchanter, or a witch. Or a charmer, or a consulter with familiar spirits, or a wizard, or a necromancer. For all that do these things are an abomination unto the LORD: and because of these abominations the LORD thy God doth drive them out from before thee. Thou shalt be perfect with the LORD thy God. (Deuteronomy 18: 9-13)

Straying away from God and being led by the pagan gods is an abomination to God and will be judged by God. There is not one verse in the Bible that supports "New Age Christianity." Isn't it time for Christians to take the Bible seriously and for pastors to preach and teach as God would have them do? A good starting point would be to go back to Genesis 1 and see what the Bible has to say about our Creator and His creation.

12

NEW WINE
OR OLD DECEPTION?

Many are saying we are living in the midst of a spiritual awakening. You can hear this everywhere. *God is pouring out His Spirit on believers and unbelievers,* they say, and *we are about to see the greatest revival in the history of mankind. Now is the time to "catch the wave" and renounce old religious ideas,* they insist. *We have arrived. This is the new era that so many have been predicting for decades. You must embrace the Holy Spirit's new strategies for revival or be left behind.*

The December 1999 *Charisma* magazine carried a feature article that foretold the future of the body of Christ. On the front cover, the following statement was made: "Fasten your seat belt. A Christian revival could sweep the world in the next 25 years."[1] Like others who espouse the final end-times great revival, *Charisma* was promoting the idea that God is now pouring out a "new wine" or new anointing to prepare an army of God to win the world for Jesus in these last days.

Experiencing "God's power" by imbibing the new wine is proof you have enlisted as a member of God's army, some also say. The more unity there is in the body of Christ, the more signs and wonders will occur. The more signs and wonders that are demonstrated, the more people will come to Christ, according to proponents of the New Wine movement.

The Fire Is Spreading

In order to understand the origin of this "new wave of the Spirit" and the impact it has had on many proclaiming Christians, it is important to discuss some of the key "visitations of the Spirit" that have occurred over the past few decades. The July 1997 issue of *Charisma* featured an article called "The Blessing Spreads World-wide." The leading paragraph stated: "Since an unusual spiritual renewal movement erupted in 1994, many Christian leaders have become convinced that a global revival is on the way."[2]

According to this New Wine theology, a "fire" that was lit at the Toronto Airport Vineyard (later named Airport Christian Fellowship and currently called Catch the Fire Toronto) in January of 1994 was transferred worldwide. Proponents say the Toronto "blessing" was transferable and contagious. Once you get "it," you can give "it" away to others.[3]

In this article, writer Marcia Ford retraced the origin of the blessing back to various sources: Pastor John Arnott and his wife Carol picked up their anointing from Claudio Freidzon while in South America.[4] Claudio Freidzon had received his anointing from Benny Hinn. Benny Hinn claims he received a special empowerment when he came in close contact with the bones of Kathryn Kuhlman.[5]

Another source of this New Wine anointing for the Toronto church came from St. Louis Vineyard pastor Randy Clark.[6] He received an "anointing" from self-proclaimed "Holy Spirit bartender" Rodney Howard-Browne.[7] Howard-Browne, who originated in South Africa, was convinced God appointed him to light the fire with this transferable anointing that would spread revival around the world.[8]

From Toronto, this "blessing" spread to many countries throughout the world. Recipients took it back to their homes in England, South Africa, Australia, and even mainland China.[9]

The Anointing

The New Wine movement and the new "transferable anointing" go hand-in-hand. When you "catch the fire," you receive "it." Nearly everyone who has had this experience has his own personal story. The following is an account given by John Arnott, senior pastor of the Toronto Airport Christian Fellowship:

> We heard about the revival in Argentina, so we traveled there in November of 1993, hoping God's anointing would rub off on us somehow. We were powerfully touched in meetings led by Claudio Freidzon, a leader of the Assemblies of God in Argentina.[10]

According to Arnott, he was touched by an encounter with a spiritual leader who had some kind of power that apparently rubbed off. This occurred when Claudio Freidzon prayed and then touched John and Carol Arnott. John fell over and then stood up. At first, he questioned whether this experience was his own flesh or from God. Then something else happened. Freidzon asked John Arnott if he wanted the "anointing." As Arnott described:

> "Oh yes, I want *it* all right," I answered. "Then take *it!*" He slapped my outstretched hands. "I will. I will take *it*," I said. Something clicked in my heart at that moment. It was as though I heard the Lord say, "For goodness sake, will you take *this*? Take *it*, *it's* yours." And I received by faith.[11] (emphasis added)

What Is the Transferable Anointing?

One of the central themes of the New Wine movement is the idea that the Spirit of God is transferrable. Once received, it is commonly believed this anointing can be given away to others. Often the word *impartation* is used by those who believe they have obtained this God-given ability.

However, it can easily be documented that the concept of impartation is not new. During the late 1940s, this doctrine was promoted by an aberrant group of experience-focused Christians from North Battleford, Saskatchewan, Canada known as the Latter Rain movement. The concept that certain individuals can receive and then impart an anointing was one of the main reasons many church leaders declared the Latter Rain teachings heretical. While this and other Latter Rain teachings had a major impact throughout North America and some parts of Europe, strong opposition by Bible teachers who supported sound biblical doctrine, forced the "manifest sons of God" belief underground. Richard Riss, a staunch supporter of the Latter Rain movement, wrote about this in his book called *The Latter Rain.*[12]

At a General Council meeting held by the Assemblies of God in Seattle, Washington in the fall of 1949, a resolution was adopted disapproving the practices of what was termed, "The New Order of the Latter Rain." Several specific concerns were listed in this document. Among these were "the overemphasis relative to imparting, identifying, bestowing, or confirming of gifts by the laying on of hands and prophecy," and "the erroneous teaching that the Church is built upon the foundation of the present-day apostles and prophets."

The official disapproval concluded by stating:

> Such other wrestings and distortions of Scripture interpretations are in opposition to teachings and practices generally accepted among us. For it be further resolved, we recommend following those things which make for peace among us, and those doctrines and practices whereby we may edify one another, endeavoring to keep the unity of the Spirit until we all come into the reality of faith.[13]

Although the Assemblies of God General Council rebuked the New Order of Latter Rain in 1949, time has a way of deleting memories. Seventy years and several generations later, it is apparent that things have changed. Impartations, the "transferable anointing," and the apostle and prophet movement all are right back in style. Only now, very few are concerned. While in the past, most evangelical Protestants would have considered such ideas heretical and the earmark of a cult, there is a large trend underway today that indicates many evangelicals are embracing similar views.

The River of God

The "river of God" has been the central focus of the teachings that spread from the Brownsville Assemblies of God in Pensacola, Florida. According to a full page advertisement in the December 1996 issue of *Charisma* magazine, over one million people had traveled to Pensacola to receive a "touch from God." Afterward, they returned home and "spread the fire" to their own churches.[14]

The fire that was transferred, according to these enthusiasts, did not come from a burning flame. The method of receiving the "fire" comes by letting "the river of God surround, uphold, refresh and at times overwhelm you."[15] The biblical basis for this new doctrine, supporters say, can be found in Ezekiel chapter 47. According to this interpretation of the Scriptures, Ezekiel saw a vision of a river that flowed from the temple of God. This river is supposed to be the river now flowing in churches where people are open to the "new thing" God is doing.

Portal in Pensacola

Renee DeLoriea is the author of *Portal in Pensacola: The Real Thing Hits Brownsville.* Her articles, reports, and stories have appeared in numerous Christian publications around the world including *Charisma* magazine.[16] In her book, she documents many of the events she personally experienced during what is commonly called the Pensacola Awakening.

DeLoriea, a student of revivals of the past, believes that God revealed to her in advance about a great revival that was to take place in Pensacola. She sold all her possessions, uprooted her family, and moved to Florida. Her book is a firsthand account of what she believes is a miraculous move of God that was happening at the Brownsville Assembly of God and around the world.[17]

In the first chapter of her book titled "The Assembling of God's Last-Days Army," DeLoriea describes what happened at the November 26, 1996 Pastor's Conference held at the Brownsville Assembly of God Church. Over 2000 pastors and their spouses had gathered there from throughout the United States and around the world anticipating an encounter with God. DeLoriea states:

> At last, there seemed to be hope for a real move of God—the kind of move they dreamed about . . . in history books and in Scripture. A portal, a grand opening in the heavens, had sovereignly opened over Pensacola, and the *shekinah* glory of God was streaming down upon His people like rays of brilliant sunshine piercing the clouds of an abating thunderstorm. These men and women of God seemed to be wondering if it might be possible that God would actually give them just a bit of the anointing they had heard God was pouring out at Brownsville.[18]

DeLoriea also gave a detailed account of the message Senior Pastor John Kilpatrick made at the Pastor's Conference. He opened his address by saying:

> God has sovereignly decided to once again replenish the parched, dry places of our hearts and lives. By His grace and mercy, He has sent in a river, and in that river is the glory, His manifest presence, and the things of God that we, for such a long time, have longed for and yearned for and cried for.[19]

Kilpatrick's comment is typical of many Christians today who are genuinely seeking to know the power of God in their lives. While enthusiasm and sincerity are important qualities of the Christian life, it is also important that believers always balance their feelings and emotions with the Word of God. Otherwise, it is very easy for them to get caught up in the hysteria of an overly experiential movement.

Jesus taught that seeking an experience in His name based upon some geographical location is part of the end-times deception and a sign He is returning soon (Matthew 24:26-27). You do not need to travel to Pensacola, Toronto, or anywhere else to encounter Jesus Christ. He says He will live in the hearts and lives of those who, by faith, through grace, invite Him in and abide in Him.

> Behold, I stand at the door, and knock: if any man hear my voice, and open the door, I will come in to him, and will sup with him, and he with me. (Revelation 3: 20)

> And he that keepeth his commandments dwelleth in him, and he in him. And hereby we know that he abideth in us, by the Spirit which he hath given us. (1 John 3:24)

The Apostle-Prophet Movement

A myriad of well-known Christian leaders claim that God has raised up an elite group of supernatural prophets and apostles, reminiscent of the claims of the Latter Rain movement of the 1940s and 1950s.[20] Called the Apostolic movement or the New Apostolic Reformation (NAR), this "mighty end-times army" of God, consisting of saints who have been trained by specially commissioned "apostles," has been called to establish the kingdom of God here on planet Earth, they say. Bill Hamon, a noted bishop, apostle, and modern-day so-called prophet wrote a book on this subject titled *Apostles, Prophets and the Coming Moves of God: God's End-Time Plans for His Church and Planet Earth*. In the dedication of the book, it reads:

> To the great company of Prophets and Apostles that God is bringing forth in these days. May it be enlightening and enabling to all those who are called and chosen to co-labor with Christ in fulfilling the coming moves of God. It is

for all those who are committed to making ready a people, preparing the way by restoring all things. This will enable Christ Jesus to be released from heaven to return for His Church and establish His kingdom over all the earth.[21]

The "Apostle John Eckhardt," pastor and overseer of Crusaders Ministries in Chicago, has traveled throughout the U.S. and around the world imparting spiritual "truths." He sees it as his job to be about the business of "perfecting the saints." He discusses his role in a chapter of the book, *The New Apostolic Churches*, compiled by the late C. Peter Wagner (d. 2016):

> It was never the will of God for the Church to go without the apostolic dimension. Because of tradition and unbelief, this dynamic did not continue from generation to generation. The good news is, though, that we are now living in times of restoration. We view ourselves as being a part of prophetic fulfillment.[22]

Eckhardt explains how vital this newly recognized office is to God's plan for the world in the last days:

> One of the first truths the Lord taught us is that the saints could not be fully perfected without the ministry of the apostle. The five ministry gifts given for equipping the saints (see Eph. 4:11) include apostles and prophets. It takes all five of these ministry gifts operating in the church to properly mature God's people for the work of the ministry. When the apostle is absent, the saints will lack the apostolic character they need to fulfill the Great Commission.[23]

When most Christians hear the title "apostle," they think of the apostle Paul or Peter, pillars of the Christian faith. Leaders of the New Apostolic Reformation believe this title is bestowed upon some today, based on such concepts as "calling," "revelation," and "gifting."

They say that today's apostle has the responsibility to establish new churches, correct error, and oversee other ministries. Bill Hamon adds to this description:

> The apostle has a revelatory anointing. Some major characteristics are great patience and manifestation of signs and wonders and miracles. We will know more and see greater manifestations concerning the apostle during the peak of the Apostolic Movement.[24]

————◆————

WITH SIGNS AND WONDERS, AND MEETINGS CHARACTERIZED BY PROPHETIC UTTERANCES, THESE APOSTLES AND PROPHETS ARE MILITANT IN URGING OTHERS TO LEAVE BEHIND THE ENCUMBRANCES OF TRADITIONAL CHRISTIANITY

————◆————

And the Apostolic movement is growing. With signs and wonders, and meetings characterized by prophetic utterances, these apostles and prophets are militant in urging others to leave behind the encumbrances of traditional Christianity and go where the Spirit takes them. Gathering at well-organized and well-attended conferences, they have a strategy for spreading their theology around the world.

Test the Spirits

Even New Wine promoters like John Arnott preach and teach that spiritual experiences need to be tested biblically. But it is apparent he is confused on this issue. It is easy to say you stand upon the Word of God. But it is quite another thing to understand what the Word of God actually teaches. Consider John Arnott's own words:

> These questions need to be asked when evaluating a spiritual experience: Is this in the Word of God? Is something similar in the Word? Is this prohibited by the Word of God? Is it within the character of God as revealed through the Bible? When we ask if something is biblical, we're really asking if it's from God, aren't we? We don't want to be deceived, and we have been given the Bible to show us who God is, what He is like and what kinds of things He does. So we evaluate things according to the Bible, as we should. Yet as we see the Spirit of God doing more and more, we may see some things that no chapter and verse in the Bible specifically describes. Why? God did not intend to describe every act He would ever do in the Bible.[25]

This statement by John Arnott is the typical defense made by New Wine promoters. I am convinced this brand of apologetics is based upon a desire to justify anything and everything in the name of God even though "it" cannot be found in the Word of God. There is no place in the Bible that justifies that recipients of God's Spirit shake and twitch like they are having an epileptic seizure. Nor do we read that the Spirit of God causes one to laugh hysterically and uncontrollably or behave like a drunkard or an animal such as a chicken or a serpent. Such behavior characterized the Toronto Blessing.

It may be worth noting here that the behaviors of jerking, twitching, convulsing, uncontrollable laughing, and animal-like behaviors *are* consistent with eastern/New Age experiences commonly and historically known to be associated with the effects of Kundalini (serpent) power. The question we should then ask is: Should we assume that the Holy Spirit is so depleted of His own resources He would look to the activities of demons as a model of how to manifest His own presence? I think not!

Oftentimes, Christians of charismatic or Pentecostal persuasion are afraid to question or challenge any or all manifestations credited to the work of the Holy Spirit for fear of being guilty of blaspheming the Holy Spirit (an idea taken from Matthew 12:31-32). Yet, they do not seem to be afraid of taking the work of demons and calling it the work of the Holy Spirit. Is this not blasphemous as well?

The truth of the matter is that these Christians have been deceived into thinking they could accidentally commit the "unforgiveable sin" when in reality, Scripture commands us to test all things ("Beloved, believe not every spirit, but try the spirits whether they are of God: because many false prophets are gone out into the world" 1 John 4:1).

As a second scenario, some are tempted to think that if the manifestations they are observing are magnificent enough, it *must* be from God. Yet, the Antichrist who is coming will do signs and wonders far beyond the scope of what we are seeing today—to the extent that the whole world will be deceived. What we should be looking at is the doctrine of these individuals and ask ourselves if it fully lines up and agrees with the pure and simple Gospel handed down to us in Scripture. So often, you will find it does not—if the Gospel is even being preached at all!

Then there is a third scenario where the church members are led to believe that if they follow the leader, then they are under an umbrella of protection where God is pleased when the congregation shows strict obedience to the shepherd. Oftentimes, this cultish mentality is compounded by the idea that the members of the church should trust the pastor's discernment more than their own because the pastor is more mature and in tune with the things of God. Again, the reality is that we should be like the citizens of Berea who "searched the scriptures daily, whether those things were so" (Acts 17:11). Jesus never taught unquestioning obedience to a pastor or leader but rather said, "[I]f the blind lead the blind, both shall fall into the ditch" (Matthew 15:14). In other words, we are all accountable for our own actions, and the pastor was never meant to be a "covering" where we are permitted to do things that violate our own conscience.

This is not to say that we should challenge a good pastor on every decision he makes, but if we are under a pastor who is a false teacher, Jesus' instruction is to "Let them alone: they be blind leaders of the blind" (Matthew 15:14).

Sometimes, if not usually, the above three scenarios are doing their havoc, all in a single church. This is a very sour formula for discernment as few have the courage to speak up, and those who do are usually exited from the church.

It is very possible for genuine sincere Christians who follow this kind of teaching to be led astray. If we are not willing to be consistent about what we believe, then we will be inconsistent in practice. Inconsistency can easily lead to apostasy. And as Paul warned, apostasy is a key factor in preparing the way for the Antichrist.

A spiritual delusion is presently underway in the name of Christ, and the church is being prepared to embrace it. The apostle Paul stated this would happen, and the current trend indicates this is exactly what *is* happening. And according to the Bible, if Christians are being deluded now, we can expect the delusion to intensify.

Bible doctrine is based on the idea that a tenet of faith must be established by the support of the whole counsel of God. Scripture must always provide the basis for biblical doctrine. The Bible teaches that all Scripture has been given by the inspiration of God.

Today, a growing number of church leaders are saying Bible doctrine is not as important as it was once thought to be. Holding firm to biblical doctrine can divide the body and hold back revival, some are saying. Other leaders have used the term *bibliolatry* to define those who put too much emphasis on the Bible.[26] And in the fall of 2016, megachurch pastor Andy Stanley (the son of Charles Stanley) told leaders and pastors at a Southern Baptist Convention "Ethics and Religious Liberty Commission" conference the following:

New Wine or Old Deception?

> I would ask preachers and pastors and student pastors in their communications to *get the spotlight off the Bible* and back on the resurrection.[27] (emphasis added)

As of the release of this book, I have heard of no public decrying of such a statement by any Christian leader.

Some leaders have claimed that we can gain new revelation apart from the Bible. They say it is important that we not judge the new revelations God is giving to mankind. While we know that God is and always has been at work in the lives of believers, the Word of God is the basis for defining all truth. And the beginning of all apostasy and deception is believing in the notion that the Word of God is not to be believed upon or trusted as His infallible standard and gauge for discerning truth.

Supporters of this experience-based brand of Christianity often use the Book of Acts to support their views that strange behavior and chaos occur in the church as God pours out His Spirit. For example, Dick Reuben, a regular speaker at the Brownsville Assemblies of God in Pensacola, Florida, states:

> If you read the Book of Acts, you will discover some pretty strange and abnormal things going on. People, they looked on and they marveled. Let me tell you, the church through the years, [has] become organized, and we've learned how to do church, and we've depended upon the hand of flesh, and we've devised programs. . . . But listen, when God shows up, it gets kind of chaotic. Did you know that?[28]

Then admonishing his critics and proposing a new doctrine based on what the Bible does *not* say, Reuben continues:

> You say, "Well, I don't see some of this happening in the Book of Acts." Listen—the Holy Spirit couldn't put everything that He did in the Book of Acts. As Steve has said, "[I]f God . . . reported everything He did on

the day of Pentecost in the Bible, you'd have to have a wheelbarrow just to carry Acts 2 around." And so God didn't put everything in the Bible that happened![29]

So what about this doctrine that has been designed to justify strange behavior in the church? Is it biblically accurate to teach that new doctrines can be fabricated that justify our feelings and beliefs? What about the Berean style of Bible study mentioned in the Book of Acts? Luke commended them for their diligence to check out the Scriptures daily to see that Paul was not feeding them a line (Acts 17:11).

Of course, it would take a wheelbarrow to carry around the Book of Acts if everything God did during that time was recorded. But God only inspired Luke to write down all He wanted us to know. The Bible indicates that Christians should be more concerned about what the Bible teaches, rather than what the Bible does not teach. However, as we have documented, the very opposite is happening within the New Wine movement. God's Word is not only being ignored, it is being completely reinterpreted to justify the signs and wonders which are touted as a prerequisite for revival.

While more than two decades have now passed since this "new wave" involving the onslaught of experiential-based Christianity began, I believe another and perhaps more powerful and deceptive wave will come and sweep over the entire land. One observation I have made is that vast numbers of churches and denominations overcome by the Toronto Blessing and the Pensacola River have since lost biblical discernment altogether and have become totally inundated by other waves related to the church-growth phenomenon we will discuss later in this book.

We are living in perilous times, and perhaps you have asked yourself as I have done so many times: Who will stand up and warn of what is happening while there is still time?

13

A SECOND PENTECOST?

W e know from the words of Jesus Christ that Satan has an agenda to deceive the world in the name of Christ. The "god of this world" (2 Corinthians 4:3-4) is the master deceiver (Revelation 12:9). We also know as we approach the return of Jesus Christ, Satan's plan intensifies (Revelation 12:12). Countless more will be deceived by those who say they are coming in the name of Christ. While the Bible has warned us in advance, the Scriptures indicate deception will be so intense even an unknown percentage of Christians will be caught in the trap (Matthew 24:24). Whether we accept this warning is our choice, but to heed the warning is a positive step to avoid being caught in this web of deceit and is the very reason why Jesus warned his disciples.

In the last chapter, we dealt with an experienced-based Christianity associated with Protestant denominations. In this chapter, my goal is to show how both Catholics and Protestants together are being deceived by embracing what many are calling a "Second Pentecost." While both groups are convinced the Holy Spirit is leading and guiding them, there are a number of serious concerns we need to uncover.

What is this so-called "Second Pentecost" so many Protestants and Catholics are referencing? What about all the ideas and teachings associated with the charismatic movement that do not have a biblical basis? Could the New Wine/charismatic movement be one of the bridges preparing a deceived Christianity for the reintroduction of the religion of Babylon predicted in the Bible for the end times?

The Latter Rain Returns

Cyclical is biblical. What has happened in the past most surely will happen again. And regarding the teachings and the practices of the Latter Rain movement that was born in the late 1940s in Canada, this is exactly what has happened.

By June of 1949, the teachings and practices of the Latter Rain movement that originated in North Battleford, Saskatchewan, divided families, churches, and fellowships of believers. Eventually, some pastors and church leaders of various denominations were willing to stand up and express their concerns about the sectarian nature of this movement. One of them was Ernest Williams, General Superintendent of the Assemblies of God in the United States from 1929 to 1949. Dealing with some of the more controversial doctrines of the Latter Rain, he wrote an article that was published in the *Pentecostal Testimony*, an official publication of the Pentecostal Assemblies of Canada. The article states:

> Does it not look like a bold step to call people out of the congregation that they might, through prophecy and laying on of hands, have gifts and callings imparted to them? Others are named who hope to get to other foreign fields. If they get there, they cannot speak the language as they hope to do, raw recruits, what may they suffer? The decay of our bodies and the inroad of disease resulting from the same are not demonism. Think of going to a weakened, afflicted person, charging that the reason the person is sick is because he is possessed of some demon, then trying to name the demon and cast it out. This could

lead to accusing poor sick people of being possessed with all sorts of demons. Think of the mental reaction on the part of the sufferer.[1]

Williams was not alone in expressing these concerns about Latter Rain doctrine. In the fall of 1949, at the General Council Meeting of the Assemblies of God held in Seattle, Washington, the Council adopted a resolution disapproving the practices of what was termed "The New Order of the Latter Rain." According to the 1949 General Council Minutes, the following statement was read and approved:

> Whereas, we are grateful for the visitation of God in the past and the evidences of His blessings upon us today, and whereas, we recognize a hunger on the part of God's people for a spiritual refreshing and a manifestation of His Holy Spirit, be it therefore resolved, that we disapprove of those extreme teachings and practices, which, being, unfounded Scripturally, serve only to break fellowship of like precious faith and tend to confusion and division among the members of the Body of Christ, and it be hereby known that this 23rd General Council disapproves of the so-called "New Order of the Latter Rain,": (1) The overemphasis relative to imparting, identifying, bestowing or confirming of gifts by the laying on of hands or of prophecy. (2) The erroneous teaching that the Church is built on the foundation of present-day apostles and prophets. (3) The extreme teaching as advocated by the "New Order" regarding the confession of sin to man and deliverance as practiced, which claims prerogatives to human agency which belong only to Christ.[2]

While the resolution made by the General Council of the Assemblies of God had a major impact on the various Pentecostal denominations throughout North America, there were those who still carried the banner of the "New Order of the Latter Rain." These Latter Rain proponents remained active and dedicated to their cause. Many revival churches that had become visible in North America during the Latter Rain remained. Most of these churches were independent and autonomous and became mother churches spawning other smaller churches that carried on and propagated the Latter Rain teachings.

In addition, various beliefs and practices of the Latter Rain movement found their way into the Charismatic Renewal. It can also be documented that the eschatological views of the Latter Rain movement were adopted by charismatics throughout the world. One of the promoters of Latter Rain doctrine was J. Preston Eby of El Paso, Texas. Richard Riss, in his book *Latter Rain: The Latter Rain Movement of 1948 and the Mid-Twentieth Century Evangelical Awakening* mentions that men like Eby taught that the Latter Rain movement would one day be revived. In a Bible study series that was published in 1976, Eby wrote the following. Although the quote is long and somewhat difficult to follow, it is important to examine his end-times views carefully:

> In 1948—the very year that Israel became a nation—
> another great deluge fell from heaven, a mighty revival
> then called the "Latter Rain." In this Restoration Revival
> God did a work which far transcended the work started
> in the Pentecostal outpouring of more than 40 years
> before. All nine gifts of the Spirit, the five-fold ministries
> of apostles, prophets, evangelists, pastors and teachers,
> spiritual praise and worship, plus the end-time revelation
> of God's purpose to manifest His Sons, a glorious church,
> to bring in the kingdom of God, all of this and much more
> was restored among God's people. And now the great
> dealings of God; the purgings, the processings, depths of
> revelation, edification and strengthening, understanding
> of the ways of the Lord, faith in the promise, waiting
> upon the Lord, development of the nature and character
> of God—all of this is being laid upon a people who
> have received the fruit of that second great visitation of

God and thus they are being prepared for the coming *third outpouring* which shall finally bring the *fullness* a company of overcoming Sons of God who have come to the measure of the stature of the fullness of Christ to actually dethrone Satan, casting him out of the heavenlies, and finally binding him in the earthlies, bringing the hope of deliverance and life to all the families of the earth. This third great work of the Spirit shall usher a people into full redemption - free from the curse, sin, sickness, death and carnality.[3] (emphasis in original)

First, Eby's statement reveals the Latter Rain movement was still alive and well a quarter century after the Latter Rain doctrines were exposed. Second, this statement illustrates that the present New Wine movement is tied to the Latter Rain teachings that were born over sixty years ago. Third, this statement shows that charismatics today are still promoting the idea that empowered men and women (manifest sons of God) can and will implement a "Church Age." And finally, a prediction is made of a new outpouring of the Holy Spirit that is extremely interesting considering current ecumenical alliances between Catholics and Protestants.

Catholic Pentecostals

Some time ago, I was handed a book to read with the following title, *As By A New Pentecost: The Dramatic Beginning of the Catholic Charismatic Renewal.*[4] Throughout my life as a researcher, writer, and speaker, I have had many papers, magazines, and books placed in my hands that have later turned out to be significant. When I browsed through this book, I could hardly believe what I was reading. The very direction my research was headed was confirmed with each page.

My first response to the book happened quickly when I read the dedication page. The author, Patti Gallagher Mansfield, dedicated her book to "Mary, Spouse of the Holy Spirit, Mother of the Church."[5] The book was written to inform readers about the events surrounding the origin of the Catholic Charismatic Renewal known as the "Duquesne Weekend." In the introduction, Mansfield states:

> The retreat of February 17-19, 1967 . . . has come to be known around the world as the Duquesne Weekend. It is generally accepted as the beginning of the Charismatic Renewal in the Catholic Church. This was the first event at which a group of Catholics experienced the Baptism in the Spirit and the charismatic gifts. While there may have been Catholics who were baptized in the Spirit prior to the Duquesne Weekend, this retreat began a widespread movement of Catholic Charismatic Renewal throughout the United States and around the world.[6]

According to Cardinal Suenens who wrote the foreword for the book, the Duquesne Weekend defined and fixed a point in the history of the Catholic Church. He also states:

> [Gallagher Mansfield] links to the Baptism in the Spirit the name and spiritual maternity of Mary, thereby reminding us that Jesus Christ continues to be born mystically "of the Holy Spirit and of Mary" and that we should never separate what God has joined together.[7]

This Marian connection with a new outpouring of the Holy Spirit is called "the Second Pentecost." This idea was not entirely new to me. Several other sources I had been reading indicated the Marian Apparition movement, the Catholic Charismatic movement, and the Protestant Charismatic movement all find common ground in the "unity movement." While I will document this further, for now it will be sufficient to state that the information I gleaned from Patti Gallagher Mansfield's book only confirmed these suspicions.

In addition, I wondered if the Latter Rain movement that predicted the "Third Wave" was what Catholics were now calling the "Second Pentecost." This Third-Wave/Second-Pentecost connection needed to be investigated further. What other ties between the two

movements were there? Could it be possible that the Marian apparitions and manifestations of Jesus in the Eucharist occurring could
play a further ecumenical role? We will examine this in a later section.

The Pope's Prayer

While Cardinal Suenens and Patti Gallagher Mansfield both
saw the Duquesne Weekend as instrumental in launching the
Catholic Charismatic movement, there is evidence the groundwork
had been laid several years before. Many who consider February 1967
as the moment the Catholic Charismatic Renewal was initiated at the
Duquesne Weekend also admit that the prayer of Pope John XXIII at
the beginning of the Second Vatican Council was significant. They
see the Catholic Charismatic Renewal as a providential answer to
the pope's prayer when he called for a new Pentecost in 1961. This
prayer states:

> Renew Your wonders in this our day, as by a new
> Pentecost. Grant to Your Church that, being of one
> mind and steadfast in prayer with Mary, the mother of
> Jesus, and following the lead of the blessed Peter, it may
> advance the reign of our Divine Savior, the reign of truth
> and justice, the reign of love and peace. Amen.[8]

Patti Gallagher Mansfield's book provides further insights into
the Catholic Charismatic movement. Apparently, Pope John XXIII
was strongly influenced by charismatic experiences he had when he
visited a small village in Czechoslovakia before he was chosen to
be pope. Anna Maria Schmidt, a former citizen of this village, told
Mansfield about the origins of the Catholic Charismatic movement
that occurred there in the eleventh century. Mansfield explains:

> [A] beautiful lady, who did not identify herself, appeared
> on the mountain and taught them how to implore the
> Holy Spirit. As they followed her instructions, they were
> all filled with the Spirit and received charismatic gifts,

such as discerning of spirits, prophecy, and the gift of tongues.[9]

Mansfield also suggested that Pope John XXIII was "influenced to pray for a new Pentecost" by Elena Guerra, a woman he called "the Apostle of the Holy Spirit." Sister Elena Guerra was the foundress of the Oblate Sisters of the Holy Spirit in Lucca, Italy. When she was fifty years old, she was "inspired to write to Pope Leo XIII urging him to renew the [Catholic] Church through a return to the Holy Spirit." Elena wrote "twelve confidential letters" to the "Holy Father" "between 1895 and 1903 calling for renewed preaching on the Holy Spirit." At Elena's suggestion, Pope Leo XIII "invoked the Holy Spirit on January 1, 1901."[10]

Finally, Mansfield sheds light on an interesting connection between the Catholic Charismatic movement and the Protestant Charismatic movement. She states:

> On the same day [January 1, 1901], an event took place in Topeka, Kansas, that marked the beginning of a great revival in the power and gifts of the Holy Spirit destined to sweep throughout this country and around the world.
>
> In Topeka, at 17th and Stone Avenue, (now the site of Most Pure Heart of Mary Catholic Church), stood a huge three-story, thirty room mansion. It was nicknamed "Stone's Folly" after the builder, Erastus Stone, discovered he could not afford to live in it. The mansion then became the home of the Bethel College and Bible School in September 1900. Rev. Charles Fox Parham and his students dedicated themselves to prayer and the study of God's Word concerning the Baptism in the Holy Spirit. In fact, the highest of the three towers in the mansion was designated as a prayer tower, and a marathon prayer vigil was organized. Twenty-four hours a day, seven days a week, these young people were asking God to baptize one or all of them in the Holy Spirit. . . .

At about 11:00 on the evening of January 1, 1901, one of the students named Agnes Ozman asked Rev. Parham to lay his hands on her head and pray that she would receive the Baptism in the Holy Spirit. That's precisely what happened. Agnes began to speak in tongues and others at the school, including Rev. Parham, had the same experience in the following days. This event is generally accepted as the beginning of Pentecostalism. . . . In 1906, a continued outpouring of the Holy Spirit occurred in Los Angeles, and is commonly referred to as the Azusa Street Revival.[11]

An additional explanation of what happened in Topeka, Kansas at the dawn of the twentieth century has also been written by Robert A. Larden in his book titled *Our Apostolic Heritage*.[12] In this book documenting the official history of the Apostolic Church of Pentecost of Canada, Larden explains how the Pentecostal doctrine of speaking in tongues was established. This doctrine claims that the evidence of one having received the "Baptism of the Holy Spirit" is speaking in tongues. He explains:

One of those who sought God for a more effective witness was Charles Fox Parham. Raised in the Congregational Church, [he] later joined the Methodists. He then associated with the revival movement which eventually separated from the Methodist body called the Holiness Movement. Charles Parham believed that while many obtained real sanctification—there still remained a great outpouring of power for Christians. In the year 1900 Charles Parham opened a Bible School in an abandoned mansion in Topeka, Kansas. Forty students gathered. Twelve ministers were among the men and women that gathered to study God's Word. The prime interest was in the Book of Acts. Parham had a speaking engagement in December of that year and instructed the students to search the book of Acts in private study for any distinctive evidence that was consistently associated with the baptism of the Holy Ghost in the early church. On his return the students were unanimous in their conviction that in each case where the baptism of the Holy Ghost was first received the evidence was "speaking in tongues."[13]

It is obvious from this account of the events leading up to the January 1901 occurrences in Topeka, Kansas, that it had already been determined speaking in tongues was not just "a" sign that someone had been filled with the Holy Spirit—it was "the" sign that must be sought. To this day, numerous Pentecostal denominations insist that speaking in tongues is "the" evidence and the "prerequisite" evidence for the baptism of the Holy Spirit.

Robert Larden's book also provides an interesting historical account that connects Charles Parham of the Topeka, Kansas group with the Azusa Revival that originated in Los Angeles, California in the early 1900s. Larden writes:

> Charles Parham never compromised his conviction in regard to revealed truth and the validity of his experience with God. A second Bible School was opened in Houston, Texas in 1905. Among the student body was one called William Seymour.[14]

William Seymour played a significant role in the Azusa Street Revival. Seymour was an ordained minister with the Holiness movement. He received an invitation to be an associate pastor of a Nazarene church in Los Angeles after the close of the Bible school that was conducted by Parham in Houston, Texas. Larden sheds further light on Seymour:

> It is said by some that he accepted the message of the baptism of the Holy Ghost with the evidence of speaking in other tongues, but had not experienced it personally when he arrived to take up his assignment. Plans were for him to speak nightly in a series of meetings and continue

as associate pastor. For his first message at the Nazarene Church he read his text from Acts 2:4, "And they were [all] filled with the Holy Ghost, and began to speak with other tongues as the Spirit gave them utterance." He emphasized the conviction that had come to them at the school in Houston and the confirmation God gave when the greater part of the student body and Brother Parham had received the Holy Ghost baptism with the same evidence as those in the upper room recorded in Acts chapter 2.[15]

Seymour's message was not acceptable to the leaders of the Nazarene church, and he was locked out of the church. One of the members of the congregation, who was an adherent of Seymour, invited him to hold a service in her home. Larden writes:

It was in that home on Bonnie Brae Street on April 9th, 1906 that seven people received the baptism of the Holy Ghost with the evidence of speaking in tongues. The joy of the Lord filled the house. They laughed and shouted, sang and worshipped the Lord all night. The word got around and early the next morning a crowd was gathering, not all could get in. They sought for a larger meeting place and acquired the rent of an old building at 312 Azusa Street. It had one time been a Methodist Church but had been out of use for many years. Old lumber and debris littered the place. They cleaned it out and swept out the accumulated dirt. Planks were acquired and placed on top of empty nail kegs to provide seating for about thirty people. There were about twelve people at that first meeting. With no instruments to lead the singing and no hymn books they worshipped God. Familiar hymns were sung by memory. One of the most common was "The Comforter Has Come." That night two more received the baptism and spoke in tongues. A little flame was lit that was destined to sweep across a nation and envelop the world.[16]

Charismatic Unity

If there are some factors indicating that the Catholic Charismatic movement and the Protestant Charismatic movement were joined together at birth January 1, 1901, then what has happened since? Over 100 years have passed by. Is it possible to examine the two different movements today, compare them, and see whether "what has been joined together" can still be found at least somewhat united?

The answer to these questions can be documented. For example, in *Charisma*, February 1995, we read that a revival that was supposedly happening in Britain was characterized by laughing and spiritual drunkenness. These kinds of experiences united Anglicans, Methodists, Pentecostals, Baptists, and Catholics.[17] Experience-based Christianity has been uniting all denominations including Protestants and Catholics worldwide. Although there is no biblical basis for this kind of human behavior, advocates of an experience-based Christianity believe it is "just people responding to God."[18]

Or consider what took place during the evening sessions at the Orlando 95 Conference, as Catholic and Protestant Charismatics abandoned their differences and worshipped together:

> Haitian Catholics danced conga-style in the aisles singing wildly in Creole. Robed monks and nuns skipped in the aisles along with Pentecostals, Methodists, Mennonites and Episcopalians. Others praised God by dancing around the convention center waving open umbrellas—perhaps to signify that the invisible rain of the Holy Spirit was falling.[19]

The Orlando 95 Conference was addressed by several key leaders, all enthusiastic about this ecumenical gathering. These included Catholic Bishop Sam Jacobs, healing evangelist Benny Hinn, and Pentecostal Bishop Gilbert Patterson. Each speaker urged churches to work together. John Buckley, a Catholic priest from Tampa, Florida, said the conference had broken down walls of prejudice between believers. "This is the greatest ecumenical movement in the Christian church," he said.[20]

Charismatic Ecumenism?

In 1985, a group of charismatic leaders got together and created the North American Renewal Service Committee (NARSC), an ecumenical entity made up of Catholic and Protestant Charismatics. The NARSC was responsible for organizing conferences on "the Holy Spirit and World Evangelism" in various cities.

"Celebrate Jesus 2000," also sponsored by the North American Renewal Service Committee, was held in St. Louis Missouri, June 22-25, 2000. This millennial conference was administered by the Franciscan University of Steubenville, Ohio, the Catholic university that had a significant influence in persuading Promise Keepers to reword their statement of faith to include Roman Catholics.[21]

The "Celebrate Jesus Conference" was advertised as "the millennium party you won't want to miss."[22] Among the 47 speakers invited to participate in the conference were John Arnott, Toronto Airport Christian Fellowship; Father Tom Forest, International Director of Evangelization 2000; Father Stan Fortuna, Evangelist, Franciscan Friars of the Renewal; Jack Hayford, The Church on the Way, Van Nuys, California; Steve Hill, Together in Harvest Ministries; Cindy Jacobs, President and Co-founder, Generals of Intercession; Bishop Sam Jacobs, Roman Catholic Diocese of Alexandria, Louisiana; John Kilpatrick, Brownsville, Assemblies of God, Pensacola, Florida; Rick Joyner, Morning Star Ministries, Moravian Falls, North Carolina; Sister Briege McKenna, International Healing Ministry; Richard Roberts, President, Oral Roberts University; Father Michael Scanlan, President, Franciscan University of Steubenville, Ohio; and Thomas Trask, former General Superintendent of the Assemblies of God.[23]

According to promoters of the conference, "the streams of Christianity are gathering" to become the "River." A promotional brochure stated:

> Join us in St. Louis June 22-25 as thousands of Christians from every stream and tradition honor the 2000th

113

anniversary of the birth of our Savior at the Celebrate Jesus 2000 Congress.

This conference promises to be the setting for powerful revival. Gifted speakers and uplifting worship will fill you anew with the living water of the Holy Spirit. International workshops and sessions will give you the tools you need to live out your faith. Fellowship among both Catholic and Protestant will foster mutual respect and remind [us] that Christ died for all. Without a doubt, you'll be prepared to "open wide the doors to Christ" in the third millennium.[24]

While the list of speakers at the "Celebrate Jesus 2000" conference looked like the "who's who" of charismatic Christianity, there is reason to believe that Steubenville administrators may have stacked the deck with fellow Catholics who have a purely Roman Catholic view of what it means to be a Christian. One of the "Celebrate Jesus 2000" speakers, Father Tom Forrest, the Vatican's representative for "Evangelization 2000," is a staunch promoter of the Catholic agenda to lure the "separated brethren" back to the "Mother of All Churches." At a special session for Catholics held at the Indianapolis conference in 1990, he went on record stating:

> Our job is to make people as richly and as fully Christian as we can make them by bringing them into the Catholic Church. So evangelization is never fully successful, it's only partial, until the convert is made a member of Christ's body by being led into the [Catholic] church.

> No, you don't just invite someone to become a Christian, you invite them to become Catholics. Why would this be so important? First of all, there are seven sacraments, and the Catholic Church has all seven. On our altars we have the body of Christ; we drink the blood of Christ. Jesus

is alive on our altars . . . We become one with Christ in the Eucharist . . .

As Catholics we have Mary, and that Mom of ours, Queen of Paradise, is praying for us till she sees us in glory.

As Catholics we have the papacy, a history of popes from Peter to John Paul II . . . we have the rock upon which Christ did build His Church.

Now as Catholics—now I love this one—we have purgatory. Thank God! I'm one of those people who would never get to the Beatific Vision without it. It's the only way to go. . . .

So as Catholics . . . our job is to use the remaining decade evangelizing everyone we can in the Catholic Church, into the body of Christ and into the third millennium of Catholic history.[25]

Will the "streams" of Christianity that were destined to form the "river" in St Louis in 2000 form a river that will flow toward Rome? Has Father Tom Forest changed his views about what it means to be a Christian since his dissertation to Catholics in 1990, or have Protestants been deluded into believing that the Catholic gospel has changed and is now compatible to the biblical Gospel?

The Alpha Factor

"Roman Catholic bishops applaud Alpha as course spreads through church."[26] This was the front-page headline I read in an article in the *Alpha News*. The subheading stated, "Cardinal Archbishop opens New Zealand conference." According to the article, an increasing number of Roman Catholic churches are using the Alpha Course. As well, many Catholic bishops and church leaders are giving the course their blessing, among them Cardinal Thomas Williams, the former Roman Catholic Archbishop of Wellington. More than 450 people packed London's Westminster Cathedral Hall in May of 1997 for the first Roman Catholic Alpha conference. Sandy Miller and Nicky Gumbel of Holy Trinity Brompton led the conference, which had received messages of encouragement from Cardinal Hume, the former Archbishop of Westminster.[27]

The late Bishop Ambrose Griffiths introduced the conference. He stated that the Alpha Course is a "powerful evangelistic tool which reaches out precisely to those whom we need." He also said the conference was very important ecumenically. "We should have the humility to learn from other Christians, and I am delighted that we are doing this today," he said.[28]

Explaining why Catholics can easily accept the Alpha Course, he further stated:

> It is not a complete exposition of Catholic doctrine. No introductory course could possibly do that. But it does not contain anything that is contrary to Catholic doctrine.[29]

In addition, he said:

> What's more, it provides in a wonderful form the basis of Christian belief which many Catholics have never cottoned up to. They have been sacramentalised, but never have been evangelized.[30]

After the conference, which included a seminar on how to run an Alpha Course in Catholic context, many delegates expressed excitement and delight at what they had heard. One delegate wrote, "This is an awesome and historic moment in the history of the Church."[31]

In Mary Danielsen and Chris Lawson's 2016 booklet, *The Alpha Course: An Evangelical Contradiction*, the authors state the following about the background of the Alpha Course leader, Nicky Gumbel:

> An important development in the historical background of Alpha's creators is that [Holy Trinity Brompton] HTB Church became the center of the "holy laughter"

movement for England and Europe in the 1990s. Eleanor Mumford, along with her husband John, carried the Vineyard movement to the UK (with grudging approval from Vineyard founder John Wimber[32]), visited the Toronto Airport Vineyard Church in Ontario in 1994, and brought back the experiences she had there. Nicky Gumbel attended a meeting in a home in May 1994 where Mumford told of her experiences in Toronto and "invited the Holy Spirit to come."

The moment she did that, strange things began to happen. One person was thrown across the room and did lie on the floor howling and laughing, "making the most incredible noise." Another man was lying on the floor "prophesying." Some appeared to be drunk. Gumbel testified that he had an experience "like massive electricity going through my body."[33]) Gumbel got himself together and rushed to a meeting at Holy Trinity Brompton. . . .When he closed that meeting with prayer and said, "Lord, thank you so much for all you are doing, and we pray you'll send your Spirit," the same strange phenomenon were again manifested. One of those present lying on the floor with his feet in the air started "laughing like a hyena." . . .

Since the Anglican Church has so much in common with the Roman Catholic Church, we have to wonder how evangelicals got the impression that the Alpha Course is compatible with Protestant/evangelical Christianity.

In the following two quotes, we can see Gumbel's acceptance and promotion of Roman Catholicism and the Catholic papacy:

"It was a great honor to be presented to Pope John Paul II, who has done so much to promote evangelism around the world. We have been enormously enriched by our interaction with Catholics in many countries."[34]

"Probably one of the strongest movements of the Holy Spirit is in the Roman Catholic Church, so there's not a huge theological difference between the official teaching of the Catholic Church and the Anglican Church, for example."[35]

For those wanting to more fully understand where the Alpha Course is taking the church, I would encourage you to read Danielsen and Lawson's booklet.[36]

Mary and the Holy Spirit

While Protestants and Catholics seem to be finding a unity centered around the "gifts of the Holy Spirit," there may be reason to be cautious, especially if you have researched the literature regarding the origins of the Catholic Charismatic movement. True Christian unity must always be centered on the finished work accomplished by Jesus' death on the Cross. The Gospel is based upon the birth, death, and resurrection of Jesus, not experiences such as speaking in tongues or being slain in the Spirit.

According to several statements made by Patti Gallagher Mansfield in her book *As By A New Pentecost,* Mary, the mother of Jesus, is the one who played a key role in the dispensation of the Holy Spirit at the "dramatic beginning of the Catholic Charismatic Renewal" at the Duquesne Weekend in Pittsburgh, February 17-19, 1967. While Jesus is mentioned from time to time in this book, a clear biblical presentation of the Gospel is absent. If a non-believer were to read the book, he or she could only assume that a "Pentecostal experience" was the essence of being a Christian. As the book is dedicated to Mary and as there are many examples of the adoration of Mary in the book, one must wonder if the Catholic Charismatic movement is more centered on Mary than it is on the Gospel of Jesus Christ. For example, regarding the Friday evening opening meeting, Patti Gallagher Mansfield states:

I believe it was significant to have our attention drawn to Mary at the beginning of our retreat. She was there at the Annunciation when the Word became flesh. She was there at the Nativity to bring forth Jesus to the world. She was there at the Cross when our redemption was won. She was there at Pentecost when the Church was born. In God's plan, it was necessary for Mary to be "*with us*" in an explicit way as we experienced a sovereign move of the Holy Spirit that Weekend. The Fathers of the Church call Mary "*the Spouse of the Holy Spirit.*" How can she fail to be present when the Holy Spirit is at work?[37]

Later that evening, Mansfield went to the chapel where she had what she describes as a supernatural experience. She states, "I knelt down too in the presence of Jesus in the Blessed Sacrament [the Eucharist]. Then something happened I wasn't expecting."[38] She continues:

I'd always believed by the gift of faith that Jesus is really present in the Blessed Sacrament, but I had never experienced His glory before. As I knelt there that night, my body literally trembled before His majesty and holiness. I was filled with awe in His presence. He was there . . . the King of Kings, the Lord of Lords, the Great God of the Universe![39]

Mansfield then begins to pray a prayer of unconditional surrender. As she knelt before the altar, she found herself prostrate, flat on her face. No one had laid hands on her. She had never had such an experience before.[40]

Later two girls who were also at the retreat, when they saw her, noticed something physically different about her appearance. Taking each of these girls by the hand, she led them into the chapel. Writing about this experience, Mansfield states:

> The three of us knelt before the Lord in the Blessed
> Sacrament, and I began to pray out loud. I didn't have the
> correct terminology; I just prayed from my heart. "*Lord
> whatever you just did for me, do it for them!*" I was asking
> the Lord to baptize them in the Holy Spirit without even
> realizing it.[41]

These statements certainly sound like the words of a genuinely
sincere person who wants to experience a closer walk with her Lord
and Savior, Jesus Christ. While Protestant Charismatics use the same
terminology when describing their experiences, there is one major
difference that needs to be pointed out. Protestants reject the idea
that Jesus is present in the Eucharist. They believe He lives in the
hearts of those who call upon His name and put their trust in Him for
salvation by grace through faith. The idea that a priest has the power
to change a piece of bread or a wafer into the actual body of Christ
is called transubstantiation. The faith to believe that this happens is
a Catholic Church dogma and has no biblical basis.

Patti Gallagher Mansfield has a theory on what she believes is
happening which fits well into the context of this book. She states:

> I don't pretend to understand it fully, but I believe the
> Lord is preparing His people for a new wave of the
> Holy Spirit. Fr. George Kosicki, C.S.B., and Fr. Gerald
> Farrell, M.M. have written an insightful book about this
> new wave of the Spirit entitled *The Spirit and the Bride
> Say "Come."* In this book they discuss the role of Mary
> in the new Pentecost. My own understanding of what
> God is calling for has been deeply influenced by their
> reflections.[42]

In the conclusion of her book, Mansfield makes a number of
statements that further reveal her understanding of the new Pentecost's focus on devotion to Mary. Speaking on behalf of Catholics,
she says:

We Catholics see in this scene a call to entrust ourselves to Mary's motherly care, to welcome her as one of the precious gifts Jesus has given us, and to ask for her powerful intercession. Just as at Cana Mary spoke to Jesus on behalf of those in need, we believe that she continues to intercede for the Church today.[43]

Then in this final statement, she explains that to be faithful to the Lord and prepare for the Second Pentecost, we need to look to "Mary" as our spiritual "Mother." Mansfield says:

To whatever measure I have been faithful to the Lord, it has been thanks to her example and to her prayer. I believe that an important element in preparing for a fresh outpouring of the Holy Spirit is our relationship with Mary as Mother.[44]

What Is This Second Pentecost?

Catholic Charismatics and Protestant Charismatics focus on the Holy Spirit. We know that the Bible is full of references to the Holy Spirit, but the Holy Spirit is a person and not a mystical force that can be invoked or manipulated. As well, while there was a Day of Pentecost that occurred as recorded in the Book of Acts, what is the biblical basis for proclaiming there is a second Pentecost? Jesus said that after He departed, the Holy Spirit would come and be with believers as the Comforter. The New Testament teaches that the Holy Spirit is with us and will continue to be with us until Jesus comes for His Church (John 14:16).

The idea there must be a special outpouring called a "Second Pentecost" or a "Third Wave" that will draw the masses to Jesus at the end of time is not biblical. If this idea is not biblical, then what is the source? Could this be a major seduction of Christianity? Are people being deceived in the name of Christ?

Consider the following messages from the "Blessed Virgin Mary" to Father Don Stefano Gobbi, the former head of the Marian Movement of Priests in the United States. He received hundreds of messages from a supernatural apparition who called itself "Mary." These messages are recorded and disseminated to 400 plus cardinals and bishops, more than 100,000 priests, and millions of religious and "faithful" around the world. Consider the following Marian messages which are contained in the book titled, *To the Priests, Our Lady's Beloved Sons*[45]:

> Enter, all of you, into the new and spiritual cenacle of my Immaculate Heart to recollect yourselves in an intense and incessant prayer made with me, your heavenly Mother, in expectation that the great miracle of the Second Pentecost, now close at hand, will be accomplished.[46]

> With an extraordinary cenacle of prayer and fraternity, you celebrate today the solemnity of Pentecost. You recall the prodigious event of the descent of the Holy Spirit, under the form of tongues of fire, upon the Cenacle of Jerusalem, where the Apostles were gathered in prayer, with me, your heavenly Mother. You too, gathered today in prayer in the spiritual cenacle of my Immaculate Heart, prepare yourselves to receive the prodigious gift of the Second Pentecost.[47]

The apparition of Mary not only predicts that she will usher in the Second Pentecost, but she also anticipates that full unity under the Catholic Church will also be achieved during this era:

> The Second Pentecost will come to lead all the Church to the summit of her greatest splendor. . . . Above all, the Holy Spirit will communicate to the Church the precious gift of her full unity and of her greatest holiness. Only then will Jesus bring into her his reign of glory.[48]

I am for you the way of unity. When I am accepted by the whole Church, then, as a Mother, I will be able to reunite my children in the warmth of one single family. For this reason, the reunion of all Christians in the Catholic Church will coincide with the triumph of my Immaculate Heart in the world. This reunited Church, in the splendor of a new Pentecost, will have the power to renew all the people of the earth.[49]

A true reunification of Christians is not possible unless it be in the perfection of truth. And truth has been kept intact only in the Catholic Church, which must preserve it, defend it and proclaim it to all without fear. It is the light of the truth which will draw many of my children to return to the bosom of the one and only Church founded by Jesus.[50]

In April of 2014, *Charisma Magazine* published an article titled "Spirit-Empowered Believers Praying for Second Pentecostal Outpouring." Charismatics came together in Jerusalem, Israel with other charismatics from around the world to pray for a second Pentecost. The article stated:

Could the world experience a second Pentecost? That's the hope of a global movement called Empowered 21, with organizers setting their sights on Jerusalem, where the first Pentecost took place. . . . "It's amazing to see how many wonderful leaders God has raised up to partner with this goal of seeing every individual touched by a real encounter with the Holy Spirit by the year 2033. It's stunning," Bill Johnson, from Bethel Church, said. Oral Roberts University President Billy Wilson, director of E21, spoke at a recent event for global movement. . . .

"Our big, big vision is bigger than all of us. It comes out of Habakkuk 2:14 that the knowledge of the glory of the Lord will cover the earth as the waters cover the sea. And the big vision is that every person on earth will have an authentic encounter with Jesus Christ through the power and presence of the Holy Spirit by Pentecost 2033," he continued.[51]

If we study Scripture, we know that this scenario is not going to happen before Christ returns. What the Bible does foretell is that in the end, Satan is going to deceive the whole world, and the world will come under the spell of the Antichrist who will demand that every person on Earth worship him.

Catholic Charismatics and Protestant Charismatics are embracing a unity based on common supernatural experiences, which are supposedly manifestations of the Spirit of God. While this chapter has dealt with some of the background behind the charismatic unification of Catholics and Protestants in the past, the trend continues at a rapid pace today. If you have not been following this trend, the next chapter will shed light on what is happening.

14

ANOTHER SPIRIT

aul's message to the church at Corinth which warned about being deceived by another spirit for another gospel and another Jesus should be very sobering for the church today. This principle remains the same. Nothing has changed. Later in the same chapter to the Corinthians, Paul explained how and why this happened:

> For such are false apostles, deceitful workers, transforming themselves into the apostles of Christ. And no marvel; for Satan himself is transformed into an angel of light. (2 Corinthians 11:13-14)

Obviously, this deception that had occurred was because shepherds who were supposedly leading their flocks in the name of Christ and claimed they were apostles of Christ were actually following Lucifer, the fallen angel also called the light bearer. While their message *seemed* to be right, it was spiritually lethal. People were being led to Hell rather than to an eternal destiny with the Jesus defined by biblical parameters.

This chapter is about events underway today happening in the name of Christ and the "Holy Spirit" that may sound good but may well be another trap set by Satan to lead the unsuspecting sheep away from the truth. First, let me make it clear it is not my intention to bash anyone or any group of believers. Nor am I writing this chapter as a person who does not believe in the work of the Holy Spirit in the believer's life or believes the Holy Spirit is not active in the church today. My concern is that just like the church at Corinth was deceived by the serpent and did not know it, so too many are deceived today into believing they are agents of truth when they are part of the deception authored by the god of this world.

It is obvious to me that my words written here will upset some to the point they will refuse to read further. However, based on the evidence presented, I challenge those who are upset to read further. The Bible teaches it is possible to believe one is "Spirit led" when instead he has fallen for a strong delusion. It is biblical to test the spirits to see if what we are following is from God or the devil (1 John 4:1).

In the last chapter, we documented examples of deception in the name of the Holy Spirit. The victims are convinced they are truly led by the Spirit when they are actually led by "another spirit" because they have not tested the spirits.

Purpose of Vatican II

A good place to start is by looking at a brief overview of one of the main objectives of Vatican II when the Roman Catholic Church established new ground rules during the early and mid '60s. Quoting a Roman Catholic source:

> The Second Vatican Council was summoned by Pope John XXIII, convening in four sessions each year from 1962 to 1965. It was his desire that the Church be brought up to date and adapt itself to meet the challenging conditions of modern times. Generally, Vatican II was an overhaul of the way the Church conducted itself and celebrated the liturgy, so that she would be more accessible to the people. Therefore, the subject was not just any given element of the Church, but rather the entire Church, period. This was no small undertaking, and by the time it was over,

it spawned four Constitutions, nine Decrees, and three Declarations. The Council was closed on December 8th, 1965 by Pope Paul VI, who had guided the council through its final three sessions.[1]

A main part of this Roman Catholic upgrade is summarized in the same source. In a section titled Vatican II: A Walk-Through-Decree on Ecumenism, several goals and objectives were listed for the purpose of bringing about unity in the name of Christ. We read:

1. All who have been "justified by faith in baptism" are members of the Body of Christ; they all have the right to be called Christian; the children of the Catholic Church accept them as brothers.

2. The Catholic Church believes that the separated Churches and communities "are efficient in some respects." But the Holy Ghost makes use of these Churches; they are means of salvation to their members.

3. Catholics are encouraged to join in ecumenical activity, and to meet non-Catholic Christians in truth and love. The task of "ecumenical dialogue" belongs to theologians, competent authorities representing different Churches.

4. Catholics should not ignore their duty to other Christians—they should make the first approach. Even so, the primary duty of the Church at the present time is to discover what must be done within the Catholic Church itself; to renew itself, to put its own house in order. Catholics sincerely believe that theirs is the Church of Christ; *everything necessary must be done that others also may clearly recognize it as Christ's Church.*(emphasis added)

5. The ecumenical movement can make no progress without a real change of heart. Theologians and other competent Catholics should study the history, teaching and liturgy of separated Churches. All Christians have a common purpose—to confess Christ before men. Practical expression must be given to this, by

relieving the distress which afflicts so many of the human race: famine, poverty, illiteracy, the unequal distribution of wealth, housing shortage [*my comment:* What is being said here is that rather than just proclaiming Christ, we must demonstrate Christianity through our good deeds. There is some truth to this, but the Bible declares that people are saved through "the foolishness of preaching" (1 Corinthians 1:21), while good deeds in and of themselves will save no one. This is why it is so important that the Gospel that is preached is true according to Scripture.]

6. In appropriate circumstances prayers for unity should be recited jointly with non-Catholic Christians. Catholics are to be directed in this by their bishops, subject to the decisions of the Holy See.

7. Between the Catholic Church and Western non-Catholic Christian communities, important differences remain; these differences are most evident in the interpretation of truth revealed by God. But the bonds of unity are already strong; their strength must be put to use. The bonds are, chiefly, the fact that Christians believe in the divinity of Christ and the fact of reverence for God's word revealed in the Bible.

8. In the cause of ecumenism, the Catholic must always remain true to the [Catholic] Faith that he has received. Impudent zeal in this matter is a hindrance to unity and not a help. So also is any attempt to achieve a merely superficial unity.[2]

A lot of things have happened in the Roman Catholic Church focused on the new emphasis to unite. For example, on April 17, 2013, an article was posted by the *Catholic News Agency* titled "Rejecting Holy Spirit's Work in Vatican II is 'Foolish,' Pope Says." Quoting from the article, we read:

> The work of the Holy Spirit at the Second Vatican Council is not yet finished, Pope Francis said, because many in the

Church are unwilling to fully embrace what God inspired in the council fathers.

In his homily at an April 16 Mass at St. Martha's Residence, the Pope observed that the Holy Spirit always "moves us, makes us walk and pushes the Church forward." However, he said, we often respond by saying, "Don't bother us."[3]

Bringing this up to date, an article titled "Pope Greets Members of the Renewal of the Spirit" provides clear insight as to how Pope Francis plans to move Vatican II forward. We read:

In his prayer at the beginning of the Audience, Pope Francis prayed that God the Father might send the Holy Spirit, Who will guide us to unity. It is the Holy Spirit, he said, who gives the various charisms within the Church, who works through the variety of gifts in the Church, and who grants unity. Pope Francis asked that Jesus, who prayed for unity in His Church, might help us to walk along the path of "unity, or of reconciled diversity."

In his address, which he delivered "off-the-cuff," the Holy Father reminded the members of the Renewal of the Holy Spirit of the words of Cardinal Leo Joseph Suenens, who called the charismatic renewal a "stream of grace." The current of grace, he said, must always flow into the ocean of God, the love of God, and must not be turned in on itself.[4]

As explained in the previous chapter, the trend for Roman Catholic Charismatics to join together with charismatics from other "streams" of faith has been going on for some time. However, as time goes by, it is becoming clearer that the streams or tributaries are now joining together to become a wide and fast-flowing river.

Tony Palmer and His Home to Rome

While many books were published in the past number of years giving testimony of those who converted from former Protestant backgrounds to Roman Catholicism, until recently not many well-known Protestant leaders have made special trips to Rome to meet with the pope. However, that has now changed. Numerous articles can be quoted proving my point. I will give one example. In an article posted in *Charisma News* and written by Rick Wiles titled "Why Did Copeland, Robison Meet With Pope Francis?," we read the following (used with permission):

> Two prominent Fort Worth-based Christian ministers led a delegation of Evangelical Christian leaders to Rome to meet privately with Pope Francis. James and Betty Robison, co-hosts of the *Life Today* television program, and Kenneth Copeland, co-host of *Believer's Voice of Victory*, met the Roman Pontiff at the Vatican on Tuesday. The meeting lasted almost three hours and included a private luncheon with Pope Francis.
>
> Mr. Robison told the *Fort Worth Star Telegram*, "This meeting was a miracle. . . . This is something God has done. God wants his arms around the world. And he wants Christians to put his arms around the world by working together."
>
> Mr. Robison said he was impressed by Pope Francis' humility and courtesy to the visiting delegation of Evangelical Protestant Christian leaders. In a written statement, Mr. Robison said he believes "the prayers of earnest Christians helped lead to the choice of Pope Francis." He described Jorge Mario Bergoglio, the Argentine Archbishop chosen as Pope, as "a humble man . . . filled with such love for the poor, downtrodden." . . .

The ecumenical meeting in Rome was organized by Episcopal Bishop Tony Palmer. Rev. Palmer is an ordained bishop in the Communion of Evangelical Episcopal Churches, a break-away alliance of charismatic Anglican-Episcopal churches. Bishop Palmer is also the Director of The Ark Community, an international interdenominational Convergent Church online community, and is a member of the Roman Catholic Ecumenical Delegation for Christian Unity and Reconciliation.

———◆———

THIS MEETING [WITH POPE FRANCIS] WAS A MIRACLE. . . . THIS IS SOMETHING GOD HAS DONE. GOD WANTS HIS ARMS AROUND THE WORLD. AND HE WANTS CHRISTIANS TO PUT HIS ARMS AROUND THE WORLD BY WORKING TOGETHER.—JAMES ROBISON

———◆———

Bishop Palmer developed a friendship with Pope Francis when the future Roman Pontiff was a Catholic official in Argentina. Prior to becoming a CEEC bishop, Rev. Palmer was the director of the Kenneth Copeland Ministries' office in South Africa. He is married to an Italian Roman Catholic woman. He later moved to Italy and began working to reconcile Roman Catholics and Protestants. Kenneth Copeland Ministries was one of Mr.

Palmer's first financial contributors over 10 years ago in support of his ecumenical work in Italy.

Earlier this year, Pope Francis called Bishop Palmer to invite him to his residence in Vatican City. During the meeting, Bishop Palmer suggested that the Pope record a personal greeting on Mr. Palmer's iPhone to be delivered to Kenneth Copeland. Mr. Copeland showed the Papal video greeting to a conference of Protestant ministers who were meeting at Mr. Copeland's Eagle Mountain International Church near Fort Worth, Texas. In the video, Pope Francis expressed his desire for Christian unity with Protestants.

Later, James Robison telecasted the video on his daily TV program, *Life Today*. "The pope, in the video, expressed

POPE FRANCIS ADDRESSING U.S. CONGRESS ON SEPTEMBER 24, 2015 IN WASHINGTON DC

a desire for Protestants and Catholics to become what Jesus prayed for—that Christians would become family and not be divided." Mr. Robison said the response to the video was very positive, and that Pope Francis asked Bishop Palmer whether a meeting could be arranged with Evangelical Protestants seeking Christian unity in the world.[5]

A few weeks after the meeting at the Vatican, Tony Palmer was killed in a motorcycle accident in England. However, the message he brought from Pope Francis to the Copeland Conference referred to in the *Charisma* article lives on. If you have Internet access, I would encourage you to watch the message and the response to the message at the Copeland conference.[6]

When Tony Palmer spoke at Kenneth Copeland's conference, he declared that the Reformation is over and has been over for the last fifteen years. While those who attended Copeland's conference (along with Copeland himself) praised and prayed for Pope Francis, the Roman Catholic Church, and former Protestants to become one, some serious problems were lurking in the background.

How can genuine Christians have unity with Pope Francis, head of the Roman Catholic Church who has now called for unity of all religions? This is not something that has been made up. It is a well-documented fact. For example, in an article titled, "In First Prayer Video, Pope Stresses Interfaith Unity: 'We are all children of God," heretical claims are being made for the sake of unity. The article states:

> The Pope's first-ever video message on his monthly prayer intentions was released Tuesday, highlighting the importance of interreligious dialogue and the beliefs different faith traditions hold in common, such as the figure of God and love.
>
> "Many think differently, feel differently, seeking God or meeting God in different ways. In this crowd, in this

range of religions, there is only one certainty that we have for all: we are all children of God," Pope Francis said in his message, released Jan. 6, the feast of the Epiphany.

At the beginning of the video, a minute-and-a-half long, the Pope cites the fact that the majority of the earth's inhabitants profess some sort of religious belief. This, he said, "should lead to a dialogue among religions. We should not stop praying for it and collaborating with those who think differently."

The video goes on to feature representatives of Buddhism, Christianity, Islam and Judaism, who proclaim their respective beliefs in God, Jesus Christ, Allah and Buddha.

Later on, after the Pope affirms that all, regardless of their religious profession, are children of God, the faith leaders state their common belief in love.[7]

The Latter Rain Charismatics and the Roman Catholic Charismatics are making the Convergence movement a reality. They do not realize that following Pope Francis or any other pope who proposes to join the religions of the world together with Christianity is inviting disaster. And very little, if any, resistance is being voiced by leaders who should know better. They simply are being swept along by the current.

It was this news item that was the impetus for *The Good Shepherd Calls*. I have been following the ecumenical movement for many years. I was part of a large fellowship of pastors who also followed current events in light of Bible prophecy and who, at one time, were diligent about warning their sheep. Since the pope's call for religious unity in the name of Christianity, only a handful have made public statements. No one wants to rock the boat even while their sheep float down the river of deception to their demise.

RICK WARREN'S DANGEROUS ECUMENICAL PATHWAY TO ROME

T he charismatic bridge to Rome is supposed to bring unity and revival in the days in which we are living. But it is not the only bridge to Rome. This chapter will examine one of the most well-known and popular pastors in the world and his efforts at forming an alliance with Rome as a basis for a social gospel program. Rick Warren, pastor and founder of Saddleback Church in California has joined the *convergence* movement, and tens of thousands of pastors are following him without any concern or question.

In 2014, Rick Warren (called "America's Pastor") was interviewed by EWTN (a Catholic TV network) host Raymond Arroyo. The interview took place at the Saddleback Church campus and was posted on YouTube by EWTN in April of 2014. Because I had written previously in 2013 about Rick Warren's connections to Rome and to the Catholic convert Tony Blair (former prime minister of Britain), I was very aware that Rick Warren was heading down the path toward Rome. But not until I saw this interview did I realize just how far he had gone in that direction.

When I wrote the 2013 commentary titled "What is Next for Rick Warren?," I provided evidence to show that Warren and Britain's prime minister Tony Blair were partnering together with the Roman

Catholic Church to form a P.E.A.C.E. Plan that would lead toward the creation of a global religion in the name of Christ. While many who read that commentary were skeptical that such a Warren-Rome connection existed, the 2014 interview leaves no doubt. EWTN made this statement about the interview on their YouTube station:

> Part II of our exclusive interview: Rick Warren, pastor of Saddleback Church in Southern California. Rick talks about the expansion of his ministry abroad, the Vatican delegation that recently came to Orange County to study his church's style of evangelization, and which television channel he finds himself watching most often and the show that draws him. [1]

If you have access to the Internet, I highly recommend you watch the entire thirty-minute interview as it is filled with information that provides further insight into Rick Warren's pathway to Rome—one he has been supporting for quite some time. For instance, in 2005, Warren created the Purpose Driven Life Catholics program. And in his best-selling book, *The Purpose Driven Life* (released in 2002), Warren makes several favorable references to well-known Catholics: page 88—Brother Lawrence, a Catholic mystic; page 108—Catholic priest and contemplative mystic, Henri Nouwen; Catholic panentheist St. John of the Cross; and twice he mentions Mother Theresa (pages 125 and 231).

But in this EWTN interview, Warren takes his views of the Catholic Church to even "greater" heights and admits he is in favor of the Roman Catholic New Evangelization program (which is set up to win the "lost brethren" back to the Mother Church). [2]

The Warren/Arroyo Interview

As I listened for the first time to the Rick Warren/Raymond Arroyo interview, thoughts and questions were racing through my mind: *What did he just say?! This is exactly the direction we predicted he would go! It will be crucial that skeptics hear and see this interview.* The comments by Warren in response to Arroyo's questions were stunning. They left no room for doubt in my mind—I knew once and for all that Warren was marching toward ecumenical unity with Rome.

The interview opened with the following question by Arroyo:

> *The Purpose Driven Life* is the best-selling book in the world—36 million plus copies. It's been translated more than any book except the Bible. What is the key to that success? Why were so many people touched by that book and continue to be?[3]

To Arroyo's question, Warren responded:

> You know, Ray, there is not a single new thought in *Purpose Driven Life* that hasn't been said for 2,000 years. I've just said it in a fresh way. I said it in a simple way. When I was writing *Purpose Driven Life* it took me seven months, twelve hours a day. I'd get up at 4:30 in the morning. I'd go to a little study. Start at 5 a.m. I was fasting til noon, and I would light some candles, and I would start writing and rewrite, rewrite, rewrite. One of the things I did before I wrote the book was, um, I'd ask the question—How do you write a book that lasts 500 years? For instance, um, *Imitation of Christ* by Thomas à Kempis, *Practicing the Presence of God* by Brother Lawrence. Ok? The Desert Fathers, St. John of the Cross, Teresa of Avila. All of these great, classic devotional works. Any one of them—I just realized that in order to be timeless you have to be eternal.[4]

Warren's answer certainly provides some understanding as to where his spiritual affinities lie, and it associates him with the Catholic contemplative prayer movement brought into the evangelical church through Richard Foster and Dallas Willard. Interestingly, in Warren's first book, *The Purpose Driven Church*, he identified (and promoted) Foster and Willard as key players in that movement.[5]

In the interview, Warren's exalting of the writers he refers to is disconcerting to say the least. They are all mystics. Brother Lawrence talked of "dancing violently like a mad man" when he went "into the presence."[6] Teresa of Avila levitated and often wrote about her numerous esoteric mystical experiences.[7] St. John of the Cross (author of the contemplative favorite, *Dark Night of the Soul*) was panentheistic in his belief that God is in all creation.[8] The Desert Fathers were ancient hermits and monks who embraced the mystical prayer practices of those from pagan religions.

For Rick Warren to list the writings of these Catholic mystics as "great" insinuating they are "eternal" is more than revealing. The Bible is the inspired Word of God. As the apostle Paul states, "All Scripture is given by inspiration of God, and is profitable for doctrine, for reproof, for correction, for instruction in righteousness" (2 Timothy 3:16). While *the Bible* is great and eternal, the books written by Roman Catholic mystics are the works of fallible humans who were misled by the fallen spiritual dimension. In their mystical writings, they promote doctrines of demons and lead Bible believers away from the faith.

Raymond Arroyo then asked Rick Warren the following question:

> What is your secret to reaching people every day, every week, not only in your writing but when you speak? What is it? What is this communication gift, if you will, if you could decode, because a lot of preachers would like to know.[9]

While Warren mentions Pope Francis several times throughout the interview with the EWTN host, he answers this question by directing attention to the pope specifically, stating:

> Well, the main thing is love always reaches people. Authenticity, humility. Pope Francis is the perfect example of this. He is a—He is doing everything right. You see,

people will listen to what we say if they like what they see. And as *our new pope*, he was very, very symbolic in, you know, his first mass with people with AIDS, uh, his kissing of the deformed man, his loving the children. This authenticity, this humility, the caring for the poor, this is what the whole world expects us Christians to do. And when we—when they go, oh, that's what a Christian does—In fact, there was a headline here in Orange County—*and I love the headline*. It said, if you love Pope Francis, you'll love Jesus. That was the headline! I showed it to a group of priests I was speaking to awhile back.[10] (emphasis added)

While loving others is a quality all Christians should embrace and promote, using Pope Francis as the perfect example seems somewhat opportunistic. For Rick Warren to call Pope Francis "our new pope" suggests that Warren has accepted the pope not only as the head of the Catholic Church but as the head of the Christian church as well. Either Rick Warren believes that or he was indeed being opportunistic.

His comments about the Orange County newspaper headline, "If You Love Pope Francis, You'll love Jesus," is no less reason for scrutiny. Can you imagine the apostle Paul referring to the head of a false religion as "our" leader and comparing this false teacher to Jesus Christ?

Rick Warren, Religious Liberty, and Catholics and Evangelicals Together

Based on Bible prophecy, the last-days one-world religion called the "harlot" will be a counterfeit to the true church, which is the Bride of Christ. Bible scholars who take this position believe the ecumenical gathering together of religions for the cause of peace will be the prerequisite. One of the key events to help bring about this abomination would be when a declaration is made that the

Reformation is over and the "separated brethren" will be welcomed back into the fold (i.e., the Catholic Church). But as we have now learned, much of this has just happened, and it will continue to unfold in greater measure.

The Rick Warren/Raymond Arroyo EWTN interview provides some significant clues indicating this scenario is presently underway. I am referring to a portion of the interview that deals with the topic of religious liberty. In fact, it was revealed that Rick Warren may have a plan laid away for the future of promoting a "religious liberty movement" that will be the equivalent of the "civil liberties movement" of the past. When Raymond Arroyo asked Rick Warren what he thought about the separation of church and state and how the Supreme Court would rule on this topic in the future, Warren responded:

> Now it's interesting that phrase today means the exact opposite of what it meant in Jefferson's days. Today people think it means keeping religion out of government or out of politics. But actually, the separation of church and state was we *are going to protect the church from the government*. I believe that religious liberty may be the civil rights issue of the next decade. And if it takes some high profile pastors going to jail, like Martin Luther King did with civil rights, I'm in. So be it. I mean, as Peter said and the apostles that we must obey God rather than men.[11] (emphasis added)

Now, while it is commendable that a pastor would be so outspoken and willing to take such a strong stand for religious liberty—especially when he shows his passion for this topic by stating he is personally willing to go to jail for such a cause, such passionate words also leave me wondering where this might take his Purpose Driven Church model. Will it have a broader agenda than previously advertised?

Arroyo then asked Warren:

Do you think events like this, moments like this, are actually sources of unity and moments of unity, particularly for Catholics and Evangelicals?[12]

When I first listened to Warren's response, I was somewhat surprised by what he said. However, after thinking about it further and comparing his answer with other statements Warren previously made about his willingness to work together with various faiths and belief systems for the common cause of good, his response made perfect sense. Warren stated:

Well, obviously we have so much in common in protecting our religious rights—and really the religious rights of other people who we disagree with on beliefs and behaviors. Muslims, for instance, don't drink alcohol. If all of a sudden they made a law that said every Muslim restaurant has to serve alcohol, I would be there protesting with that. If they made a law that said every Jewish deli in New York City has to sell pork, I'm going to be there protesting. I don't have a problem with pork. But I am going to protest that. If they make a law that says every Catholic school has to provide contraceptives, if you're morally convinced you shouldn't have contraceptives, I stand with you, firm with you on your belief on that because you have a right to train your children the way you want to.[13]

It is difficult to challenge Warren's argument as he states his case. Religious freedom is a major pillar that America was founded upon. To attack religious freedom or rights could well spark a religious liberty movement if this is the direction political leaders are headed.

However, it is also possible that a so-called religious liberty movement championed by "America's Pastor," who is willing to go to jail for standing up for the religious rights of all religions, could be a stepping stone to something else—especially when it is so obvious this would be another effective way to join evangelicals and Catholics together; the current common trend is going in that direction with each passing day.

While it may seem like a stretch to suggest Rick Warren will become the pied piper who unites all the world religions for a common cause, it is certainly within the realm of possibility that Warren could be a major spokesperson for persuading evangelicals to join with Roman Catholics. This whole movement has been in place for some time and has received endorsements from such well-known leaders as Bill Bright, J. I. Packer, and Charles Colson.

In the past, Rick Warren has made numerous statements about his willingness to join forces with Rome to establish the kingdom of God here on Earth. In a message Warren gave at the Pew Forum on Religion in Key West, Florida, May 23, 2005, he stated:

> Now when you get 25 percent of America, which is basically Catholic, and you get 28 to 29 percent of America which is evangelical together, that's called a majority. *And it is a very powerful bloc,* if they happen to stay together on particular issues. . . . I would encourage you to look at *this evolving alliance between evangelical Protestants and Catholics.*[14] (emphasis added)

Without question, Warren's "evolving alliance" with Rome has come a long way since he made that statement. The interview with Raymond Arroyo of EWTN is proof of that. When a pastor of Warren's stature and influence refrains from warning his followers about the dangers found in the extra- and non-biblical teachings of Roman Catholicism, discerning Christians should *not* remain silent.

Rick Warren, Jean Vanier, and the New Evangelization

One significant revelation brought to light during the Warren/Arroyo interview was that Rick Warren and Saddleback Church had hosted a delegation from Rome to discuss the New

Evangelization program. According to the interview, a number of Roman Catholic delegates were observing the Warren-Saddleback Purpose-Driven model in order to gain ideas and insight for the Roman Catholic New Evangelization plan initiated by Pope John Paul II and continued by Pope Benedict and now Pope Francis. I have discussed this New Evangelization plan and the serious implications of it in several articles over the years as well as in my book *Another Jesus: the eucharistic christ and the new evangelization.*

With regard to the Catholic delegation visit to Saddleback, Raymond Arroyo asked Rick Warren the following question:

> The Vatican recently sent a delegation here to Saddleback—the pontifical council—the academy for life. Tell me what they discovered and why did they come? This is a sizable group.[15]

Rick Warren enthusiastically answered:

> They were about thirty bishops from Europe. One of the men had been actually trained and mentored by Jean Vanier, which is an interesting thing because we have a retreat center here and *my spiritual director, who grew up at Saddleback, actually went and trained under Jean Vanier too.* So I am very excited about that.[16] (emphasis added)

While the term *spiritual director** or the name Jean Vanier may not mean much to you unless you are versed on contemplative mystical spirituality, this admission by Warren provides conclusive evidence of his endorsement of Roman Catholic monastic mysticism (i.e., contemplative prayer). The fact he mentions he has his "own" spiritual director located at Saddleback who was trained under the leadership of Jean Vanier is even more significant and further unveils Warren's journey to Rome.

---

*A term used in contemplative spirituality as one who can help "discern" the voices one is hearing in the contemplative "silence."

A brief look at Jean Vanier, the man who trained Rick Warren's spiritual director, will provide important insights. Vanier (b. 1928) is the Canadian Catholic founder of L'Arche, which is a humanitarian community for disabled people. It is L'Arche where Catholic priest Henri Nouwen spent the last ten years of his life. Vanier is a contemplative mystic who promotes interspirituality and interfaith beliefs, calling the Hindu Mahatma Gandhi "one of the greatest prophets of our times"[17] and "a man sent by God."[18] In the book *Essential Writings*, Vanier talks about "opening doors to other religions" and helping people develop their own faiths be it Hinduism, Christianity, or Islam.[19] The book also describes how Vanier read the Catholic mystic and interspiritualist Thomas Merton and practiced and was influenced by the spiritual exercises of the Jesuit founder and mystic St. Ignatius.

Now think about this: To learn through Rick Warren's interview with Raymond Arroyo that Warren's own "spiritual director" was trained under Jean Vanier is, at the very least, a key to understanding the long history where Rick Warren has expressed support for contemplative mystics and ecumenical/interspiritual efforts. In Ray Yungen's book, *A Time of Departing*, he points out that both Rick and Kay Warren very much admire the writings of Henri Nouwen. As a matter of fact, Yungen has devoted an entire chapter chronicling Rick Warren's contemplative interest including his instructions in *The Purpose Driven Life* on breath prayers (a type of contemplative prayer). Now that Warren has revealed that his own spiritual director was trained under someone like Jean Vanier, we can better understand the direction Warren is heading.

The New Roman Catholic Evangelization

If the delegation sent to Saddleback from Rome consisted of thirty Bishops, obviously this was a very significant event. What were the delegates discussing with Warren and his team? Warren provides the answer to that question in the interview:

> *[T]hey were talking about the New Evangelization,* and
> Saddleback has been very effective in reaching [the]
> secular mindset. Our church is 33 years old. Easter
> 2014 at Saddleback is our 34th anniversary. And in 34
> years, we've baptized 38,000 adults. Now, these are adult
> converts. People with no religious background. People
> who say, "I was nothing before I came to Saddleback."
> So we figured out a way to reach that mindset. And *I
> fully support your Catholic Church's New Evangelization*
> which basically says we've got to *re-evangelize people who
> are Christian in name but not in heart.* And *they need a
> new fresh relationship to our Savior.*[20] (emphasis added)

While Warren provides his stamp of approval on the Roman
Catholic New Evangelization program and makes it sound like the
purpose is to win converts to Christ, there is much more to the
picture than Warren describes. The Roman Catholic New Evangelization program is dedicated to winning converts to the Roman
Catholic Eucharistic Christ and obedience to the sacraments of the
Roman Catholic Church. While Warren may call this "a new fresh
relationship to our Savior," he is overlooking what Catholics must
believe in order to be a member of the Catholic Church. Either
he is oblivious to this fact, or he is ignorant of it. For a man who
claims to be a voracious reader and who has a doctorate degree from
a theological seminary, it's hard to believe it's the latter.

In a commentary I wrote called "Mysticism, Monasticism, and
the New Evangelization," I was able to document that contemplative mysticism provides the catalyst for the New Evangelization.
Thus, Rome and Babylon join together to form a new ecumenical
Christianity that fits the description of the harlot—the counterfeit
bride—described in the Book of Revelation, chapter 18.

The facts stare us in the face. Warren's pathway to Rome is
dangerous! Why do so few recognize what is happening? Do you
know someone who is caught up in the deception but does not
see what is going on? Maybe this would be a good time to pray

God's grace would open their eyes, and they would see the truth of God's Word.

Rick Warren and the Chaplet of the Divine Mercy

Thus far in this chapter, I have laid out critical documentation indicating how Warren is headed down the road to Rome. Now, I would like to address what is possibly the most blatant endorsement of Roman Catholicism revealed in Warren's entire interview with EWTN. It was so revealing that even Raymond Arroyo expressed surprise when he asked Warren to comment on the following topic:

> Tell me about your—the little breather you take in the day when you watch television. When we first met, you came up to me afterwards—I can't believe you watch Chaplet of the Divine Mercy.[21]

In response to Arroyo's comment, Rick Warren expounded:

> I'm an avid fan of EWTN. I make no bones about it. I probably watch it more than any Christian channel. Well, you know what? Because you have more, more, uh, shows that relate to history. And if you don't understand the roots of our faith, that God had been working for 2,000 years, regardless of what brand of believer you are, God has been working for 2,000 years in His church. And if you don't have those roots, you're like the cut flower syndrome. Or you're a tumbleweed.[22]

If Warren's main reason for watching the Roman Catholic Eternal Word Television Network is to gain a knowledge and understanding of Christian history, then there is no question he is getting a biased one-sided view. While I admit I do not watch EWTN as much as Warren apparently does (and certainly not for the same reasons), I do know that a major part of Christian history dealing with the Reformation and the Counter-reformation is not one of the favorite topics presented. Perhaps a quick review of *Foxe's Book of Martyrs* would be a good balance for Warren and a reminder of what happened to Christians who stood up against the pope of Rome and his Jesuit enforcers in the past for believing the Word of God rather than the word of man. People were burned at the stake for saying that Jesus could not be found in a wafer (the Eucharist).[23]

In the interview, Warren not only stated that EWTN was his favorite Christian television network, he further offered that he had a favorite program he and his wife watch regularly on that network. If Arroyo was shocked by this revelation, the best way to describe *my* reaction to his response would be astonished and angry. In Warren's own words:

> One of my favorite shows, which you repeat often is the Chaplet of the Divine Mercy, which I love. And when I've had a very stressful day, I'll come home, I've got it taped, and Kay and I will both, we'll listen. We'll put it on and just sit back, relax and worship. And in the time of reflection, meditation and quietness, I find myself renewed and restored. So thank you for continuing to play the Chaplet of the Divine Mercy.[24]

Arroyo responded to Warren's statement, "Thank Mother Angelica."

Warren then echoed, "Thank you, Mother Angelica." "Mother" Mary Angelica (1923-2016) was the founder of EWTN (Eternal Word Television Network). Among the programs making up the daily broadcasting schedule is "The Chaplet of the Divine Mercy." A description of this program provides background information:

The Chaplet of the Divine Mercy is a Christian devotion based on the visions of Jesus reported by Saint Mary Faustina Kowalska (1905-1938), known as "the Apostle of Mercy." She was a Polish sister of the Congregation of the Sisters of Our Lady of Mercy and canonized as a Catholic saint in 2000. Faustina stated that she received the prayer through visions and conversations with Jesus, who made specific promises regarding the recitation of the prayers. Her Vatican biography quotes some of these conversations. As a Roman Catholic devotion, the chaplet is often said as a rosary-based prayer with the same set of rosary beads used for reciting the Holy Rosary or the Chaplet of Holy Wounds, in the Roman Catholic Church. As an Anglican devotion, The Divine Mercy Society of the Anglican Church states that the chaplet can also be recited on Anglican prayer beads. The chaplet may also be said without beads, usually by counting prayers on the fingertips, and may be accompanied by the veneration of the Divine Mercy image.[25]

Note the reference to "the veneration of the Divine Mercy image," which is an essential component of the Chaplet of the Divine Mercy. Consider this further documentation that will clarify that idolatry is the only way to describe what is taking place:

The earliest element of the Devotion to the Divine Mercy revealed to St. Faustina was the Image. On February 22nd, 1931 Jesus appeared to her with rays radiating from His heart and said, Paint an image according to the pattern you see, with the signature: Jesus I trust in You. I desire that this image be venerated, first in your chapel, and throughout the world. (Diary 47)

I promise that the soul that will venerate this image will not perish. I also promise victory over its enemies already here on earth, especially at the hour of death. I myself will defend it as My own glory. (Diary 48) I am offering people a vessel with which they are to keep coming for graces to the fountain of mercy. That vessel is this image with the signature "Jesus, I trust in You." (Diary 327)[26]

One could contend that Warren was just "making conversation" with Arroyo or even making a joke when he made the claim that *The Chaplet of the Divine Mercy* was his favorite "Christian" television program. But he has never made a public statement refuting or withdrawing his statements. Plus, he gave such detail in his account. If this is what he truly believes, if he was speaking the truth to Arroyo, then he is defying the God of the Bible and willingly ignoring the commandment in the Bible that states:

Thou shalt not make unto thee any graven image, or any likeness of any thing that is in heaven above, or that is in the earth beneath, or that is in the water under the earth. (Exodus 20:4)

While researching this issue, I took the time to watch several Chaplet of the Divine Mercy programs posted on the Internet. Staring at images of "Christ" or worshipping a monstrance containing the supposed body of Christ while repeating the rosary apparently brought peace and relaxation for Warren. However, it does not take a great deal of discernment to realize these unbiblical practices are rooted in paganism.*

---

* I believe the best way for me to confirm this point is to provide an Internet link to an actual Chaplet of the Divine Mercy service so you can see with your own eyes what Warren and his wife Kay consider a "Christian" devotional. This is only one of many programs that you can watch that all show the same thing. Please check out this 8-minute video clip of a Chaplet of the Divine Mercy program: https://www. youtube.com/watch?v=__RbWgxA2G0 (unusual hyperlink: there are two underscores: __).

The Bottom Line

There's no other way to put it, Rick Warren is on a dangerous path away from sound biblical doctrine toward an ecumenical apostate form of Christianity with Rome that has the potential to lead many astray.

What does it mean "to earnestly contend for the faith"? Is sound biblical doctrine being compromised for the sake of unity in the church today? When a pastor endorses a television program that promotes idolatry, shouldn't that pastor be called out or at least asked to give a public repeal of his earlier endorsements?

The facts have been presented and a hypothesis can be formulated that leads to a reasonable conclusion. My prayer is that the damage done to biblical Christianity can be corrected through open repentance and public statements that set the record straight by Warren himself and those who follow him.

The Warren/Arroyo EWTN interview provides many insights regarding the "New Evangelicalism" presently unfolding. Rather than lines being drawn in the sand, walls are coming down, and ecumenical unity is being established. If Rick Warren and his followers represent the direction many Protestants are heading, it is only a matter of time for the coming one-world ecumenical religion to be established. The Jesuit plan to bring the "separated brethren home to Rome" will have been accomplished. Those who refuse to follow will be singled out and considered "heretics" who are ruining the P.E.A.C.E. process. Is it possible that persecution for these "resisters" is in store?

While charismatic unity and Rick Warren joining hands with Rome to work together for the cause of good are two of the ways the Gospel according to the Scriptures is being compromised, there is another danger we have yet to discuss—"signs and wonders" of the deceptive variety will have the potential to deceive billions of people on the planet if they refuse to accept the warnings found in Scripture.

16

THE KINGDOM OF GOD ON EARTH WITHOUT THE KING

A cleverly devised plan is underway declaring the Reformation is over. The "Holy Spirit" is supposedly uniting the church for a mighty revival before Jesus returns. Ecumenical madness is spreading like a virus. Few pastors take the time to listen carefully to what the present pope himself is saying. He is all for unity with anyone and everyone who will join with Rome. This is what the Jesuit agenda[1] is all about, to unite all people and all religions under the authority of Rome. And for the first time in history, the Roman Catholic Church has a Jesuit pope! When you consider that the first Jesuits five hundred years ago were commissioned by the pope to do whatever it takes to bring an end to the Reformation and then consider the efforts being made today by the papacy and some Protestants (such as Tony Palmer) to end the Reformation, it's a chilling scenario.

The ecumenical wheel has many spokes, but all the spokes lead to the hub. The hub is the Vatican located in Rome with the pope on the throne of "Peter." From there, the kingdom of God will be established. In an article titled, "Pope's Mass: We're not Christian Without the Church," reporting on Pope Francis speaking to a large group assembled for Mass, we read:

There is no such thing as a Christian without the Church, a Christian who walks alone, because Jesus inserted himself into the journey of His people: This was Pope Francis' reflection at Mass this morning in Casa Santa Marta. Beginning with the first reading of the day, Pope Francis said that when they proclaimed Jesus the apostles did not begin with Him, but the history of the people. In fact "Jesus does not make sense without this history" because He "is the end of this story, [the end] towards which this story goes, towards which it walks."[1] (brackets in original)

Obviously, with Pope Francis speaking to a group assembled before him as he is presiding over the Mass, when he says "church," he is talking about the Catholic Church. Anyone who doubts he was addressing the Roman Catholic "faithful," the following quote will confirm this:

Looking forward, the Christian is a man, a woman of hope. And in this, the Christian follows the path of God and renews the covenant with God. He continually says to the Lord: "Yes, I want the commandments, I want your will, I will follow you." He is a man of the covenant, and we celebrate the covenant, every day in the Mass: thus a Christian is "a woman, a man of the Eucharist."[2]

Or consider the following information available at the Catholic website Catholicism.org:

"Outside the Church there is no salvation" (extra ecclesiam nulla salus) is a doctrine of the Catholic Faith that was taught by Jesus Christ to His Apostles, preached by the Fathers, defined by popes and councils and piously believed by the faithful in every age of the Church. Here is how the Popes defined it:

- "There is but one universal Church of the faithful, outside which no one at all is saved." (Pope Innocent III, Fourth Lateran Council, 1215.)

- "We declare, say, define, and pronounce that it is absolutely necessary for the salvation of every human creature to be subject to the Roman Pontiff." (Pope Boniface VIII, the Bull Unam Sanctam, 1302.)

- "The most Holy Roman Church firmly believes, professes and preaches that none of those existing outside the Catholic Church, not only pagans, but also Jews and heretics and schismatics, can have a share in life eternal; but that they will go into the eternal fire which was prepared for the devil and his angels, unless before death they are joined with Her; and that so important is the unity of this ecclesiastical body that only those remaining within this unity can profit by the sacraments of the Church unto salvation, and they alone can receive an eternal recompense for their fasts, their almsgivings, their other works of Christian piety and the duties of a Christian soldier. No one, let his almsgiving be as great as it may, no one, even if he pour out his blood for the Name of Christ, can be saved, unless he remain within the bosom and the unity of the Catholic Church." (Pope Eugene IV, the Bull Cantate Domino, 1441.)[3]

Who Has the Keys to the Kingdom

If you have ever walked around St. Peter's Square in Rome, you will know there is a statue of Peter before you enter the basilica, illustrating one of the main pillars of the Roman Catholic Church. The statue represents Peter, the disciple Catholics claim was the one Jesus chose to become the first Pope. The claim is that Roman Catholicism is the only true representation of Christianity because its beliefs can be traced back to the appointment of Peter as the successor of Jesus. He was handed the "keys to the Kingdom" by Jesus, they say.

In order to trace the origin of this claim, we need to go to the Scriptures and check out if this claim is valid. It is based on the portion of Scripture found in Matthew chapter 16 when Jesus asked the disciples the question *who do they say I am?*:

> When Jesus came into the coasts of Caesarea Philippi, he
> asked his disciples, saying, Whom do men say that I the

Son of man am? And they said, Some say that thou art John the Baptist: some, Elias; and others, Jeremias, or one of the prophets. He saith unto them, But whom say ye that I am? And Simon Peter answered and said, Thou art the Christ, the Son of the living God. And Jesus answered and said unto him, Blessed art thou, Simon Barjona: for flesh and blood hath not revealed it unto thee, but my Father which is in heaven. And I say also unto thee, That thou art Peter, and upon this rock I will build my church; and the gates of hell shall not prevail against it. And I will give unto thee the keys of the kingdom of heaven: and whatsoever thou shalt bind on earth shall be bound in heaven: and whatsoever thou shalt loose on earth shall be loosed in heaven. Then charged he his disciples that they should tell no man that he was Jesus the Christ. From that time forth began Jesus to shew unto his disciples, how that he must go unto Jerusalem, and suffer many things of the elders and chief priests and scribes, and be killed, and be raised again the third day. (Matthew 16: 13-21)

While Roman Catholics avidly believe Jesus chose a man to succeed Him to head the Church, that is not what Jesus said. Jesus was responding to the question He had asked and Peter had answered. Peter said, "Thou art the Christ, the Son of the living God." The rock or the foundational belief that Christianity would be based on would not be following a man. The foundation was about knowing who Jesus is and the role He plays in history. This key was the key to the Kingdom of Heaven, not a key to a kingdom established here on Earth by a man even though it might be in the name of Jesus.

According to Roman Catholic dogma, the succession of popery throughout the ages has made the claim that salvation can only be dispensed by Rome. From the beginning, at Philippi, Jesus made it clear to the disciples and Peter that in no way should any man be followed and given a title to indicate he is a form of Jesus Christ in the flesh.

When Jesus told the disciples what would happen to Him and that He would suffer, die, and be resurrected, Peter refused to believe this vital message which fulfills the Gospel according to the Scriptures: The Bible states: "Then Peter took him, and began to rebuke him, saying, Be it far from thee, Lord: this shall not be unto thee" (Matthew 16: 22).

Jesus immediately responded to Peter's heretical claim by saying: "Get thee behind me, Satan: thou art an offence unto me: for thou savourest not the things that be of God, but those that be of men" (Matthew 16: 23).

Therein lies the error that has been passed down through the generations and has impacted not only the Roman Catholic Church but many Protestant pastors and leaders who profess to believe the Gospel of Jesus. It is man that gets between God and man. Men not only misunderstand what Jesus said about the rock or foundation that Christianity should be built upon, men take the position of the Good Shepherd and make the claim that they, and only they, have been given custody over the keys to the kingdom.

Kingdom-Now Evangelicals

While Rome leads the way with the bold claim that God chose Peter and the succeeding popes to take the title of "Vicar of Christ" and determine what the sheep should or should not believe, other groups believe they have been called to usher in or even prepare and set up the kingdom of God here on Earth without the presence of the King. Often taking the position that Jesus will not actually physically return to rule and reign for a period of one thousand years, this group sees itself as chosen by God to be human vessels for this purpose.

Common names for this teaching are: Kingdom Now, Dominion Theology, and Reconstructionism. It is the idea that before Christ can return, the world must be brought together in unity and perfection, and this work will be done by the Christian church. Rick Warren's Purpose Driven P.E.A.C.E. Plan, Jim Wallis' social gospel agenda, and Tony Campolo or Brian McLaren's emergent church are a few of the avenues through which this is being propagated. The goal is to basically eradicate all the world's ills (e.g., disease, poverty, terrorism, and pollution) and thus, we will have created a "Heaven on Earth" Utopia.

While creating such a world sounds very good, it is not what the Bible says is going to happen. Many Scriptures, in both the Old and New Testaments, describe a very different scenario, such as the following:

> Then shall they deliver you up to be afflicted, and shall kill you: and ye shall be hated of all nations for my name's sake. And then shall many be offended, and shall betray one another, and shall hate one another. And many false prophets shall rise, and shall deceive many. And because iniquity shall abound, the love of many shall wax cold. But he that shall endure unto the end, the same shall be saved. And this gospel of the kingdom shall be preached in all the world for a witness unto all nations; and then shall the end come. (Matthew 24:9-14)

The following list of the some of the erroneous teachings in Kingdom-Now theology illustrate how dangerous this belief system is, yet it has tremendously pervaded the church today:

- Prophetic Scriptures are denied or fulfilled in 70 AD (as is also the belief of preterism).

- The church is the new Israel (replacement theology).

- Armageddon is the *ongoing* battle between the forces of light and darkness.

- The Antichrist is a spirit, not an actual person.

- We are already in the Tribulation, but at the same time, we are in the Millennium. It doesn't get any stranger! It's one or the other.

- Rather than following traditional Bible prophecy, they follow "new revelations."

- Modern-day prophets must be obeyed and not judged for their inaccuracy.

- They want to restore the Edenic nature even though Eden is where sin began.[4]

This movement has swept the planet, and those who refuse to join hands are considered "colonial," "militant fundamentalists," and "narrow-minded crackpots" who are not willing to catch the "new wave" and get on board with the mighty revival that is moving the world toward unity and peace. Many of the leaders in this movement have no problem whatsoever joining with the pope in Rome and the kingdom-of-Earth plans he has for joining together with other religions, including Islam.

While some discerning Christians can see how this trend plays a role in light of Bible prophecy, there is a huge portion of Christianity that does not. These are those who are reading books by authors who promote emerging church (or "progressive Christianity") ideas for the postmodern generation that reject the teachings of the Bible and embrace establishing the kingdom of God on Earth right now. They are willing to join hands with other religions by reinventing Christianity into a "broad-way" spirituality where all are saved and part of God's Kingdom. No longer do they believe in the "narrow road" to eternity. The kingdom of God is for all religions, they say (and even for those who believe in nothing). Unity, peace, connectedness, and oneness is all that matters, while biblical doctrine is being set aside as irrelevant to the "new reformation" at hand. Obviously, such a view leaves little room for the Cross and the biblical Gospel. And Scriptures such as this one are overlooked:

> And he [Jesus] went through the cities and villages, teaching, and journeying toward Jerusalem. Then said one unto him, Lord, are there few that be saved? And he said unto them, Strive to enter in at the strait gate: *for many, I say unto you, will seek to enter in, and shall not be able.* When once the master of the house is risen up, and hath

> shut to the door, and ye begin to stand without, and to
> knock at the door, saying, Lord, Lord, open unto us; and
> he shall answer and say unto you, *I know you not whence
> ye are.* (Luke 13:22-25; emphasis added)

Unfortunately, while there may be many pastors, like Rick Warren, who still hold to a personal belief in Jesus Christ as their Savior, the time will come when the path they are now taking may cost them dearly. It is my hope that these leaders might wake up to see what they are doing before it is too late. And let us not forget the countless number of people following these shepherds who may never embrace a saving knowledge of Jesus Christ because of the truths being withheld from them for the sake of "peace" and "unity."

It is also grievous to know that a good number of "Christian" leaders no longer believe (or have never believed) in the Cross as a propitiation for sin but maintain their belief that such a concept is both archaic and barbaric. They hold to the view that Christianity needs to be reinvented for our times. Brian McLaren, who in 2015 represented "Christianity" at the Parliament of the World Religions in Utah, holds to just such a view. In one interview, he said that the idea of God sending His Son to a violent death is "false advertising for God" and he equally rejected the doctrine of Hell as well.[5]

In addition, McLaren has played a significant role in promoting kingdom-now theology as can be seen in his book *The Secret Message of Jesus: Uncovering the Truth That Could Change Everything*. McLaren, who was once listed by *Time Magazine* as one of the top 25 most influential persons associated with evangelical Christianity, has sought to upgrade the Christian faith in order to make it relevant for today. He asks a number of questions at the beginning of his book that imply the church has misrepresented Jesus' core message and promotes the idea that Christians need to be honest with themselves even if that means altering their faith. In this book, he makes the following statement:

> Sadly, for centuries at a time in too many places to count,
> the Christian religion has downplayed, misconstrued, or

forgotten the secret message of Jesus entirely. Instead of being about the kingdom of God coming to earth, the Christian religion has too often been preoccupied with abandoning or escaping the earth and going to heaven . . . We have betrayed the message that the kingdom of God is available for all, beginning with the least and last and the lost—and have instead believed and taught that the kingdom of God is available for the elite, beginning with the correct and the clean and the powerful.[6]

In McLaren's 2016 book titled *The Great Spiritual Migration: How the World's Largest Religion is Seeking a Better Way to be Christian,* he describes this all-inclusive "kingdom of God" that incorporates "multifaith [i.e., all religions] collaborations." He states:

This kind of collaboration leads to a fresh understanding of what it means to evangelize. I was taught that it meant converting people to the one true religion, namely, my own [Christianity]. Now I believe evangelism means inviting people into heart-to-heart communion and collaboration with God and neighbors in the *great work of healing the earth*, of building the beloved community, of seeking first the kingdom of God and *God's justice for all*. Members of *each tradition* bring their unique gifts to the table, ready to share and receive, learn and teach, give and take, in a spirit of generosity and vulnerability. Neither my neighbors nor I *are obligated or expected to convert*. . . . As we work together *for the common good*, we are *all* transformed. Those who haven't experienced this kind of transforming collaboration simply don't know what they're missing. . . . Through *multifaith collaborations*, I have come to see how the language Paul used about *one body with many members* (1 Corinthians 12, Romans 12: 4– 5) applies not only to differing gifts among individual Christians *but also to differing gifts among religions*.[7] (emphasis added)

While many evangelicals have now pushed Brian McLaren to the sidelines of evangelical Christianity, others have continued carrying on his message, sometimes in more subtle ways. But as the Bible says, there is nothing new under the sun. Satan's devices are always in play. His goal is to destroy the message of the Cross, and while he cannot ever actually destroy it, he can cause untold numbers to reject it by offering them substitutes. But we know there is no substitute for the finished work on the Cross by Jesus Christ, who is the only Savior for mankind.

What Does This Tell Us?

There is a common cliché: if it quacks like a duck, walks like a duck, and has feathers like a duck—it *is* a duck! In this chapter, we have touched on three different areas with regard to establishing the kingdom of God on Earth right now without the King. Is this what Jesus intended would happen, or are we being misled by human beings who are following the thoughts of their own imagination or worse yet the inspiration of Satan?

While the idea that the kingdom of God is being established here on Earth by human leaders has been around for centuries, we should pay special attention when current events reveal that though the world gets worse and worse, we are being told it is getting better and better. When false religions become part of the kingdom, then clearly, this is not God's kingdom, but rather it is the kingdom that belongs to the god of this world. Jesus made it very clear there are two kingdoms—one of God and one of this world—when he told Pontius Pilate shortly before He was crucified, "My kingdom is not of this world" (John 18:36). Jesus also said to Pilate in that same conversation "Every one that is of the truth heareth my voice." Ask yourself this, are you hearing the voice of the Good Shepherd, or is it the voice of the god of this world who leads a kingdom that is not of God?

17

LYING SIGNS AND WONDERS

The Bible is full of references regarding the miraculous working power of God. God, because He is God, is not limited to His natural laws. The creation of the universe is the first great miracle recorded in the Bible. Numerous other Old Testament miracles show God's supernatural intervention into the affairs of man. The fact that God was manifest on Earth in the form of Jesus Christ is the greatest miracle of history. While Jesus Christ walked this Earth, He performed many miracles that are recorded in Scripture.

There are those today who deny that God performed miracles in the past and others who say God cannot perform miracles now. A belief in the supernatural power of God is scoffed at and denied. However, many others, including professing Christians, seek after signs and wonders carelessly. They are obsessed with the miraculous and often do not realize Satan is in the business of intervening in the affairs of men and can interject what appears to be miraculous signs and wonders of the deceptive variety.

Regarding last days spiritual signs and wonders, a search of the Scriptures will find only two references. In both cases, signs and wonders are mentioned as a warning relating to the strong delusion that will be underway at that time.

The first instance is recorded in Matthew chapter 24 where Jesus warned about the appearance of false Christs, false prophets, and appearances of false Jesus' that will be able to perform false miracles. He said:

> Then if any man shall say unto you, Lo, here is Christ, or there; believe it not. For there shall arise false Christs, and false prophets, and shall shew great signs and wonders; insomuch that, if it were possible, they shall deceive the very elect. Behold, I have told you before. Wherefore if they shall say unto you, Behold, he is in the desert; go not forth: behold, he is in the secret chambers; believe it not. (Matthew 24:23-26)

Jesus was making a prophetic statement. He was asked to describe the signs indicating His return, and He provided signs. He did this in advance so those who took Him seriously would pay attention and be prepared when these signs came about. One of the major signs He warned about was the fact there would be "signs and wonders" of the deceptive variety, and many would be deceived.

The second example regarding a warning about lying signs and wonders is found in Paul's letter to the Thessalonians. He describes a period that will set up the arrival of the Antichrist characterized by lying signs and wonders. He writes:

> For the mystery of iniquity doth already work: only he who now letteth will let, until he be taken out of the way. And then shall that Wicked be revealed, whom the Lord shall consume with the spirit of his mouth, and shall destroy with the brightness of his coming: Even him, whose coming is after the working of Satan with all power and signs and lying wonders, And with all deceivableness of unrighteousness in them that perish; because they received not the love of the truth, that they might be saved. And for this cause God shall send

them strong delusion, that they should believe a lie. (2 Thessalonians 2: 7-11)

Note that although Satan's work is being accomplished through false miraculous signs and wonders, it is God allowing this to happen because those being deceived refuse the truth of God's Word. Instead, they will come under a strong delusion that God will allow to happen. The last days will be characterized this way. This should be a sobering thought for those who scoff at biblical prophetic statements warning the sheep and the world of what is coming.

Power Evangelism

The term "power evangelism" was coined by John Wimber and is based on the following succession of ideas:

Unity of the body of Christ will provide the environment for the manifestation of numerous signs and wonders and these signs and wonders will draw many unbelievers to Christ.

Power Evangelism is also the title of a book Wimber wrote to explain this technique.

An evangelist is someone who proclaims the Gospel—the good news that Jesus Christ died to save us from our sins. A "power evangelist," according to Wimber, is someone who proclaims the Gospel and demonstrates the truth of the Gospel with "signs and wonders." In essence, "power evangelism" is predicated upon the supposition that the Gospel message in itself is largely ineffective unless accompanied by the miraculous.

Wimber believed that for Westerners to understand "power evangelism," their worldview must be modified. In his book, he explains how people who live in third-world countries are more open to God's power because they have different beliefs and expectations.

It was Wimber's view that a Western materialistic worldview holds people back from experiencing the miraculous. For example, in *Power Evangelism,* he states:

Most Western Christians must undergo a shift in perception to become involved in a signs and wonders ministry—a shift toward a worldview that makes room for God's miraculous intervention. It is not that we allow God's intervention: he does not need our permission. The shift is that we begin to see his miraculous works and *allow* them to affect our lives.[1]

Although Wimber claimed God will do what He wants despite ourselves, it doesn't seem as if that is what he really means. When one reads through his entire book, it becomes apparent that signs and wonders can be induced if a particular method is used. In fact, Wimber believes Jesus taught His disciples how to perform signs and wonders. He states:

But Christ's method of training is difficult for Western Christians to understand. There are several reasons for this. Evangelicals emphasize accumulating knowledge about God through Bible study. . . . Christ's method of training was . . . more oriented to learning a way of life through doing than through the accumulation of knowledge about God.[2]

Wimber further elaborates on how the disciples learned to become miracle workers. He states:

He trained them to do signs and wonders. They were hitched together for three years, and when released, the disciples continued to walk in his way. They performed signs and wonders and trained the next generation to perform them also.[3]

Did Jesus "train" his disciples to perform signs and wonders? Such a statement assumes that man can learn how to initiate and imitate God's power. God is not some cosmic puppet that operates based on our demands. God performs signs and wonders according to His sovereign plan. Power evangelism may well be part of a "paradigm shift" or a "third wave" as Wimber claims. However, it would be well to check out the warnings from the Scriptures. It will be "false signs and wonders" that will deceive people from the truth in the last days.

The promotion of Wimber's power evangelism methods and ideas continues to impact a large portion of Christianity today. This premise that *unity* of all those who profess to be Christian is a prerequisite for more and more miracles to occur drawing more and more to Christ is somewhat alarming. Many today who profess Christianity embrace apparitions of Mary and manifestations or appearances of what they believe is "Jesus." Could these supposed "signs and wonders" be what Jesus and Paul were warning about?

Apparitions of a Woman Claiming to Be the Mother of Jesus

She appears as a beautiful translucent woman surrounded by brilliant light. Her countenance is peaceful, her eyes kind and loving. Those who see her relate feeling such joy and pleasure that the term ecstasy is often used to describe the experience. She is believed to be the Virgin Mary, the mother of the Lord Jesus, and the sightings of her image may be more widespread than most people realize. She has been seen all over the globe—in Medjugorje, Bosnia; Fatima, Portugal; Lourdes, France; Guadalupe, Mexico; Egypt; Russia, and all across the U.S.A. Wherever she has appeared, millions upon millions of faithful followers flock to the shrines built in her honor.

Often when the apparition comes, she is accompanied by miraculous signs—healings, bleeding or crying statues, oil extruding from Marian statues and images, rosaries that turn gold, strange lights in the sky, and unusual phenomena in the sun. And she has much to say to her followers. Her words are scrupulously written down and distributed among the faithful. She speaks of future events, and most of what she says can be found in the pages of Scripture. However, a critical examination of her messages reveals she is preaching a false gospel.[4]

While her messages of peace and unity seem harmless, is it possible she has an agenda that is anticipated in the Bible?[5] What if these apparitions of Mary are not actually Mary? What if the master deceiver is the inspiration behind these extra-biblical and anti-biblical messages? There is no doubt people all over the world are experiencing some sort of supernatural phenomenon. The question is, however, what are they experiencing? What is the source of these experiences? And how can we know?

A PHOTO OF A PERCEIVED APPARITION OF THE
VIRGIN MARY ABOVE THE CHURCH OF VIRGIN MARY
IN ZEITOUN, CAIRO, AFRICA (1968; PUBLIC DOMAIN)

While most believe that the Marian Apparition movement is primarily for Catholics, there is reason to suggest that the Protestant/Catholic Charismatic ecumenical alliance based on an experience-focused foundation may soon provide a bridge for a much wider acceptance. For example, consider an article that appeared in *Charisma* in March 1999 titled "Pentecostal Evangelist Calls Christians to Expect the Unusual When Revival Hits."[6] According to this article, Pentecostal evangelist Ruth Heflin has been challenging churches to stop limiting what God can do. "I know revival is coming," Heflin said, "because I see unity developing in the body of Christ. People are so hungry for God that they are willing to forget their doctrinal differences and come together."[7]

Heflin also believes that all mainline churches like the Catholic Church will be involved in the coming revival she is predicting. The article states that "she has even ministered recently in a Roman Catholic church in Philadelphia."[8] Heflin also believes that the church in the United States will begin to experience more supernatural signs and wonders as we move closer to a season of revival. "We are beginning to see more miracles at our camp meetings in Virginia," she said. "In addition to healings we've seen oil appear on people's hands and have literally felt the rain of the Holy Spirit come down during the service."[9]

The July 1999 issue of *Charisma* explains that Catholic Charismatics and Protestant Charismatics have many common beliefs. Both groups are embracing signs and wonders, and both believe they are setting a precedent for a special spiritual event about to happen. According to Catholic bishop Sam Jacobs, a respected leader in the charismatic movement from Alexandria, Louisiana, "many charismatic leaders expect something to happen."[10] He further states:

> The power of God is going to fall in a fresh new way in the world, not just in the charismatic renewal, but in the church and in the world.[11]

Bishop Jacobs based his predictions on the words of Pope John Paul II, who predicted a new springtime for Christianity beginning with the new millennium. In Jacobs' own words, "Something new is going to happen. The next century (21st century) is going to open up a new spiritual movement."^{12}

The Lady of All Nations

While the "messages from heaven" are somewhat diverse, some common factors can be identified. One of these is the extra-biblical idea that peace in the world can only occur if the pope proclaims a dogma that Mary shares in the act of redemption with her son, Jesus.

Amsterdam is one of the locations where apparitions of this nature have been received, its messages recorded and exported to the world. Advocates believe that Mary, the mother of Jesus, appeared to visionary Ida Peerdeman on March 25, 1945. This was the first in a series of about sixty apparitions which supposedly took place from 1945 until 1959 and became known as the "Messages of the Lady of All Nations."^{13}

According to a *Lady of All Nations Worldwide Action* pamphlet, the reason the messages of Amsterdam are so unique to the history of the Marian Apparitions movement is that "Mary is coming in our modern times under a new title THE LADY OF ALL NATIONS and is requesting a final Marian dogma."^{14} This dogma, it is stated, will contain a threefold truth:

> The Father and the Son wish to send Mary, the Lady of All Nations, in this time as Coredemptrix, Mediatrix, and Advocate. When the dogma is proclaimed, the LADY OF ALL NATIONS will grant peace, true peace to the world.^{15}

The Lady of All Nations doctrines are spreading worldwide. A publication titled *Third International Day of Prayer in Honor of the*

LADY OF ALL NATIONS states that the Lady of All Nations is not just for one country, she is destined for the people of the world.[16]

Six cardinals and forty-seven bishops from thirty-five different countries attended the Third International Day of Prayer held in Amsterdam in 1999, along with over 12,000 other delegates that came from every continent. Even the former Archbishop of New York, Cardinal John O'Connor, sent his greetings from the United States and expressed his regrets that he could not participate in the "celebration to the glory of Our Lady."[17]

The main thrust of the Lady of All Nations movement is for participants to focus on a prayer. On February 11, 1951, Peerdeman claimed the "Lady" taught her a prayer to the Lord Jesus Christ imploring Him to send the Holy Spirit. In the very next apparition, March 4, 1951, the "Lady" appeared to Peerdeman as "the Lady before the Cross." She was standing upon the globe. Peerdeman claimed that the "Lady" made the following request: "You shall have this image made and spread together with the prayer I recited."[18]

The prayer and the image were to be spread throughout the whole world for the preparation and illustration of a new dogma. According to the "Lady," this new dogma would be the final and greatest dogma: Mary, Coredemptrix, Mediatrix and Advocate. The "Lady" also foretold a great controversy and conflict that would arise over this dogma, which when finally accepted would usher in "a new era for humanity."[19]

This prayer usually is printed along with a painting of the image of the Lady of All Nations. She appears standing on the world. Her arms are extended, and three bands of light are projected downward to a large flock of sheep being illuminated. A very prominent cross appears behind the "Lady." The prayer states:

> Lord Jesus Christ, Son of the Father, send now Your Holy Spirit over the earth. Let the Holy Spirit live in the hearts of all nations, that they may be preserved from degeneration, disaster and war. May the LADY OF ALL NATIONS, who once was Mary, be our Advocate.[20]

The *Worldwide Action* pamphlet distributed by the Lady of All Nations Action Center in St. Louis, Missouri encourages all people to pray this prayer. The pamphlet states:

> Let the people pray this short, simple prayer every day. This prayer is short and simple, so that everyone in this quick and modern world can pray it. It is given in order to call down the True Spirit upon the world.[21]

Many of the Peerdeman messages warn the Church of Rome of the seriousness of impending dangers if the new dogma is not adopted and promoted. The "Lady" asks all humanity to take heed of these messages. She calls upon all Christians to unite and to encounter the world with the cross in their hands. Furthermore, the "Lady" commands that the Church be united and become one large community of all peoples.[22]

Who Is This Queen?

The Book of Revelation warns about a counterfeit religious system. Bible-believing Christians call this global religion the "counterfeit bride." John, the apostle, labeled this false church the harlot. The Scriptures also indicate the harlot is associated with a "queen." In Revelation, we read:

> For all nations have drunk of the wine of the wrath of her fornication, and the kings of the earth have committed fornication with her, and the merchants of the earth are waxed rich through the abundance of her delicacies. And I heard another voice from heaven, saying, Come out of her, my people, that ye be not partakers of her sins, and that ye receive not of her plagues. For her sins have reached unto heaven, and God hath remembered her iniquities. Reward her even as she rewarded you, and double unto her double according to her works: in the cup which she hath filled fill to her double. How much

she hath glorified herself, and lived deliciously, so much torment and sorrow give her: for she saith in her heart, I sit a queen, and am no widow, and shall see no sorrow. Therefore shall her plagues come in one day, death, and mourning, and famine; and she shall be utterly burned with fire: for strong is the Lord God who judgeth her. (Revelation 18:3-8)

What is Christianity? Is Christianity based upon the Word of God and the teachings of Jesus Christ, or is Christianity founded upon messages from Heaven attributed to the so-called apparitions of Mary? Or what about other extrabiblical dogmas that have been expounded by church leaders in the past? Who has the authority to add to the canon of Scripture? It is important that we consider the answers to these questions seriously. Humans are designed to be rational thinking beings and to make choices. It is also important we make correct choices. If we do not, then the Bible teaches there will be serious consequences.

Throughout this book, the premise has been presented that all teachings in the name of Christ should be tested and scrutinized against the Word of God. At this point, I want to make another plea for Christians to consider the Word of God as the final authority on all topics relating to Christianity. If we say we are Christians and do not do this, then we willingly open the door for deception. As I mentioned earlier in this book, like the citizens of Berea who "searched the scriptures daily" (Acts 17:11), we are instructed to test all things against the Word of God. Nowhere in Scripture are we instructed to unquestioningly believe the opinions of men without careful examination. Regarding the Marian movement and other experience-based movements that embrace non-biblical teachings in the name of Christ, the time has come to make a stand. If we do not, then we may well become a part of the counterfeit church. Extra-biblical Christianity can become Babylonian in nature, and the harlot John wrote about in the Book of Revelation can and will materialize.

The Eucharistic Jesus

The apparition of Mary conveys numerous messages given to thousands of visionaries that deal with a variety of topics. One of the main themes consistently reported by those who receive messages from "Mary" is the great importance of the Eucharist. Not only are Catholic apologists, like Peter Kreeft, stating that experiences centered around the "Host" are important for unity, so are the apparitions of Mary and even so-called manifestations of "Jesus."

The following quote is from a message from an apparition of Mary that occurred in Rome, Italy. Rome, of course, is where the "Mother of All Churches" is located. It was here that "Mary" stated that she is the "Mother of the Eucharist":

> Speak about the Mother of the Eucharist, because the Mother of the Eucharist closes history. The Immaculate Conception* opens the History, and the Mother of the Eucharist closes it. . . . All the messages come from God and everywhere that I am appearing, I am speaking about the same things, because through the triumph of the Eucharist the Mother wants all the Churches to be reunited, so that there will be only one Church for all the people.[24]

At this apparition site in Rome, the visionary Marisa Rossi has also received many messages from "Jesus" in the Eucharist. Interest-

---

*The Immaculate Conception, sometimes confused with the virgin birth, is the doctrine that upholds a sinless view of Mary, declaring that she was free of original sin from the moment of conception.[23] This doctrine is upheld with an ecclesiastical anathema (curse to Hell) to anyone who denies this doctrine. Yet, the real Mary declared her need of a Savior (Luke 1:47). Why would she need a Savior if she were sinless? The ecclesiastical hierarchy of the pope committed grave error when they burned people at the stake over such issues.

ingly, he is also speaking about his great desire for unity, particularly religious unity:

> It is God the Father's wish to reunite all the religions and the races, for them to become only one community and the Eucharist to become the center of all the religions and races . . . I want all religions to be reunited, the races to be reunited, I want only one religion, only one love, because God is love.[25]*

In addition, the apparition of Mary spoke to Father Gobbi, the leader of the Marian movement of Priests, and stated the importance of the Eucharistc reign of Jesus:

> Today I ask all to throw open the doors to Jesus Christ who is coming. I am the Mother of the Second Advent and the door which is being opened on the new era. This new era will coincide with the greatest triumph of the Eucharistic reign of Jesus. . . . The Eucharistic Jesus will release all his power of love, which will transform souls, the Church and all humanity.[26]

From these messages and many others, we can see that "Mary" and the Eucharistic Jesus are preparing the world for a new era of unity under the Roman Catholic Church. They will usher in this new period with mighty signs and wonders. This fact is well supported

---

* If this were the real Jesus speaking, has he completely changed his mind over what he said in the New Testament? Jesus held the view that where there is no truth, there can be no love, for love can never be nurtured by compromising the truth. That is why He said to His disciples, "Suppose ye that I am come to give peace [unity] on earth? I tell you, Nay; but rather division" (Luke 12:51). Jesus was not divisive, but He never promoted unity at all costs either—especially when the cost meant exchanging Jesus for another Jesus, the Gospel for another gospel, and the Spirit for another spirit.

as Marian author and researcher Thomas Petrisko makes clear in his book *Call of the Ages*:

> While the Blessed Virgin Mary is indeed the great sign spoken of in Chapter 12:1 of the Book of Revelation, the numerous apparitions of Jesus to so many visionaries throughout the world is another phenomenon that deserves close examination. Like Mary's apparitions, these reported visions are not to be taken lightly, for they carry with them incredible miracles and profound messages reportedly from the Lord Himself.[27]

Eucharistic Experiences

"Eucharistic Experiences" are extremely interesting in light of an explanation made by Peter Kreeft, author of *Ecumenical Jihad: Ecumenism and the Culture War*. In a chapter titled "The Eucharist and Ecumenism," Kreeft, a former Dutch Reformed Calvinist, now Catholic, makes the following statement in support of the Catholic dogma of the Eucharist. He writes:

> Once you have swallowed the camel of the Incarnation, why strain at the gnat of the Eucharist? If the eternal Creator-Spirit can become a flesh-and-blood-man, why can't that man's body take on the appearances of bread and wine? The gap between bread and human flesh is only finite; the gap between man and God is infinite. If God can leap the infinite gap, He can certainly leap the finite one.[28]

Of course, it is not a matter of whether God is able to take on the appearance of bread; the question is: does the Bible teach this? In Kreeft's pilgrimage from Dutch Reformed Calvinism to Roman Catholicism, it was the dogma of the Eucharist that was the most important for his conversion process. "No Catholic dogma is so distinctive and so apparently anti-ecumenical as the dogma of the Real Presence of Christ in the Eucharist," Kreeft writes. "Yet this dogma may be the greatest cause of ecumenism and eventual reunion," he continues.[29]

Kreeft also explained in his book how he came to this conclusion. He writes:

> If I was to become a Catholic, it would be out of love of Christ; and if Christ was really present in the Eucharist, as the Church said He was, then my love for Him would have to draw me there like a magnet, away from a church where Christ was present only subjectively, in the souls of good Protestant Christians, into the Church where He was more fully present, present also objectively, in the Eucharist.[30]

Since his conversion, Peter Kreeft now believes that Protestants are really missing what true Christianity is all about. He states:

> When I think how much my Protestant brothers and sisters are missing in not having Christ's Real Presence in the Eucharist; when I kneel before the Eucharist and realize I am as truly in Christ's presence as the apostles were but that my Protestant brothers and sisters don't know that, don't believe that—I at first feel a terrible gap between myself and them. What a tremendous thing they are missing! It is as if Christ paid a visit to Capernaum, and a resident of Capernaum didn't bother to come out of his house to see Him. What a point of division the Eucharist is! One of the two sides is very, very wrong. I said before that if Protestants are right, Catholics are making the terrible mistake of idolatrously adoring bread and wine as God. But if Catholics are right, Protestants are making the just-as-terrible mistake of refusing to adore Christ where He is and are missing out on the most

ontologically real union with Christ that is possible in this life, in Holy Communion.[31]

Now that Peter Kreeft has become an avid supporter and member of the Catholic Church, he holds out hope that other Protestants will be transformed like himself. He even sees that these *separated brethren* may one day be drawn back to the Catholic Church by the Eucharistic Jesus along with help from Mary whom he believes may also play a key role. He explains:

> I found that this doctrine, which seemed to repel and divide, at the same time attracted and united. The same with Mary: she—who is a point of division between Catholics and Protestants—she may bring the churches together again and heal the tears in her Son's visible body on earth, she, the very one who seems to divide Catholics from Protestants. The most distinctive Catholic doctrines, especially those concerning the Eucharist and Mary, may prove to be the most unifying and attracting ones.[32]

I find it quite troubling that many Christian figures favorably quote Peter Kreeft in their books. One of them, Kenneth Boa, a popular evangelical teacher and author promotes Kreeft in his book *Faith Has Its Reasons* and admits that Kreeft is "popular among Protestants as well as Catholics."[33]

Such endorsements and other signs taking place illustrate that Kreeft's hopes are being fulfilled. More and more Protestants are testifying that they are being drawn to the Catholic Church, especially through the Eucharist. Some say they have encountered the presence of Christ in a new and exciting way.

One such person is Presbyterian pastor Steven Muse. Muse is one of the contributing authors of *Mary the Mother of All: Protestant Perspectives and Experiences of Medjugorje*, published by the Loyola University Press and edited by Sharon E. Cheston.

According to Muse, his visit to Medjugorje was life changing, especially after he encountered the Eucharistic Christ. He writes:

> The fact remains that never before or since in my life have I had such an encounter with Christ in the Eucharist. I believe this is because I never received the bread and the wine as the Body and the Blood of Christ, so what I loved in my heart and believed in my mind were never experienced as real in the here and now of my bodily presence as I encountered him again and again for the entire week. Sometimes this happened twice a day as I received Communion both in the morning at English Mass, and again in the evening at the Croatian Mass, where I did not even understand what they were saying or singing but only prayed the rosary in my own language with the others as if I had been saying "Hail Marys" all my life. What was true was that the Father, Son and Holy Spirit were real. *And Mary was real.*[34]

While Muse testified of a real encounter with "Christ" and "Mary" while visiting Medjugorje, other well-known Protestants like Benny Hinn have made predictions that "Christ" will be showing up on stage at his crusades. On March 29, 2000, Hinn made the following statement:

> I'm gonna show you the power of God on young people. . . . Now, what you're gonna see happens usually at the last night at the end of the service for the young people. It's gonna be a powerful crusade, great, great things. Let me tell you something. The Holy Spirit has spoken, He told me He is about to show up. Oh, I gotta tell you this just before we go. I had a word of prophecy from Ruth Heflin, you know who Ruth Heflin is? Ruth prophesied over me back in the seventies. Everything she said has happened. She just sent me a word through my wife and said: The Lord spoke to her audibly and said . . . tell

Benny I'm going to appear physically on the platform
in his meetings. Lord, do it in Phoenix, Arizona in the
name of Jesus! And in Kenya too, Lord, please, Lord, in
fact, do it in every crusade in Jesus' name.[35]

Could the entity that sometimes appears as Christ in the
Eucharist eventually appear to Protestants in the flesh? Would these
signs and wonders fulfill Bible prophecy? Remember what Jesus said:

> For there shall arise false Christs, and false prophets, and
> shall shew great signs and wonders; insomuch that, if it
> were possible, they shall deceive the very elect. Behold, I
> have told you before. Wherefore if they shall say unto you,
> Behold, he is in the desert; go not forth: behold, he is in the
> secret chambers; believe it not. For as the lightning cometh
> out of the east, and shineth even unto the west; so shall also
> the coming of the Son of man be. (Matthew 24:24-27)

Are signs and wonders the evidence that a great revival will
soon take place? If "Mary" and the Eucharist provide such signs and
wonders, is it reasonable to assume they may represent phenomena
that will draw Protestants and Catholics together? If so, then could
"Mary" draw all "Christians" under the umbrella of the Roman
Catholic Church, which according to her, she alone holds the truth?
If these apparitions are deceptive in nature, can we predict that the
religions of the world will unite together as well and become the false
Babylonian-like church mentioned by John in Revelation 17 and 18?
Finally, can we predict that many who profess "the faith" will fall
away to embrace lying "signs and wonders" instead?

ISRAEL, THE JEWS, AND THE CHURCH

Anyone who has read the Bible knows the God of Israel is the God of the Bible. The Old Testament lays out the history of the Jews from creation to the time of Christ. The nation Israel started from one man, Abraham. Israel was a real historical place on planet Earth with real people who suffered and survived throughout time. It remains in existence today. Jesus, the founder of the Christian church, was a Jew. The church is not a nation but a body of believers who follow Jesus their Savior. The church and Israel are two separate and very different entities.

Many today refuse to see the significance of Israel from God's perspective. In fact, a large portion of the church has removed Israel and replaced it with the church. This is called replacement theology, and it has been around for some time. The Roman Catholic Church, in its endeavor to establish its version of the kingdom of God on Earth, has always promoted the idea that the Roman Catholic Church has replaced Israel. However, it is not just the Roman Catholic Church that embraces this teaching. A high and increasing percentage of evangelical Protestants (especially those in the Reformed camp and the emerging church) also agree. They see the kingdom of God as being established by the church. And some reformers, like Luther and Calvin, did not offer a biblical understanding of Israel and the

Jews but simply accepted what Rome taught rather than what the Scriptures taught.

Now, you may be wondering, why would such an interpretation of the Bible, relegating Israel to a place in history and elevating the church to a position of power, be so popular now? Especially when the prophecies found in the Old Testament make it clear that God has a special plan for Israel.

In this chapter, we will examine various aspects of this issue. While many books have been written about this, I will just be giving an overview. But anyone who truly studies God's Word can see for himself that Israel is Israel, past, present, and future.

They Were Scattered

If you are a Christian, you have heard an argument that goes something like this: "Christianity is a faith for the weak-minded. People believe without using their minds." One of the best ways to confront a person who believes that the Bible is foolishness is to present them with the reality of the scattering of the Jews. God, through His prophet Ezekiel, warned the Jewish people that they would be cast out of their homeland before it happened.

> Yet will I leave a remnant, that ye may have some that shall escape the sword among the nations, when ye shall be scattered through the countries. (Ezekiel 6:8)

Later in Ezekiel, God said the scattering would be throughout the whole world:

> And I will scatter toward every wind all that are about him to help him, and all his bands; and I will draw out the sword after them. And they shall know that I am the LORD, when I shall scatter them among the nations, and disperse them in the countries. (Ezekiel 12: 14-15)

And I will scatter thee among the heathen, and disperse thee in the countries, and will consume thy filthiness out of thee. And thou shalt take thine inheritance in thyself in the sight of the heathen, and thou shalt know that I am the LORD. (Ezekiel 22:15-16)

As already stated, the Old Testament is a written record about certain events in Jewish history. According to the Bible, the Jews were and are God's chosen people. However, when they refused to be obedient to God's plan for their lives, God used His prophets to warn them about the judgments that were to come. Although the Jewish people thought they were free to worship as the heathen did, God had a different idea. Ezekiel, under God's leading, warned the Jews of judgment that history has proven to be true.

The scattering of the Jewish people around the world stands as sufficient proof alone. Next time you see a Jew, think about how they have been scattered all over the world, and yet they manage to retain their identity. It's one more reason to believe the God of the Bible.

Moses Saw the Scattering

Ask people if they know about Moses. Nearly everyone will tell you he is the man in the Bible God used to lead the Jewish people out of the bondage they were experiencing in Egypt. Although his mother and father were Jewish, he was brought up as an Egyptian. The Pharaoh's daughter found him in a wicker basket in the Nile and then raised him from a baby. She named him Moses, which means she had drawn him out of the water.

The other aspect of Moses' life, which people remember, is the leadership he provided to his people before they came into the Promised Land. Although these Jews experienced all kinds of difficulties because of their grumbling and disbelief, Moses made it clear to them before they arrived that their sufferings had just begun. Their future would be filled with trials, he prophesied, and that included being scattered all over the world. On one occasion, Moses said:

> And the Lord shall scatter you among the nations, and ye shall be left few in number among the heathen, whither the Lord shall lead you. (Deuteronomy 4: 27)

Then predicting an even more terrible demise, Moses prophesied:

> The Lord shall cause you to be defeated before your enemies; you shall go out one way against them, but you shall flee seven ways before them, and you shall be an example of terror to all the kingdoms of the earth. (Deuteronomy 28: 25)

Finally, one more example showing the clarity of this amazing prophecy:

> And the Lord shall scatter thee among all people, from the one end of the earth even unto the other; and there thou shalt serve other gods, which neither thou nor thy fathers have known. (Deuteronomy 28: 64)

Keep in mind, all the prophecies were written about 3500 years ago, before the Jews had arrived in the land of Israel. They were told that their home would only be temporary. Because of their sins, they would be scattered throughout all the kingdoms of the world.

Once more, we can see the accuracy of Bible prophecy: Are there any Jews in Russia? How about Argentina, Chile, or Peru? What about the United States and Canada? Are there any Jews in Australia? Or how about South Africa? How about Mexico? El Salvador? England? Eastern Europe? The answer to all these questions is affirmative; the Jewish people have been scattered throughout the nations of the world, just as God said would happen!

Moses was a prophet of God. What he prophesied has come true. Bible prophecy and the Jewish people show we can believe in the Bible.

The Bible Records the Scattering

As we have seen, God used Moses to prophesy that the nation of Israel would be scattered throughout the world. These words were spoken and written down before the actual dispersion occurred. This would mean that for Moses to have this kind of knowledge about the future, he would have to be inspired by an intelligent being who knows the end from the beginning. The Bible states this is possible. The source of this knowledge is God.

Another amazing aspect of the Bible is the fact it was written over a period involving thousands of years. Not only does the book tell us about events before they happen, it later records them historically documenting that God means what He says.

For example, in the Book of Esther we read:

> And Haman said unto king Ahasuerus, There is a certain people scattered abroad and dispersed among the people in all the provinces of thy kingdom; and their laws are diverse from all people; neither keep they the king's laws: therefore it is not for the king's profit to suffer them. (Esther 3:8)

Notice the words that Haman used: "scattered" and "dispersed." He was referring to the Jews who had been relocated to Persia. They were a portion of a larger group who had been forced to leave their homeland as prophesied by Ezekiel.

But as Bible history records, other waves of the scattering occurred at other periods of time. The Gospel of Luke records Jesus speaking of a further scattering after His departure:

> And they shall fall by the edge of the sword, and shall be led away captive into all nations: and Jerusalem shall be trodden down of the Gentiles, until the times of the Gentiles be fulfilled. (Luke 21: 24)

Once more, all we have to do is look to history to see that Bible prophecy has been fulfilled. In 70 AD, the Romans demolished Jerusalem. The Temple was burnt and every single stone making up the walls was toppled to the ground. Not one was left in its original place fulfilling Jesus' words: "There shall not be left here one stone upon another that shall not be thrown down" (Matthew 24:2).

Finally, turn to the Book of James, which states, "James, a servant of God and of the Lord Jesus Christ, to the twelve tribes which are scattered abroad, greetings" (James 1:1). They were dispersed because they had been scattered. Bible prophecy has been confirmed repeatedly. The Bible is not just a storybook. It is historically accurate and true.

The Rebirth of Israel

The biblical prophets foretold that Israel would be scattered as a nation, and history has revealed these prophecies were one hundred percent accurate. The suffering and pain that God's chosen people have experienced is unprecedented in all of history.

Think about what occurred during the Nazi Holocaust and the repression and secularization of the survivors that followed. It seems unbelievable that this group of people could have possibly survived. But the Jewish people are with us today—an incredible testimony to the fact that God keeps His promises.

Since 1948, the year the nation of Israel was born, hundreds of thousands of Jews have moved to Israel from all over the world. Current events show that Israel is at the center of world attention. It is fascinating to see Bible prophecy being fulfilled. Consider this 1995 report about the Jewish people in Eastern Europe:

> In Budapest, Prague, Warsaw, Moscow, Berlin, in hundreds of towns and villages from the Baltic to the Black Sea, Jewish communities are coming together. Synagogues and schools are rising again, some on the foundations of Jewish institutions dating from the Middle

Ages. Jews are proudly calling themselves Jews once more, reviving traditions and cultures long buried in the ashes of Hitler's ovens.[1]

While in the past, most Jews immigrating to Israel came from Eastern Europe, North Africa, and the Middle East, a 2016 *Newsweek* article reports that thousands of Jews are emigrating from Western Europe (France, Belgium, etc.) now as well.[2] Since the Iron Curtain was lifted, a lost generation has been found. Renewed interest in Judaism is part of a broad search for spirituality that has sprung up in a desert created by the demise of an ideology. Although some may see the revival and gathering together of the Jewish people as a mystery or just a passing trend, anyone who has knowledge of the Old Testament Scriptures will know exactly what is going on. We are living in the very days that the prophets spoke about. This is what Ezekiel said God would do in the last days:

> And ye shall know that I am the LORD, when I have opened your graves, O my people, and brought you up out of your graves, And shall put my spirit in you, and ye shall live, and I shall place you in your own land: then shall ye know that I the LORD have spoken it, and performed it, saith the LORD. (Ezekiel 37: 13-14)

God is reviving the Jewish people and bringing them back to their land. We are reading about it in the news every day. Sad to say, while Bible prophecy is being fulfilled, the church is being seduced into believing Israel no longer has any significance, and God has forgotten about them and handed over the promises He gave Israel to the church instead.

Israel and the Last Days

The Jews are not a perfect people, by any means. Like other nations, they too have rebelled against God. Nevertheless, they remain God's chosen people because of the everlasting covenant

God made with them (Genesis 17:7), and the Bible has a lot to say about how the nations of the world will view Israel in the last days. History reveals Jews have experienced anti-Semitism everywhere they were dispersed. Now that many have returned to their homeland as the Bible foretold, they are hated and despised even more. It is not possible to understand what is happening today in the Middle East without understanding the biblical perspective of what lies ahead. Ezekiel foretold what will happen when the nations of the world come against Israel in the last days in an attempt to wipe Israel off the map:

> [A]nd thou shalt come up against my people of Israel, as a cloud to cover the land; it shall be in the latter days, and I will bring thee against my land, that the heathen may know me, when I shall be sanctified in thee, O Gog, before their eyes. (Ezekiel 38:16)

Is there any wonder why events in the world are unfolding as we see them happening today? Even nations that were once allies of Israel are now changing their views and becoming indifferent or even hostile. We are seeing this in our own country, the United States. What is even more deplorable is the change in the attitude of many in the church. Not only have they fallen for replacement theology, many now believe that the "God" of Islam is the same as the God of Israel and that Israel has no significance whatsoever when it comes to Bible prophecy and the last days.

Islamic Favor by the Church That Has Rejected Israel

While it should be clear to proclaiming Christians who read the Bible that Israel plays an important role in history, the present, and the future, apparently it is not. An alarmingly increasing number of those who claim to be Christian believe God is finished with Israel and that the church has replaced Israel and will receive the blessings that Israel supposedly lost.

To take this a step further, and with the help of a liberal anti-Israel media, many have now come to believe that not only does Israel have no significance in the world today, Israel and the Jews are a detriment to the world, and Islam and the Muslims are what is significant. In an article titled "The Left's Muslim Replacement Theology for Jews," New York writer Daniel Greenfield explains what the media is trying to convince people of:

> Muslims are the new Jews. You can find this offensive claim repeated everywhere in the media. The Jews, a small ethnic minority of millions that was stateless for thousands of years, are a terrible analogy for a global Muslim population of 1.6 billion and around 50 countries that do not comprise a single ethnicity or race. Comparing the two makes as much sense as comparing the Finns to all of Asia. . . .
>
> In this twisted historical revisionism, the Jews, a beleaguered minority hanging on to a country slightly bigger than Fiji, who have spent the last 40 years cutting pieces off their small slice of the world to hand over to the region's massive Muslim majority in the hopes of being left alone, are the new Nazis.
>
> And the Muslim billion ruling over vast territories where human rights for non-Muslims are rarer than hen's teeth, where non-Muslim populations decline year after year as they are forcibly converted or are forced to flee their Muslim oppressors, are somehow the new Jews. . . .
>
> The analogy makes no sense. But that hasn't stopped the media from embracing it anyway. . . .[3]

Greenfield says that the media is trying to portray the Jews as the Nazis and the Muslims as the "new Jews" persecuted as in the Holocaust. He says that the claim that "Muslims are the new

Jews carry with them a whiff of progressive replacement theology."
Greenfield continues:

> The old Jews have been found wanting. Setting up a country and defending it against Muslim terrorism made them bad victims. The Muslims are superior replacement victims. They have the right to Israel and to Jewish history. . . .
>
> The final act of one people replacing another is genocide. Just ask Herod or Mohammed, whose final deathbed wish was that Jews and Christians should be purged from Arabia. Or ask the latest pundit explaining why Jews can't live near Bethlehem, but Muslims must be brought to live in New York.
>
> Muslims are not the new Jews. And the idea that Muslims have replaced the Jews and are entitled to appropriate their land and history for their own use is not only anti-Semitic, it's genocidal.[4]

Incredibly, people are buying into this Islamic replacement theology by the droves. Such a view will help draw the nations of the world against Israel in the great battle of Armageddon predicted in the Bible.

Tony Blair, former prime minister of the United Kingdom and former Anglican convert to Roman Catholicism came up with an interesting slant on replacement theology. In an article published by The Council on Foreign Relations titled "A Global Battle for Values," he writes:

> To me, the most remarkable thing about the Koran is how progressive it is. I write with great humility as a member of another faith. As an outsider, the Koran strikes me as a reforming book, trying to return Judaism and Christianity to their origins, much as reformers attempted to do with the Christian church centuries later. The Koran is inclusive. It extols science and knowledge and abhors superstition. It is practical and far ahead of its time in attitudes toward marriage, women, and governance.[5]

In case Tony Blair's words sound strange to your ears, you are not alone. How could a man who became a spokesperson for world powers including Russia, USA, the European Union, and the United Nations make a statement like this? But it gets worse, yet. Blair continues:

> Under its guidance, the spread of Islam and its dominance over previously Christian or pagan lands were breathtaking. Over centuries, Islam founded an empire and led the world in discovery, art, and culture. The standard-bearers of tolerance in the early Middle Ages were far more likely to be found in Muslim lands than in Christian ones.[6]

Blair's comments are from one who claims to be a Christian but who is not versed in the Bible or secular history. When one does not understand Israel and what God says about Israel, it is easy to be misled.

A Sad Conclusion

From what we read in the Bible, it is clear that Satan hates God's chosen people. The devil can read God's Word, and he also knows what God has said about blessing those who support His people. This is what God told Abraham:

> And I will make of thee a great nation, and I will bless thee, and make thy name great; and thou shalt be a blessing: And I will bless them that bless thee, and curse him that curseth thee: and in thee shall all families of the earth be blessed. (Genesis 12: 2-3)

God is committed to the people of Israel as is described in Romans:

> Hath God cast away his people? God forbid. For I also am an Israelite, of the seed of Abraham, of the tribe of Benjamin. (Romans 11:1)

In Mike Oppenheimer's discussion on replacement theology, he states:

In Ezekiel 36, God makes it very clear that He will never abandon Israel—not for their sakes alone, but because His name and His reputation are on the line. Jeremiah writes immediately after the promise of a New Covenant:

"Thus saith the Lord, which giveth the sun for a light by day, and the ordinances of the moon and of the stars for a light by night, which divideth the sea when the waves thereof roar; The Lord of hosts is his name: If those ordinances depart from before me, saith the Lord, then the seed of Israel also shall cease from being a nation before me for ever." (Jeremiah 31:35–36)

God is so adamant about His covenant with Israel here that He would sooner revoke the existence of the stars and planets than He would withdraw His covenant with Israel.[7]

What is so incomprehensible is that those who profess to be followers of Jesus Christ would like to reinterpret what God has said and replace Israel with the church. This is so dangerous and is a sign we are in the end times where the world and the church are being conditioned by the one who will deceive the whole world into thinking that God no longer has a special plan (or covenant) with the Jews, but has rejected them and their right to be their own nation. This lie puts a special distortion to all of Scripture and will indeed fuel the fire of growing anti-Semitism.

When Christians become despisers of the Jews, we know the time is short because the spirit of antichrist is already at work in those who profess to know God but have fallen victim to part of the delusion that will beset the world in the last days. It is prophecy being fulfilled; unfortunately, these Christians are on the wrong side of the equation.

19

HOW TO BUILD
A CHURCH

The subject of church growth is a popular topic in Christian circles. The success of a denomination or a church is often measured by tabulating numbers of individuals. Size has become the indicator of how well a church or denomination is doing. It makes perfect sense that this is happening because now that biblical doctrine is being set aside, a quest for numbers has become all important. Directly along this line, a valuable gauge for viewing the success of such a ministry is how much money is going into the offering plates. Bottom line, it is not *what* is being preached that counts but what will draw the crowds.

The great commission, as presented in the last chapter of the Book of Matthew, outlines the obligation handed down through the generations of believers of Jesus Christ. What Jesus stated should be very clear:

> Go ye therefore, and teach all nations, baptizing them in the name of the Father, and of the Son, and of the Holy Ghost: teaching them to observe all things whatsoever I have commanded you: and, lo, I am with you alway, even unto the end of the world. (Matthew 28:19-20)

Certainly it should be understood that the great commission is about spreading the good news of the Gospel of Jesus Christ far and wide. No one could ever deny that the times have changed, but the basic message remains the same as it was when Jesus challenged His disciples some two thousand years ago. And it is obvious from the statement Jesus made, the command to be constantly reaching out to the lost should go on fervently until the end of the age when He will return.

By most of today's standards within the evangelical/Protestant church, the larger the church or the denomination the more successful that organization has been in fulfilling the great commission. However, that is not necessarily so. A brief analysis of some of the church-growth programs indicates a lot of church activities don't actually produce permanent spiritual fruit. In other words, a church might have people filling the pews and the church building, but if they are not being fed, nourished, and discipled through the Word of God but are rather being stuffed with man-made products, they will not be permanently affected.

One of the new popular strategies that has been sold by the church-growth "experts" is the concept we are living in a market-oriented society. Often pastors and church boards are advised to survey their surrounding communities to see what kinds of programs or activities people would like or what would make them feel comfortable and not threatened if they were to come to their churches. When they determine what these needs or desires are, they then come up with the appropriate programs, entertainment, or services to which the crowds are drawn.

Although getting people to come to church may be an important step in having them eventually hear the Gospel, a candy-coated version of Christianity was never part of the New Testament church. Paul wrote that the Gospel was not something to hide and disguise or completely alter altogether. Instead, he said it is powerful, and it transforms lives.

Today, too many churches attempt to become large by telling people what they want to hear rather than telling them what

God wants said. Shouldn't we get back to the bold preaching and teaching of the Word of God which will produce mature well-fed Christians who can share their faith with others and live out their faith according to the Word of God?

What Is Church Growth About?

We are living in a period of time where massive changes are underway in the way pastors do church. There are churches which remain biblically based, but such churches are becoming more difficult to find. There are those that claim to be biblically based but have incorporated worldly principles to make church more acceptable to our generation. Then, of course, there are churches that almost eliminate the teaching of the Scriptures, the mention of sin and Hell and the fact that Jesus died on the Cross as a substitute for us (He paid the price that we should have paid).

Church growth, in essence, is now linked with humanistic methods of marketing. If a church is getting bigger and bigger, that is all that is important, church-growth teachers say. However, growth from a biblical perspective, if it is healthy growth, must be dependent on God's people being taught the truth. Biblical faith comes by hearing God's Word and acting upon it. So what happens then, if church-growth methodology incorporates humanistic methods that attract people based on what is appealing to the carnal mind and the flesh?

With regard to church-growth, two major camps exist. There are those who say it is necessary to find out what people want and then provide the atmosphere or attraction that will meet their needs. This style tends to appeal to a self-centered "what's in it for me" brand of consumer. On the other hand, there are those who say we need to point people to the Word of God and be Christ-centered based on the systematic and Spirit-led teaching of the Scriptures.

Obviously, these two philosophies of ministry are headed in opposite directions. But is one right and the other wrong? What is wrong with getting people to come to church even if sin and repentance are never mentioned? Can't we be open to new methods of introducing people to Christianity? After all, we are living in the 21st century, not in the dark ages?

Perhaps you are familiar with all the arguments that support church growth man's way. However, let me ask a question? If the Gospel must be disguised or watered-down to make it more appealing and effective, is this altered "Gospel" the Gospel at all?

It is interesting to note that the apostle Paul was a strong proponent of boldly proclaiming the Gospel. Writing to the church in Rome he stated:

> For I am not ashamed of the gospel of Christ: for it is the power of God unto salvation to everyone that believeth; to the Jew first, and also to the Greek. For therein is the righteousness of God revealed from faith to faith: as it is written, The just shall live by faith. (Romans 1: 16-17)

Paul was not ashamed of the Gospel. He called the Gospel the "power of God" because it has the power to transform lives and change hearts. Man-inspired, market-driven programs may appear to do this for a season, but if it is to be a lasting and true change of the heart, it can only be done through the genuine article. Man's ways can give the *appearance* of good, but God's ways actually produce true good.

> There is a way which seemeth right unto a man, but the end thereof are the ways of death. (Proverbs 14:12)

Druckerism and Church Growth

The term "Druckerism" may be foreign to you. You will not find the word in the dictionary. Druckerism is a word I use to describe the church-growth movement that has devastated what we still call the evangelical church. Druckerism will help us to explain what is happening in the church-growth movement, why this is happening, and where much of the church will head in the future. The word is based on the concepts prompted by Peter Drucker (1909-2005), an Austrian born business-growth management guru who had a huge impact on the world and now the church.

The Drucker Institute states the following:

> Peter F. Drucker was a writer, professor, management consultant and self-described "social ecologist," who explored the way human beings organize themselves and interact much the way an ecologist would observe and analyze the biological world.
>
> Hailed by *Business Week* as "the man who invented management," Drucker directly influenced a huge number of leaders from a wide range of organizations across all sectors of society. Among the many: General Electric, IBM, Intel, Procter & Gamble, Girl Scouts of the USA, The Salvation Army, Red Cross, United Farm Workers and several presidential administrations.
>
> Drucker's 39 books, along with his countless scholarly and popular articles, predicted many of the major developments of the late 20th century, including privatization and decentralization, the rise of Japan to economic world power, the decisive importance of marketing and innovation, and the emergence of the information society with its necessity of lifelong learning. In the late 1950s, Drucker coined the term "knowledge worker," and he spent the rest of his life examining an age in which an unprecedented number of people use their brains more than their backs.[1]

Drucker's humanistic church-growth consulting ideas have reshaped modern-day Christianity from fellowships of believers that once gathered to be taught God's Word into corporations that now are run for profit with a focus on the accumulation of property.

Drucker believed megachurches were the most fertile ground for his humanistic ideas and would have the most influence in reshaping spirituality on a planetary basis.

Although Drucker is now deceased, his church-marketing schemes are not. He was a well-known globalist who had an emphasis on one-world government and one-world religion. His concept was better known as the three-legged stool plan. He was a famous consultant for three well-known present-day American pastoral super-heroes: Robert Schuller, the late founder and pastor of Crystal Cathedral in Orange, California; Bill Hybels, founder and head pastor of the Willow Creek Church near Chicago, Illinois; and Rick Warren, senior pastor of Saddleback Church in Lake Forest, California and founder/author of the Purpose Driven books and affiliated churches worldwide.

In 2011, Robert Schuller's empire collapsed, and bankruptcy was declared after years of success. Some have wondered if this was a sign that the church-growth era was coming to an end. Others have discovered that surviving megachurches are looking for new ways to expand by joining what is called the emerging-church movement, which we will examine in the next chapter of this book.

It is unlikely that the church-growth, Druckerism era is over, and at the very least, its effects will be felt for years to come. One thing we are clearly witnessing though—the Bill Hybels seeker-friendly model and the Rick Warren purpose-driven model are morphing into a New Age mystical madness that is a revival of ancient Babylonianism. There is also strong evidence that both movements mentored by Peter Drucker are merging together with Roman Catholicism and the plan to build the kingdom of God here on Earth without the King.

This, of course, is what Rome has planned for centuries. This is the plan of the Jesuits who have intricate plans to infiltrate every Bible-based church and organization with the goal of establishing a one-world religion headed by the papacy. This can easily be seen.

Rick Warren and Tony Blair's Global Peace Plans

A lso in 2011, Rick Warren and Tony Blair met at Saddleback for the Peace in a Globalized Society Forum to discuss their plan for the globalization of religion for the cause of peace.[2] Warren and Blair spoke about Warren's P.E.A.C.E. Plan and his "Three Legged Stool Plan." Tony Blair spoke about his interfaith Faith Foundation. Both speakers were noticeably excited about what they were doing for the world.

At the forum, both Warren and Blair stated that the only way a global peace could happen on planet Earth in the future would be for all faiths to work together and do good together. The audience at the forum appeared to be mesmerized and awe-struck as they were wooed with discussion on faith, good works, democracy, and coming together.

It seems apparent that neither Rick Warren nor Tony Blair understand that their Peace Plan goals are fulfilling Bible prophecy, which speaks of a peace that is not from God but will deceive many.

Warren and Blair share much in common when it comes to plans for the world. Warren has his P.E.A.C.E. Plan, and Blair had his Peace Forum, and they are ultimately heading in the same direction. There is a peace plan coming on the Earth; but it is not the Lord's peace plan. There is a false peace, and it will deceive many.

> Because, even because they have seduced my people, saying, Peace; and there was no peace. (Ezekiel 13:10)

> Destruction cometh; and they shall seek peace, and there shall be none. (Ezekiel 7:25)

> And in those times there was no peace to him that went out, nor to him that came in, but great vexations were upon all the inhabitants of the countries. (2 Chronicles 15:5)

Megachurch Marketing

Drucker's model now incorporated by a multitude of churches crossing every denomination works on the assumption that a church should operate as a business. A successful business operates according to the following principles: find out what the needs are, manufacture a product or come up with a service that will meet those needs, and then let the masses know.

This has had a major impact on pastors and church leaders who desire to be successful, often under the pressure of congregations and church boards who believe the size of the church indicates how good the pastor is. Because we are living in an age where the Bible states many will want to have their ears tickled rather than being convicted of sin and serving the Lord, being entertained in a non-threatening environment is often what church goers desire.

When older generation pastors are replaced by younger leaders who have been trained in the church growth/management techniques taught at Bible schools, colleges, and seminaries, suddenly the Bible is watered down or takes on new meaning.

Pastors and churches that once faithfully taught God's Word and warned their flocks now look for messages that are more like stories than sermons. Because the emphasis is now on appealing to the younger postmodern generation, the pastor is obligated to become postmodern himself. No longer can he declare "thus saith the Bible." He must find ways to reinvent Christianity to make his message more appealing.

These methods have been effective and churches have even grown. When a pastor is successful, he becomes famous, and many others start to follow him, read his books, and go online to obtain outlines of his messages so they can find out how to be successful as well.

The larger the church the bigger the business and the bigger the staff. A big business requires a big budget, and a big budget requires a big offering. This limits the pastor and elders from addressing controversial issues that the sheep need to hear, in order to avoid offending the big donors at the church; hence, the shepherd remains silent.

Perhaps as you are reading this, you will recognize this is exactly what has happened in a church you know of or maybe even once attended. The fact is, this trend has happened all over the world. Many sheep, once part of Bible-believing churches, have been driven out of their flocks. When they shared their concern with their pastors or members of the elder board, they were told that if they did not like the way leadership was going, they should leave and find another church. The problem they often discover is that no other churches in their town or city have *not* been impacted by "Druckerism" in the same way.

Like Sheep Led to the Slaughter

The Bible is full of illustrations that make it easy for us to understand some of the basic principles of Christianity. For example, Jesus spoke using parables. He used an example from agriculture that can easily be understood with regard to the farmer who sowed seed. Some seed fell on good soil and germinated while some fell on rocky ground and did not.

Jesus also said He was the Good Shepherd. Most people understand what it means to be a good shepherd. Unfortunately, there are pastors who are supposed to be shepherds, who apparently are not familiar with the characteristics of a good shepherd.

While I was on a speaking tour in England, a pastor told me a story that very well illustrates what a good shepherd is and what he is not. Apparently, a group of Christians were touring Israel by bus. Their guide was taking them from place to place and describing the different things they were seeing. During the tour, the guide told them about how shepherds lead and protect sheep in Israel.

At one of the bus stops in a rural region, the guide was providing information to the group. As he was speaking to the group, a flock of sheep passed behind him. The group's attention was drawn to the sheep, and there was one thing obvious. The shepherd was not leading the flock; rather he was behind them and driving them by slapping his staff on the ground.

Somewhat dismayed, the tour guide asked the group for permission to leave for a moment and walked over to the shepherd. "What are you doing?" he asked emphatically. "I have just told this group of Christians that a shepherd leads the flock. You are behind the flock, and you are driving them."

"Oh, what makes you think I am a shepherd," the man asked the tour guide. "I'm not a shepherd. I'm the butcher. I am taking these sheep to slaughter."

This illustration shows what is wrong in many churches today. Sheep should be led, not driven. This is why a Christian should always be Spirit led. When we get our eyes off Jesus and on to a man, it is easy to lose sight of the importance of being led by the Lord, especially if church growth is the priority.

At some point in their ministries, these purpose-driven, seeker-friendly, Drucker-influenced pastors stop guiding, directing, and protecting their flocks and are overcome by human methods.

Is it possible for a shepherd to become a butcher and not know it happened? There is a worldwide movement taking place that is an orchestrated plan by man to drive the sheep away from the fold by many false shepherds. Claiming that the church must change in order to reach this present generation, apostasy in the name of Christ is forming a spirituality that embraces anything and everything. Best described as "Christian Babylonianism," the counterfeit bride, of which the Bible warns, is being prepared for the counterfeit "Christ," and few seem to be aware.

20

HOW TO KNOW WHEN THE EMERGING CHURCH EMERGES IN YOUR CHURCH

There was a time—not that long ago—when the Bible was considered to be the Word of God by the majority of evangelical Christians. Now that we are well into the third millennium and the postmodern, post-Christian era, the term evangelical can mean almost anything. What has happened? Why is this happening? And what is the future for mainstream Christianity?

For the past several years, I have been speaking around the world on current trends impacting Christianity. After these presentations, I am approached by Christians who come from many different church backgrounds. Many are expressing their concerns about what is happening in their churches, troubled by the new direction they see their churches going. While they may not always be able to discern what is wrong, they know *something* is wrong and that it needs to be addressed.

Further, many have told me they have attempted to express their concerns with their pastors or church elders. In almost every case, they were told they had a choice to make—get with the new program, or get out of the church.

This move toward a reinvented Christianity or a "new" Christianity is not just a passing fad. While some within this emerging church movement have attempted to change the name because of criticism that has outed the dangers and non-biblical focus of the emerging church, it is nevertheless the same dangerous movement. Whether it is called the *emerging church, the emergent church, vintage Christianity, ancient faith, organic church, the progressive church, red-letter Christianity, a social gospel,* or *the new spirituality,* it is the same reinvented, reimagined Christianity that has been altering the face of Christianity for many years.

I am often asked by concerned brothers and sisters in Christ to provide an explanation to help them understand what they have encountered. They want to know why these changes are underway and what to expect in the future. As well, they want to know what, if anything, can be done to stem this tide. It is for this reason I have written this chapter—to provide biblical insight regarding the emerging church and where it is heading in the future.

The Gospel According to the Scriptures

Throughout church history, various trends have come and gone. While culture changes from place to place, biblical Christianity has always been based upon the central message of the Bible which is the Gospel of Jesus Christ, and the message never changes.

This Gospel message is about who Jesus Christ is and what He has done. A child can understand the Gospel message, which is a message that proclaims that life here on planet Earth is finite and that life after death is eternal and that Jesus died on the Cross for our sins that we may be with Him in Heaven. In Acts chapter 2, Peter proclaimed a simple Gospel message by stating who Jesus is and urging the people to repent, receive "remission of sins" through Christ by faith, and to follow Him (Acts 2: 36-38).

How we respond to the Gospel message during the time we have on Earth determines where we spend eternity—Heaven or Hell. Jesus, the Creator of the universe, provided a way (and the *only* way) we can spend eternity with Him. It is a matter of making a personal decision whether we will accept the plan He has provided.

God's adversary does not want mankind to understand the simple message. His plan is to deceive the world. If he can blind people to the Gospel or convince them that they believe the Gospel when indeed they do not, his plan has been successful.

The Gospel According to Postmodernism

Times change! However, the Gospel must remain the same no matter what else changes. We are living in a postmodern era.* In a sincere attempt to reach the postmodern generation with the Gospel, many Christians have become postmodern in their thinking. In other words, they have allowed the present culture to influence *them* rather than *they* influencing the culture.

Perhaps the term postmodern is new to you. Let's examine what it means. First, the modern era was characterized by a time of rational thinking based on factual observation. Many claim the modern era ended in the mid-1900s.

The postmodern mindset moves beyond the rational and the factual to the experiential and the mystical. In other words, in the past it was possible to know right from wrong and good from evil. In the postmodern era, all things are relative to the beholder. What may be right for you may be wrong for someone else. There is no such thing as absolute truth, they say. The only thing absolute is that there are no absolutes.

We now live in a time in history that is characterized as postmodern. Professors at universities teach students there is no right or wrong. All things are relative. The Gospel message to the postmodern mindset is far too dogmatic and restrictive. They say it is necessary to find a more moderate gospel that can be accepted by the masses and allows everyone to go to Heaven regardless of beliefs.

---

*Some are saying that the "postmodern era" is over and that we are now living in a "post-postmodern era," but this is still a relatively new concept that we only wish to acknowledge but not address in this book. We will save this for a future project.

Many church leaders are now looking for ways to reach the postmodern generation. They believe they can find the appropriate methods to do so without changing the message. However, in their attempt to reach this postmodern generation, they have become postmodern themselves and have changed the message. As the Gospel is fixed upon the Scriptures, the Gospel cannot change, unless of course it becomes "another gospel," as Scripture warns. This is what is happening in the emerging (or emergent) church.

He Didn't Come

Many have noticed that since the turn of the millennium, their churches have changed positions on Bible prophecy and the second coming of Jesus. Many have given up on the return of Jesus altogether. During the '60s and '70s, there was an excitement about the imminent return of Jesus. The young people in "the Jesus Movement" were excited about Bible prophecy and could see signs that Jesus would descend from the heavens for His Bride at any moment.

The year 2000 was of particular importance. When Jesus didn't show up, many were disappointed. "Perhaps Jesus has delayed His coming," some said. Others took the position that He may not be coming at all, at least not in the manner we have been taught. They are now convinced that we need to be busy, "building His Kingdom" here on Earth by "whatever human effort is required."

The Gospel of the Kingdom

One of the main indicators that something has changed can be seen in the way the future is perceived. Rather than urgently proclaiming the biblical Gospel and believing the time to do so is short, the emphasis has now shifted. No longer are "signs of the times" significant. The battle cry is very different. A major emphasis among evangelicals is the idea that the world can be radically improved through social programs and peace plans.

This concept, while on the surface may sound good, has some serious flaws from a biblical standpoint. According to the Scriptures, there will be no kingdom of God until the King arrives. All the human effort man can muster up will fall short of bringing Utopia. In fact, according to the Scriptures, fallen man will lead us further down the road to a society of despair and lawlessness just like it was in the days of Noah. Jesus said, "For as in the days that were before the flood . . . so shall also the coming of the Son of man be" (Matthew 24:38-39). In other words, Jesus is saying that when He returns, the state of the world will be marked by immorality and lawlessness of the same caliber as when God had decided to destroy the whole Earth.

Thus, this purpose-driven view of establishing global Utopia may be a plan, but it is "driven" by humanistic reasoning and not led by the Holy Spirit. While it is, of course, right and pleasing to the Lord to do good to others, strive for peace with all men, and exhibit Christian charity whenever possible, all the goodness we can do will not be good enough. [1]

Books or the Bible?

It should be apparent by now that this book is written to point shepherds and the sheep to Jesus Christ and His Word. The Word of God (the Bible) is the most important book in the world. It is inspired. Books written by men and women, including the book you are reading, are not. Humans are fallible beings who have incomplete knowledge and wisdom, but the Bible has always proven to be totally accurate!

How tragic it is then that shepherds and sheep are so easily influenced by books written by humans. Since the printing press was invented around 1440 by Johannes Gutenberg, humans have been influenced by the written word. Until the advent of the Internet, the printing press was the most powerful tool on the planet to shape the minds and actions of others. "Give me 26 lead soldiers, and I can change the world," is a quote often attributed to either Gutenberg, Karl Marx, or Benjamin Franklin. Who first coined the statement is not what is important. The significance of this declaration speaks for itself. The printed word is a powerful and effective way to spread either propaganda or the truth.

Gutenberg's printing press opened the door for printing Bibles that could be translated into various languages and distributed around the world. Obviously, this was one of the major factors that contributed to the Reformation. With the Bible available in a printed form, the Word of God was accessible to the common man. This, of course, was upsetting to the Roman Catholic Church that had maintained only the priests and the hierarchy of the Catholic Church had the authority to read the Word and the ability to properly interpret it for others. The problem was that the people remained in darkness because the Word was forbidden to them or superseded by dogmas and man-made traditions.

Those today who love truth and love the Word of God and teach it diligently know we are entering another period similar to the Dark Ages. The Bible has been set aside, and people are reading and studying books written by human beings who have ideas and motives that often contradict the Scriptures. Large Christian publishing companies, in order to be financially successful, are looking for a sure seller from authors who are able to tickle the ears of their readers.

Then, when we find pastors recommending books for "Bible study" which are written by popular authors who seldom quote the Bible or take it out of context when they do, or use paraphrased versions of the Bible perverting the message of the Bible, we know the church is in deep trouble. Without going into detail, I will mention three of the most troubling and dangerous books that have swept the world like a storm: *The Purpose Driven Life* by Rick Warren, *The Shack* by William P. Young, and *Jesus Calling* by Sarah Young.[2] Publishers have made millions of dollars while millions and millions of sheep are being deceived.

Further, books are flooding the Christian market promoted by publishers with an agenda to re-structure Christianity by introducing eastern-religious practices and the ideas and teachings that come from Roman Catholic mystics and church founders. I have every reason to believe that most evangelical and Protestant pastors' libraries are full of books written by such people as Henri Nouwen, Richard Foster, Richard Rohr, Brennan Manning, and Thomas Merton, all promoting what is called Spiritual Formation. Other books loaded with quotes that are often inserted into pastors' messages come from the writings of the Desert Fathers, Augustine, Bernard of Clairvaux, Thomas Aquinas, Madam Guyon, Julian of Norwich, Thomas à Kempis, Teresa of Avila, Ignatius of Loyola, Brother Lawrence and *The Cloud of Unknowing*.[3]

While these individuals helped shape the traditions and dogmas of the Roman Catholic Church such as Mariology and the worship of the Eucharist, they also played a huge role in changing the course of biblical Christianity and what it means to follow Jesus Christ alone. Surely, when their names are mentioned from the pulpit as role models for the truth, every Bible-believing Christian should cringe.

Spiritual Formation and Transformation

Much of what I have described provides the formula for a dumbing-down of Christianity that paves the way for an apostasy that will only intensify in the future. This trend away from the authority of God's Word to the "reimagined" form of Christianity has overtaken most evangelical denominations like an avalanche (and has influenced *all* denominations to one degree or another). Few Bible teachers saw this avalanche coming. Now that it is underway, few realize it has even happened.

However, there is another big piece to the puzzle that must be identified in order to understand what is emerging in the emerging church. Believing in the Word of God has given way to chasing after experiences that God's Word forbids. As focus and trust in the Word of God becomes less and less important, the rise of mystical experiences is alarming, and these experiences are being presented to convince the unsuspecting that Christianity is about feeling, touching, smelling, and seeing God. The postmodern mindset is the perfect environment for the fostering of what is called "Spiritual Formation." This teaching suggests there are various ways and means to get closer to God. Proponents of Spiritual Formation, like Richard Foster and Dallas Willard, erroneously teach that anyone can practice these "spiritual disciplines" and become more "Christ-like." Having a relationship with Jesus Christ is not a prerequisite and is certainly not the focus. Spiritual Formation is a works-based program that lessens (or even extinguishes) the emphasis on the study of God's Word and the actual relationship the believer has with Jesus Christ. And rather than focusing on being led by the Holy Spirit and transformed by the person of Jesus Christ living in the believer, the focus is on "disciplines" and mystical prayer practices (what Spiritual Formation advocates call "going into the silence" or "sacred space"). These contemplative teachers say we cannot really know God without stilling our minds into neutral (the same thing done in eastern meditation). Once we still our minds, we get rid of thoughts and distractions, and then we can really hear from God, they say.

These teachings, while actually rooted in ancient wisdom (the occult), were presented to Christianity post-New Testament and are not found in the Word of God. The Spiritual Formation movement is based upon experiences practiced by desert monks and Roman Catholic mystics. These mystics encourage the use of rituals and practices, that if performed would enable the practitioner to experience God's presence. In truth, these hypnotic, mantric-like practices were leading these monks into altered states of consciousness through the same methods used by Buddhists and Hindus to encounter a spiritual realm forbidden in Scripture, hence occupied by deceiving spirits.

Such methods are dangerous and are forbidden in the Old Testament (Deuteronomy 18:9-13) and by Jesus Himself in the New Testament (Matthew 6:7). The Bible warns severely against divination, which is practicing a ritual or mind-altering method in order to obtain information from a spiritual source. While proponents of Spiritual Formation (like Richard Foster who wrote the classic *Celebration of Discipline*) say these methods show that the Holy Spirit is doing something new to refresh Christianity, I would suggest that what is happening is not new and is not the Holy Spirit.

The Spiritual Formation movement is being widely promoted at colleges and seminaries as the latest and the greatest way to become a "christ-like" spiritual leader in these days. These ideas are then being exported from seminaries to churches by graduates who have been primed to take Christianity to a "new" level of enlightenment.[4]

Signs the Emerging Church Is Emerging

Specific warning signs are symptomatic that a church may be headed down the emergent/contemplative road. In some cases, a pastor may not be aware he is on this road nor understand where the road ends up. Here are some of the warning signs:

- Scripture is no longer the ultimate authority and the basis for the Christian faith.

- Sound biblical doctrine is seen as outdated (even dangerous) and divisive, and the experiential is given a greater role than doctrine. Images and sensual experiences are promoted as the key to experiencing and knowing God.

- Bible prophecy is no longer taught and is considered a waste of time.

- Bible study is replaced by studying someone's book and his or her methods.

- The centrality of the Gospel of Jesus Christ is being replaced by humanistic methods promoting church growth and a social gospel.

- More and more emphasis is being placed on building the kingdom of God now and less and less on the warnings of Scripture about the return of Jesus Christ and a coming judgment in the future.

- The teaching that the church has taken the place of Israel and that Israel has no prophetic significance is embraced.

- The Book of Revelation is promoted and presented as having been already fulfilled in the past and consequently has no real bearing on future events.

- An experiential mystical form of Christianity begins to be promoted as a method to reach the postmodern generation. These experiences include meditative repetitive beats of music, icons, candles, incense, liturgy, labyrinths, prayer stations, contemplative and centering prayer, lectio divina, and experiencing the sacraments—particularly the sacrament of the Eucharist.

- The view that Christianity needs to be reinvented is promoted by ideas designed to provide "relevance" for this generation.

- Church health is evaluated on the quantity of people who attend.

- God's Word, especially concepts like Hell, sin, and repentance, is eventually downplayed so the unbeliever is not offended when he comes to church.

- The pastor may implement an idea called "ancient-future" or "vintage Christianity" claiming that in order to take the church forward, we need to go back in church history and find out what experiences were effective to get people to embrace Christianity.

- A strong emphasis on ecumenism indicating that a bridge is being established that leads in the direction of unity with the Roman Catholic Church.

- Some evangelical Protestant leaders are saying that the Reformation went too far. They are reexamining the claims of the "church fathers" saying that communion is more than a symbol and that Jesus actually becomes present in the wafer at communion.

We are currently witnessing a growing trend toward an ecumenical unity for the cause of world peace claiming the validity of other religions and that there are many ways to God.

Members of churches who question or resist the new changes that the pastor is implementing are reprimanded and usually asked to leave.

Is the Emerging Church History?

Recently I read a Facebook post by a southern California pastor that the "emerging church" was no longer a problem for him or his church. He stated that the emerging church was just another passing fad that had come and then disappeared never to be heard of again. His church was going to focus on what was positive and insinuated that "hyper-discernment ministries" were scaring his sheep into believing they were living in the last days and that apostasy was rampant.

The comments by this pastor are not uncommon. In fact, fewer and fewer shepherds today are warning the sheep in their flocks of the dangers lurking not only outside the fold but also within the fold. A good shepherd must keep watch over his flock as many wolves are lurking around seeking whom they may devour. Ignoring these dangers does not make the problems go away. Sheep can easily be misled by false unbiblical teachings that are like a grain of arsenic in a milk shake. The milk shake may look and taste good but the grain of arsenic will be enough to kill someone.

When a pastor makes the claim that the emerging church is a thing of the past, this shows he is either uninformed or he is willingly ignorant. Sad to say, it can be both, and he may not even know it. The emerging church has many stealth methods to find its way under the radar. Satan is a master deceiver and knows what he is doing. In the early stages of the emergent church takeover, the methods may have been somewhat more obvious, at least to those with God-given discernment.

Now that the clear majority of churches have been inoculated with the poison, it appears that the majority of sheep have fallen victim to the poison and have fallen asleep. Discernment is diminishing. Worse yet, the shepherds (i.e., pastors and teachers), who are supposed to protect the sheep, have fallen asleep. They are still looking for ways to replace the older generation who "smelled a rat" and left. Now these pastors are looking for ways to fill the pews with novel ideas that appeal to the "carnal mind" (Romans 8:7).

There is one area that will illustrate that the emerging church is still alive and active in many churches, ministries, Christian colleges, and seminaries. One of the most effective ways for contemplative mysticism, along with other eastern mystical beliefs, to creep in is through recommended books for the women of the church in the "Ladies Ministry." Millions of Christian women are reading books like *Jesus Calling* by Sarah Young, and books by Beth Moore are read and studied more than the Bible.

In fact, in many churches, these books replace the Bible altogether. Rather than teach verse-by-verse through a book of the Bible, the leader of the women's study teaches page-by-page through a book that is very appealing to the flesh and provides additional revelation to the Bible. When a discerning woman in the study goes to the pastor and expresses her concerns, she is often chided for being divisive, or her concerns are totally overlooked.

One of the problems is this: often the pastor's wife is the leader of the women's study. He may or may not recognize that his own wife is off track. Whatever the case, recognizing the danger of what is going on and taking action is not in his portfolio—he doesn't want to rock the boat. Soon the women have their husbands reading the books they are reading, and they too become inoculated with unbiblical ideas. Before long the church that was once right on, is right off.

Emergent apostasy is spreading like wildfire around the world. The only way to slow this delusion down is to shine the light of God's Word on Satan's plan. However, therein lies the problem. Human pride will never be corrected by the truth unless leaders will humble themselves. Unfortunately, most who have chosen the path they are on have no intention to change. Even when they are chided with love, they hurl back nasty names rather than repent.

What Does the Future Hold?

If this emerging, progressive, new spirituality church continues to unfold at the present pace, traditional evangelical Christianity will disappear altogether, and the Gospel of Jesus Christ according to the Scriptures will be considered too narrow and too intolerant. In other words, the narrow way to Heaven that Jesus proclaimed will eventually be abandoned for a much wider way that embraces pagan experiential practices. I call this form of Christianity that is unfolding—"Christian Babylonianism."

This "new" Christianity will replace biblical faith with a "faith" that says man can establish the kingdom of God here on Earth. The Word will continue to become secondary to a system of works motivated and propelled by experiences.

An ecumenical pattern toward unity with Rome will become more apparent. Those who refuse to embrace this direction will be considered spiritual oddballs that need to be reprimanded.

Those who stand up for biblical faith will be considered the obstructions to the one-world spirituality being promoted as the answer for peace.

The best way to be prepared for what is coming is to gain an understanding of what is happening now. While not many seem to discern the trend underway, there are some. Without the Bible and the Holy Spirit as our guide, the darkness coming would be overwhelming. However, the light of God's Word penetrates the darkness, and there are those who are being delivered from deception and understand what is taking place.

I am convinced we are seeing apostasy underway, exactly as the Scriptures have forewarned. This means that this current trend is not going to disappear. We must continue to proclaim the truth in the midst of deception with love. As Paul instructed Timothy:

> And the servant of the Lord must not strive; but be gentle unto all men, apt to teach, patient, In meekness instructing those that oppose themselves; if God peradventure will give them repentance to the acknowledging of the truth; And that they may recover themselves out of the snare of the devil, who are taken captive by him at his will (2 Timothy 2: 24–26).

There are still pastors and churches dedicated to proclaiming the truth. Find out where they are, and support them. If you are in a location where this does not seem to be possible, seek out materials available from solid Bible-based Christian ministries and hold Bible studies in your own home.

> I charge thee therefore before God, and the Lord Jesus Christ, who shall judge the quick and the dead at his appearing and his kingdom; Preach the word; be instant in season, out of season; reprove, rebuke, exhort with all long suffering and doctrine.

> For the time will come when they will not endure sound doctrine; but after their own lusts shall they heap to themselves teachers, having itching ears; And they shall turn away their ears from the truth, and shall be turned unto fables. But watch thou in all things, endure afflictions, do the work of an evangelist, make full proof of thy ministry. (2 Timothy 4:1-5)

THE UNIFICATION OF CHRISTIANITY UNDER THE POPE

t is difficult not to like Pope Francis. He appears to be a humble man who cares for the poor and lowly. He is constantly building bridges. He has even apologized on behalf of the Catholic Church for the persecution and suffering experienced by the hundreds of thousands who stood up against Rome in the past. In an article published by the *Christian Post*, "Pope Francis Asks Protestants for Forgiveness for Catholic Mistakes," the following statement is made:

> Roman Catholic Church leader Pope Francis has asked Christians of other traditions to forgive Catholics who have offended them in the past, and called on Catholics to offer the same in return.

> "As Bishop of Rome and pastor of the Catholic Church, I want to ask for mercy and forgiveness for the behavior of Catholics towards Christians of other Churches which has not reflected Gospel values," Francis said at the closing Vespers of the Week of Prayer for Christian Unity in the Basilica of St. Paul earlier this week.

"At the same time, I invite all Catholic brothers and sisters to forgive if they, today or in the past, have been offended by other Christians. We cannot cancel out what has happened, but we do not want to let the weight of past faults continue to contaminate our relationships." . . .

The pope talked at length about the nature of forgiveness, and said: "Beyond the differences which still separate us, we recognize with joy that at the origin of our Christian life there is always a call from God Himself. We can make progress on the path to full visible communion between us Christians not only when we come closer to each other, but above all as we convert ourselves to the Lord, who through His grace, chooses and calls us to be His disciples," he continued.[1]

Pope Francis' words of forgiving others are based on Jesus' own words that we are to forgive those who have sinned against us. He has let it be known as head of the Roman Catholic Church that the time has come to lay aside differences and have communion with those who "departed" from the Roman Catholic Church. In a time in history when there is so much violence, turmoil, poverty, and suffering in the world, how can someone who wants to bring peace, tranquility, and forgiveness to Earth not be admired?

The pope's influence on Protestants and evangelicals has been profound. Consider the following article by Lisa Cannon Green, managing editor for *Facts & Trends* magazine (a Southern Baptist publication) called "From Antichrist to Brother in Christ: How Protestant Pastors View the Pope." Green writes:

More than half of evangelical pastors say Pope Francis is their brother in Christ.

More than one-third say they value the pope's view on theology, and 3 in 10 say he has improved their view of the Catholic Church.

Those are among the findings of a new study of 1,000 Protestant senior pastors, released this week from Nashville-based LifeWay Research.

Overall, the survey found that many Protestant pastors have taken a liking to Pope Francis.

Nearly 4 in 10 say the pope, known for his humility and concern for the poor, has had a positive impact on their opinions of the Catholic Church.[2]

These statistics reiterate what I have said; the pope's influence on Protestants and evangelicals has been profound!

The Pope and Lutherans

For a number of years, Rome has been welcoming home those who departed because of the Reformation. It is not uncommon today to hear comments coming from the Vatican inviting these "separated brethren" home. While superficially the welcome mat seems wide and without any restrictions, it is important to read the fine print carefully. Has Rome reformed, or is there a stealth effort to disguise the road home without stating the rules clearly? A *New York Times* article titled, "Pope Francis, Catholics and Lutherans Will Recall Reformation," provides evidence in this regard. Quoting from the article:

Nearly 500 years ago Martin Luther nailed his 95 Thesis to the door of a German Church beginning the Protestant Reformation that led millions to break with the Roman Catholic Church and ushered in more than a century of conflict and war. On Monday the Vatican announced that Pope Francis will participate in a Lutheran-Roman Catholic worship service in Sweden this October, kicking off a series of events planned for

2017 to commemorate the 500th anniversary of the Reformation.

> The agenda to mend relations with Protestants has been on the agenda of many popes before Francis, but it is a delicate endeavor. The worship service in Sweden was billed by its sponsors, the Vatican and the World Lutheran Association, as a "commemoration," not as a "celebration" in order to avoid any inappropriate note of triumphalism. Some Catholics have criticized the notion of a pope celebrating the anniversary of a schism.[3]

This same article further expounds on a message given at a basilica in Rome by Pope Francis at an ecumenical meeting he was addressing on the closing day of The Week of Prayer for Christian Unity:

> He appealed for forgiveness for the "sin of our divisions, an open wound in the body of Christ." He added that "when together the Christians of different churches listen to the word of God and try to put it into practice, they achieve important steps toward unity.[4]

In case this sounds too good to be true, do a search of the news on Google like I did for Lutherans, Pope Francis, and Eucharist. You will come across an article that describes a road leading back to unity with Rome, but it is a one-way road. A March 6, 2015 article I came across in that Google search carries a headline that reads "Church Unity is Found in Christ, Eucharist, Pope Francis Tells Bishops." This article states:

> Pope Francis on Wednesday reminded bishops to turn their sights to the Eucharist—rather than themselves— as the source of unity for the Church.

"The bishop does not gather people around himself, or his own ideas, but around Christ, present in his word and in the Sacrament of his Body and Blood," the Pope said Mar. 4 during an audience with bishops taking part this week in a gathering of the Focolare movement.

"The Bishop is the principle of unity in the Church, but this does not take place without the Eucharist," he said; otherwise, "unity would lose its divine pole of attraction, and would be reduced [to] a solely human, psychological, and sociological dynamic."[5]

The Vatican and Pope Francis, without making it clear to the "separated brethren," have one thing in mind: There will never be unity unless those who have "departed" from the "One True Mother Church" will acknowledge the presence of Jesus in the wafer dispersed at Mass. If you remember only one thing from this chapter, remember *that*. But keep in mind also that the Catholic Church holds firmly to the belief that only the Catholic priest

POPE FRANCIS LEADING AN ECUMENICAL VESPERS SERVICE IN ROME IN JANUARY 2016. CREDIT: EPA/CLAUDIO PERI

has the power to transform the bread and wine into the body and blood of Jesus Christ; and priests will not dispense the Eucharist to non-Catholics, although sometimes Catholic priests have been known to do this without papal consent. In other words, the only way to achieve this ecumenical unity is for the "lost brethren" to be absorbed into the Catholic Church. In an example given below, exception was given to this closed-communion rule at a Mass in the Vatican, so perhaps this rule may be stretched more in the future. But, one thing is for certain, the Catholic Church cannot recant its literal view of the Eucharist, for to do so would dissolve the whole meaning of the Mass, and if the Catholic Church lost the Mass, its theological structure of working out one's salvation would collapse. Know this for certain, if Protestants think that the papacy suggests we can remain Protestant, they are very mistaken.

Remember that next time you hear Christian leaders like Rick Warren, Beth Moore, James Robison, or Kenneth Copeland suggest that the Catholic Church is a part of the body of Christ and that we need to be united together with them.

Lutheran/Roman Catholic unification is happening so rapidly right now, it is impossible to keep track of the progress. A January 2016 *Christianity Today* article titled, "Lutherans Receive Holy Communion at the Vatican Despite Ban on Intercommunion" stated:

> A group of Lutherans have received Holy Communion at the Vatican after meeting Pope Francis, according to reports coming out of Rome.
>
> The Lutherans from Finland, led by Bishop Samuel Salmi of Oulu, indicated by the traditional method of crossing their arms over their chests that they should not be offered the sacrament at Mass in the Basilica. But the priests went ahead and gave it to them regardless, Edward Pentin in Rome reported for NCRegister. "Catholics shared the Eucharist. I also got to be part of it," said Bishop Salmi, who made it clear the Catholic

priests had known who the Lutherans were so they had not been invited to partake by mistake. He also spoke of the Pope's opponents who oppose any move towards relaxing the rules on who can receive Communion.[6]

With 2017 marking the 500th year anniversary of Luther nailing the 95 Theses to the door at Castle Church in Wittenberg, Germany, Lutherans are coming back to the Roman Catholic fold. As just described, transubstantiation requires an ordained Catholic priest. The unity that Pope Francis is promoting is unity based on the Roman Catholic understanding of the sacrament of the Eucharist. Perhaps you may not agree with this assessment, but further documentation will show that Pope Francis has an even wider agenda. He would like to see unity of the Roman Catholic Church with the Orthodox Church as well.

The Pope and the Orthodox Church

While the Reformation began in the mid-1400s, the split from Rome that resulted in the formation of the Orthodox Church occurred four centuries before. Dr. George T. Dennis, professor of history at Catholic University of America in Washington. D.C, presents a brief overview of what happened. While 1054 AD is usually given as the date when the schism occurred, many problems occurred before this date. Dr. Dennis explains:

> On Saturday, July 16, 1054, as afternoon prayers were about to begin, Cardinal Humbert, legate of Pope Leo IX, strode into the Cathedral of Hagia Sophia, right up to the main altar, and placed on it a parchment that declared the Patriarch of Constantinople, Michael Cerularius, to be excommunicated. He then marched out of the church, shook its dust from his feet, and left the city. A week later the patriarch solemnly condemned the cardinal.

Centuries later, this dramatic incident was thought to mark the beginning of the schism between the Latin and the Greek churches, a division that still separates Roman Catholics and Eastern Orthodox (Greek, Russian, and other). Today, however, no serious scholar maintains that the schism began in 1054. The process leading to the definitive break was much more complicated, and no single cause or event can be said to have precipitated it.[7]

Notable differences have separated the Roman Catholic Church and the Eastern Orthodox Church (Russian and Greek). I will not take time discussing their differences in this book. The point is that both sides have disputed with each other over the years often with a vengeance. However, Pope Francis and his recent predecessors have been making tremendous strides to bring about unity. News items constantly report on this progress. For example, on June 19, 2015, an article titled "Pope, Orthodox Patriarch Express Commitment for Unity" appeared in the *National Catholic Inquirer*. Quoting from the article:

> Pope Francis and the patriarch of the Syriac Orthodox Church of Antioch expressed their desire to work toward full communion of the two churches. The pope met with Patriarch Ignatius Aphrem II at the Vatican Friday. This was Aphrem's first official visit with Francis. The two church leaders spoke privately after which each gave a public discourse.
>
> "We express our desire and readiness to look for new ways that will bring our churches even closer to each other, paving the way for Antioch and Rome, the only two apostolic sees where St. Peter preached, to establish full communion," Aphrem said.[8]

The events happening today, as we see Christianity coming together under one canopy with headquarters in Rome, would have never been considered possible even just a few years ago. No one can deny that something is happening, yet you will hear virtually nothing from Christian leaders warning about it.

In January of 2016, as I was writing this very chapter, a Google alert came through on my e-mail indicating an article had just been posted dealing with the Roman Catholic Church and the New Evangelization. I opened the article titled, "Evangelization Deformed or Delayed: A Danger of the Quest for Religious Unity," written by Dr. Jeff Mirus for Catholicculture.org and read it immediately. How interesting! Here was a timely piece of evidence, vividly confirming the plans Pope Francis has to gather Rome's scattered flock under the guise of Christian unity.

Dr. Jeff Mirus quoted Pope Francis who had just made a statement at a homily as he was closing The Week of Prayer for Christian Unity. The pope said:

> Beyond the differences which still separate us, we recognize with joy the path to full visible communion between us Christians not only when we come closer to each other, but above all as we convert ourselves to the Lord. . . . And converting ourselves means letting the Lord live and work in us.[9]

Then Dr. Mirus continued with this comment:

> But it seems to me that the Pope has an advantage in these matters which the rest of Catholics lack, and which we can be sure is never far from the minds of Protestants, the Orthodox and Jews. These know, in an oppositional way sometimes overlooked by Catholics, that the Pope stands for the fullness of faith and authority of the Catholic Church. In attending to the Pope's quest for unity, none of these other believers supposes for a moment that the Pope will eliminate differences by abandoning the Catholic Faith. He will

not deny that Christ is God to promote unity with the Jews, nor abandon his ecclesiastical jurisdiction to eliminate divisions with the Orthodox, nor declare the seven sacraments optional to conciliate Protestants.[10]

Pope Francis and the Evangelicals

In July of 2016, an event called Together 2016 took place at the National Mall in Washington, DC where tens of thousands of people showed up. Some of the speakers and musicians included Ravi Zacharias, Luis Palau, Michael W. Smith, Josh McDowell, Francis Chan, Ann Voskamp, Mark Batterson, Sammy Rodriguez and Hillsong. Nick Hall, the organizer of the event who had hoped to draw one million people, stated, "Together 2016 is about laying aside what divides us to lift up Jesus who unites us."[11]

While this was an evangelical event, one other person who was invited to speak was Pope Francis. According to a *Christian Post* article, the pope spoke via video to the mostly millennial-aged crowd:

> "God does not leave anyone disillusioned. Jesus is waiting for you. He is the One who planted the seeds of restlessness in your heart." "Give it a try! You have nothing to lose! Try it. Then you can tell me," the pope added.[12]

It's been over fifteen years since contemplative pioneer Richard Foster shared his vision of Catholics and evangelicals coming together[13] and over two decades since Chuck Colson helped author a document titled "Evangelicals/Catholics Together."[14] It's been over a decade since Rick Warren announced his hopes to bring about a second reformation that would include people of different religions.[15] In more recent days, evangelical leaders such as Beth Moore,[16] Franklin Graham,[17] and Kenneth Copeland have played

their parts in helping to remove the barriers between the evangelical/
Protestant church and the Roman Catholic Church.

Another event that took place in 2016 in the U.S. was called
The Gathering and included speakers Jonathan Falwell, Kay Arthur,
Tony Evans, Greg Laurie, Anne Graham Lotz, Max Lucado, and
Priscilla Shirer. The Gathering mission statement was "One Vision,
One Voice, One Agenda." The statement read:

> The Gathering has one purpose: to unite the Body of
> Christ in America—all believers, regardless of race, age,
> or denomination—in prayer for forgiveness, wisdom,
> and provision for our nation.[18]

———◆———

**WHAT KIND OF GREAT AWAKENING IS
AWAITING THE WORLD AND THE CHURCH IF
TRUTH HAS TO BE LAID ASIDE FOR UNITY AND
PEACE? CAN THERE REALLY BE A REVIVAL OR
A "NEW REFORMATION" OR A GREAT AWAKENING
WHEN THE PREMISE OF IT IS ECUMENICAL,
INTERSPIRITUAL, AND EVEN PANENTHEISTIC?**

———◆———

This "one purpose" sounds very noble. Certainly, America
desperately needs help from God. But sadly, when the church says
"all believers," this no longer means just evangelical or Protestant.
I have shown you in this chapter how evangelical and Protestant
leaders have included in that definition of "the Body of Christ," the

Catholic Church. The Gathering is no exception. One of the speakers at The Gathering was Bishop Ray Sutton, Dean of the Province and Ecumenical Affairs of the Anglican Church in North America. Sutton is involved in ecumenical, road-to-Rome activities such as the Ecumenical Meeting with the Polish National Catholic Church in 2016.[19] Sutton also advocates for the Catholic transubstantiation of the communion elements (an ongoing resacrificing of Christ on an altar in contradiction to Hebrews 9:24-28; 10:10, 12, 14).[20] In essence, Sutton is doing what Tony Palmer was trying to do in his work to bring Protestants and Catholics together.

Evangelical and Protestant leaders, whether knowingly or unknowingly, are helping the pope with his New Evangelization Program to end the reformation, remove the separation between the Protestant and Catholic Church, and unite the "lost brethren" by reabsorption into the "Mother Church." What these leaders are doing is willfully ignoring major doctrinal differences (i.e., the Gospel) for the sake of unity, peace, and togetherness.

The motto for The Gathering was "Before every great awakening, there was a solemn assembly." But what kind of great awakening is awaiting the world and the church if truth must be laid aside for unity and peace? Can there really be a revival or a "new reformation" or a great awakening when the premise of it is ecumenical, interspiritual, and even panentheistic? It can happen, but it won't be one that is from God. Rather it will be a fulfillment of Bible prophecy of what will happen in the days prior to Christ's return.

Isn't it time to take off the blinders and see what is happening? The ecumenical agenda to unite Christianity under one banner should be obvious. However, this is just the tip of the iceberg.

22

CHRISTIAN BABYLONIANISM UNITES ALL RELIGIONS

T he word "Gospel" is used by Paul to define what it means to understand who the Good Shepherd is and what He has done for us. The Gospel explains the relationship that occurs as a result of accepting and acknowledging the Savior's sacrifice, repenting from our sins, and then following Him. When Paul wrote to the Romans, he began the following way:

> Paul, a servant of Jesus Christ, called to be an apostle, separated unto the gospel of God . . . Concerning his Son Jesus Christ our Lord, which was made of the seed of David according to the flesh; And declared to be the Son of God with power, according to the spirit of holiness, by the resurrection from the dead: By whom we have received grace and apostleship, for obedience to the faith among all nations, for his name: Among whom are ye also the called of Jesus Christ. (Romans 1:1, 3-6)

Christianity is about the Gospel of God. This is a message that is passed down to us today though the Bible. It is a unique message that must be defined by the Bible alone. The Gospel is about Jesus alone.

Earlier in this book, we established the fact that history unfolds in repetitive cycles. Whatever has happened before can and almost always happens again (Ecclesiastes 1:9). We are living at such a time once more. The events that occurred during the Babylonian era when mankind joined together politically and economically and was obsessed with a spirituality that worshipped Satan rather than the Creator, are upon us again (Revelation 18:1-5). While the Bible warns us in advance this is what will happen in the last days, few see the events underway, and even fewer are willing to sound the alarm.

While Babylon was a city in a region located on planet Earth, this time we are seeing the Babylonian plan unfold on a global basis. It would take another entire book to deal with this subject properly. The political and economic alliances unfolding, along with the global system of technology that has advanced via the Internet and satellite technology, have provided the modern-day foundation for the new Babylon as a three-legged global-wide infrastructure being set up and currently unfolding. As we will be looking at in this chapter, the third leg of the Babylonian three-legged stool is a global spirituality based on a revival of ancient Babylonianism. A spirituality is unfolding in the name of Christ, but it is embracing the beliefs of many different gods. This spiritual paradigm is not rooted in biblical Christianity but is rather the religion of the Antichrist.

Never in history has this occurred at such a level nor has it even been possible before. The pressure to find a global solution for religious differences under the shadow of the global threat of terrorism has been the catalyst that has brought this about. Further, growing concerns to resolve the global problems created by the byproducts of our technology have also become an incentive. The potential for destroying the planet is a real and present danger.

While numerous governments, organizations, and even individuals are playing a role in the establishment of a modern-day world-wide Babylon, there is one individual and one organization that leads the way. At the risk of offending some who may be reading this book, I want to make another heartfelt attempt to share my heart. Please examine the facts presented in the rest of this chapter with an open mind and more importantly with your eyes focused on the Word of God. It may seem that seeking to unite all religions together for the cause of peace is the right thing to do, but it is not biblically sound. If you claim to be a Christian, remember what Jesus said:

> Enter ye in at the strait gate: for wide is the gate, and broad is the way, that leadeth to destruction, and many there be which go in thereat: Because strait is the gate, and narrow is the way, which leadeth unto life, and few there be that find it. (Matthew 7: 13-14)

For the *narrow way* Jesus described to become the *wide way* traveled by the majority of the world's population, Satan would have to devise a plan to deceive many (a vast number) spiritually. Obviously, this would not happen overnight nor would it be easily detected by the unsuspecting.

The Political Pope

The pope is perhaps the most influential man in the world. When he shows up, the world, the church, and the media pay attention. At one time, before worldwide travel was possible, the pope was confined to Europe and spent most of his time in Rome. The past three popes have traveled extensively, but now with modern technology, the pope has a global dominion he can daily access via the media.

It is also important to note that popes today have become much more politically involved than they've been since the close of the Counter Reformation. The greatest example of this is Pope Francis, who is continually making statements about how the world should be run by the governments and leaders of nations and has even visited the United Nations and the U.S. Congress to deliver his messages. Following is a news item describing his message given to the United Nations on September 25th of 2015. In an article titled "The Pope Pleads to the UN: The Planet Is Ours to Save," we read:

On Friday, the pope stood before the United Nations and declared that the organization has failed. He urged UN members to care for the environment and the humans living in it, and to take on challenges ranging from human and drug trafficking to extreme poverty and government corruption. "We cannot permit ourselves to postpone certain agendas for the future," he said.

This speech, which marks the fifth time a pope has addressed the international body, follows the themes of the pope's past writings and homilies. Last June, Pope Francis released an encyclical on the environment, Laudato Si. In it, he wrote of drought and flood and pollution and waste; he talked about the cultural obsession with technology and the man-made causes of climate change. At the center of this argument was a call to care for humanity, but it was also laced with an accusation: International institutions have done far too little to protect the environment.[1]

Of course, this was not the first time a well-known religious leader has addressed the United Nations bringing a message for peace centered on politics. It is apparent the pope has taken the leadership as a spiritual leader to address global problems with global solutions and mix these ideas with a spirituality that transcends Roman Catholicism. In a previous message given June 18, 2015, an article titled, "Pope Francis: 'Revolution' Needed to Combat Climate Change" states:

As a former teacher, Pope Francis knows how to deliver a stern lecture. On Thursday, he gave one for the ages. While slamming a slew of modern trends—the heedless worship of technology, our addiction to fossil fuels and compulsive consumerism—the Pope said humanity's "reckless" behavior has pushed the planet to a perilous "breaking point."

"Doomsday predictions," the Pope warned, "can no longer be met with irony or disdain."

Citing the scientific consensus that global warming is disturbingly real, Francis left little doubt about who to blame.

Big businesses, energy companies, short-sighted politicians, scurrilous scientists, laissez faire economists, indifferent individuals, callous Christians and myopic media professionals. Scarcely any area of society escaped his withering criticism.

"The Earth, our home, is beginning to look more and more like an immense pile of filth," Francis said. "In many parts of the planet, the elderly lament that once beautiful landscapes are now covered with rubbish."

Francis' bracing manifesto came Thursday in the form of an encyclical, a letter traditionally addressed from St. Peter's Square to the more than 1 billion Catholics across the globe. Derived from the Greek word for "circle," an encyclical is among the church's most authoritative teaching documents.[2]

This message from Pope Francis sounds strangely familiar to a comment given in a message by Pope Benedict in 2007. In an article titled "Pope: Creation vs. Evolution Clash an 'Absurdity,'" we read that Pope Benedict downplayed biblical creation. He also made this very significant statement:

Benedict also said the human race must listen to "the voice of the Earth" or risk destroying its very existence.[3]

"Listening to the voice of the Earth" is a phrase of utmost significance. Such a practice was common to all pagan beliefs that originated in Babylon. The term for the goddess of the Earth the

Greeks worshipped was Gaia. "Gaia" is a term reintroduced to our generation by James Lovelock and defines the Earth as a living, self-regulating evolving entity.

Evolution is the foundation for eastern religions such as Buddhism and Hinduism that do not believe in a personal God. Instead they believe that evolution is God.

The Pope and Buddhism

While the pope and others who direct the Roman Catholic New Evangelization program that has been active in the third millennium claim they are building bridges to other religions for the sake of love, unity, and friendship, countless items in the news indicate there is much more in the making. Hardly a day passes when some item is not reported in the news indicating that another bridge has been constructed somewhere in the world. For example, an article titled "Pope Francis Makes Surprise Visit to Buddhist Temple" documents what I mean:

> COLOMBO, Sri Lanka—Pope Francis is legendary as a man of surprise and outreach, and on a Wednesday evening in Sri Lanka he found a way to combine both, making an impromptu visit to a Buddhist temple in the country's capital city. While there, according to a Vatican spokesman, Francis was shown a room with a statue of the Buddha and two other holy figures in Buddhist tradition. His hosts also showed him a jar containing relics that are only opened occasionally, but which they opened for him.

> There was also singing, during which the spokesman said the pope "listened respectfully." While not an absolute first, given that Pope John Paul II called upon a Thai Buddhist leader named Vasana Tara in a Buddhist center during a visit to Bangkok in 1984, Francis' stop was certainly unusual.

> A Vatican spokesman said that one of the Buddhist authorities who greeted Francis upon his arrival at the

airport in Sri Lanka on Tuesday had invited him to drop by, and that Francis "wanted to demonstrate his friendship and positive attitude" toward Buddhists. The unscheduled stop, which the Vatican spokesman said lasted roughly 20 minutes, came after Francis had returned from an excursion earlier on Wednesday to a Marian sanctuary in northern Sri Lanka which had been a major conflict zone during the country's 30-year civil war.[4]

Several things come to my mind after reading the above statement. As I travel at least once a year to Myanmar for our Bryce Homes Program, I am very familiar with Buddhism and its similarity to Roman Catholicism. Statues such as those of Mary and Jesus are comparable to statues that Buddhists bow down to in an act of worship. Catholics and Buddhists both have prayer beads they use to count repetitious chants that seem to give them the confidence that they are in communication with the spirit world.

Certainly, there is nothing wrong with the fact that Pope Francis "wanted to demonstrate his friendship and positive attitude towards Buddhists" as the article states. However, since this encounter with Buddhists in Sri Lanka, the pope has declared that Buddhists worship the same God that Christians worship as we will show in this chapter. There is more transpiring with the "friendship" evangelism that the pope is advocating than what is being advertised.

It takes a vivid imagination to be able to justify why the pope is not reaching out to Buddhists with the Gospel of God. The foundation of Buddhism is the belief that man is evolving onward and that through meditative techniques a human can become a higher being. This is completely opposite of what the Bible teaches. The pope may mention the word Christ when he is speaking with Buddhist leaders, but from their perspective, the only "Christ" they would understand comes in the form of "christ consciousness," which is one of the mystical pathways they believe leads to godhood.

Why would the pope not speak to Buddhists about their need for accepting the only true God and the sacrifice Jesus made to save them from Hell? No amount of "friendship evangelism" will lead them to this truth. Only the Gospel according to the Scriptures presented in love will convict them of their sin.

The Pope, Islam, and Peace

It is not just the Buddhist religion where the pope can be found building bridges. Over the years, we have been following the evidence showing that various Roman Catholic popes are reaching out to the religion of Islam claiming they are brothers and sisters who worship the same God. To illustrate this, consider an article titled "Pope: Christians, Muslims Are 'Brothers'" published November 30, 2015. The article states:

> Pope Francis said on Monday that Christians and Muslims were "brothers," urging them to reject hatred and violence while visiting a mosque in the Central African Republic's capital which has been ravaged by sectarian conflict.[5]

Francis said his visit to CAR "would not be complete if it did not include this encounter with the Muslim community," saying all those who believed in God "must be men and women of peace."[6]

Some of the comments by Catholics who were interviewed in this article are shocking unless you understand the Bible and the direction the world is headed toward—a one-world religion for peace:

> "We should eat together, we should live together with Muslims," said Clarisse Mbai, a mother who lost all her possessions in inter-religious violence. "They looted everything, they burnt my house and I have nothing but I am ready to forget," she said.

> Nicole Ouabangue, whose husband was hacked to death with an axe, said she had heard many speeches before but the pope's words were "different." "Pope Francis has

more influence. If there is anybody who can resolve our problems on Earth, it is him," she said.[7]

Do All Religions Worship the Same God?

In the preface of this book, I mentioned I previously had no intention of writing another book. That was until I read a January 2016 *Catholic News Agency* article and saw a video that broadcast to the world Pope Francis' claim that all religions worship the same God. The article, which turned out to be the catalyst for this book, is titled "In First Prayer Video, Pope Stresses Interfaith Unity: 'We are all children of God." It reads:

> The Pope's first-ever video message on his monthly prayer intentions was . . . highlighting the importance of interreligious dialogue and the beliefs different faith traditions hold in common, such as the figure of God and love.
>
> "Many think differently, feel differently, seeking God or meeting God in different ways. In this crowd, in this range of religions, there is only one certainty that we have for all: *we are all children of God*," Pope Francis said in his message. . . . At the beginning of the video, a minute-and-a-half long, the Pope cites the fact that the majority of the earth's inhabitants profess some sort of religious belief.
>
> This, he said, "should lead to a dialogue among religions. We should not stop praying for it and collaborating with those who think differently." The video goes on to feature representatives of Buddhism, Christianity, Islam and Judaism, who proclaim their respective beliefs in God, Jesus Christ, Allah and Buddha.[8] (emphasis added)

Pope Francis Proposes New Beatitude— To See God in Every Person

Shortly before this book went to press, the *Catholic News Service* released a news article that had an equally strong impact on me. The November 2016 article reported that Pope Francis has proposed six new beatitudes. Four of the "new beatitudes" had to do with forgiving others, caring about the Earth, and helping the poor and needy. One of them was ecumenical in nature: "Blessed are those who pray and work for full communion between Christians [meaning Christians and Catholics]."[9] But the one that stunned me was "Blessed are those who see God in every person and strive to make others also discover him."[10] Pope Francis' earlier comments that all religions worship the same God were certainly enough to show the direction he is going, but this beatitude (as if the beatitudes in Scripture need to be expanded) absolutely confirms that this pope is not only ecumenical, he is also interspiritual (all paths lead to God) and panentheistic (God is in all). But as author and speaker Warren Smith points out in his booklet *Be Still and Know That You Are Not God,* this is what the Catholic Church has believed all along. It's just that most people don't know it because it hasn't been broadcasted as it is now with Pope Francis. This is what the Catholic Catechism says:

> Let us rejoice then and give thanks that we have become not only Christians, but Christ himself. Do you understand and grasp, brethren, God's grace toward us? Marvel and rejoice: we have become Christ.[11]

> For the Son of God became man so that we might become God.[12]

The question is, will anyone speak up, or will there just remain silence from leaders and shepherds in the Christian church? Biblically, we are headed toward the fulfillment of prophecy indicating we are in the last of the last days where all religions culminate together, where man will declare his own divinity, and where preparations are made for the world to worship the Antichrist.

23

COME OUT OF HER

The Bible refers to the body of Christ as *the bride*. Revelation states:

> And there came unto me one of the seven angels which had the seven vials full of the seven last plagues, and talked with me, saying, Come hither, I will shew thee the bride, the Lamb's wife. (Revelation 21:9)

Paul further explained to the church at Ephesus:

> For the husband is the head of the wife, even as Christ is the head of the church: and he is the saviour of the body. (Ephesians 5:23)

The church is married to the Lamb. The Lamb is Jesus Christ, and the bride of Christ is the Church of Jesus Christ. The Church is made up of born-again believers who understand that Jesus is a narrow way and the only way. The Church is not made up of a mixture of Christianity and pagan religious beliefs for the purpose of establishing a global ecumenical spirituality for the cause of peace.

Christians are called to follow Jesus Christ (Mark 8:34). Following Jesus means to hear and believe His Word (Romans 10:17), as it is not possible to please God without faith (Hebrews 11:6). And if we believe His Word, it follows that we will obey His Word (John 15:7), we will teach His Word—as the basis of sound doctrine (2 Timothy 4:2), and we will expose false doctrine—a characteristic of the perilous last days where Satan and the fallen spirit realm are at work to deceive the whole world (1 Timothy 4:1).

The above Scriptures are vital to understanding some of the basic principles of what it means to be a Christian. Over the past several chapters, we have been documenting various trends presently underway in what most would term as the body of Christ. The ideas and practices being promoted contradict the very teachings revealed in God's Word.

Given the fact that these trends can be understood as signs of the end times and that we are very near to the events foretold that will judge the world as described in the Book of Revelation, now is the time to be alert and to take action.

A Counterfeit Bride

In the Book of Revelation, John warns about a global false Babylonian religious system. Bible-believing Christians call this religious system that impacts the entire planet the *counterfeit bride*. John, the apostle, labeled this false church the *harlot* and warned that it would be judged:

> And there came one of the seven angels which had the seven vials, and talked with me, saying unto me, Come hither; I will shew unto thee the judgment of the great whore that sitteth upon many waters: With whom the kings of the earth have committed fornication, and the inhabitants of the earth have been made drunk with the wine of her fornication. So he carried me away in the spirit into the wilderness: and I saw a woman sit upon

a scarlet coloured beast, full of names of blasphemy, having seven heads and ten horns. And the woman was arrayed in purple and scarlet colour, and decked with gold and precious stones and pearls, having a golden cup in her hand full of abominations and filthiness of her fornication: And upon her forehead was a name written, MYSTERY, BABYLON THE GREAT, THE MOTHER OF HARLOTS AND ABOMINATIONS OF THE EARTH. (Revelation 17:1-5)

In chapter 18 of the Book of Revelation, as I mentioned in an earlier chapter, John presents more information regarding this false religion described as the "harlot" and associated with a "queen." He said that "*all nations* have drunk of the wine of the wrath of her fornication, and *the kings of the earth* have committed fornication with her, and *the merchants of the earth* are waxed rich through the abundance of her delicacies" (vs. 3, emphasis added). Then John heard a voice from heaven saying, "*Come out of her*, my people, that ye be not partakers of her sins, and that ye receive not of her plagues" (vs. 4, emphasis added). The passage says that the harlot's sins "have reached unto heaven, and God hath remembered her iniquities" (vs. 5). It then describes the judgment that will come upon this harlot:

How much she hath glorified herself, and lived deliciously, so much torment and sorrow give her: for she saith in her heart, I sit a queen, and am no widow, and shall see no sorrow. Therefore shall her plagues come in one day, death, and mourning, and famine; and she shall be utterly burned with fire: for strong is the Lord God who judgeth her. (Revelation 18: 7-8)

So what did John see in the vision he received from God?—Verse three indicates that a global spirituality had formed based on a revival of ancient Babylonianism. He is appealing to those who *have been* seduced and deceived by the harlot to get out of the system because His words are, "Come out of her."

John is not the only prophet who foretold of a harlot queen who would be judged for the whole world to see at the end of the age. Isaiah also warned about a deceiving woman called the "virgin daughter of Babylon" who would be judged by God. In Isaiah, we read:

> Come down, and sit in the dust, O virgin daughter of Babylon, sit on the ground: there is no throne, O daughter of the Chaldeans: for thou shalt no more be called tender and delicate. Take the millstones, and grind meal: uncover thy locks, make bare the leg, uncover the thigh, pass over the rivers. Thy nakedness shall be uncovered, yea, thy shame shall be seen: I will take vengeance, and I will not meet thee as a man. As for our redeemer, the Lord of hosts is his name, the Holy One of Israel. Sit thou silent, and get thee into darkness, O daughter of the Chaldeans: for thou shalt no more be called, The lady of kingdoms. (Isaiah 47:1-5)

Who is this "Lady of Kingdoms" of whom Isaiah is prophesying? Apparently, she is a female entity who has played a deceptive role in the past and is somehow connected to the pagan religious practices of ancient Babylon. Isaiah's words bring a strong retribution and condemnation upon those who have rejected the true Redeemer, the "Holy One of Israel"—the LORD of hosts is His name.

We know from biblical history that a queen, the Queen of Heaven, played a significant role in deluding people of the past (Jeremiah 7 and Jeremiah 44). Is it possible this same Queen of Heaven will play a role in deluding the world once more as the counterfeit bride sets up the counterfeit Christ and all religions come together under the canopy of an apostate Christianity that deceives the world in the name of the Savior, Jesus Christ?

Come Out of Her

How is it possible for so many people to be deceived in the name of Jesus? This is the question I have been asked over and over. Even though Christians seem to have a problem understanding why this is the case, there is a simple biblical answer.

We have tried to emphasize the importance of following the Good Shepherd, Jesus Christ, Savior and Lord. Without accepting the Gospel of Jesus and understanding the finished work of Jesus on the Cross, there is no salvation for anyone—past, present or future. Before Jesus, people looked ahead to the Cross and what the Savior would do in the future. Now in the present, salvation requires looking back to the Cross. This is the way it will be until the second coming of Jesus.

With the importance of the Cross in mind, let us remind ourselves of Satan's goal to deceive the world (e.g., Revelation 12:9). As the one who hates the Gospel, what would be the most effective and devastating way to attempt to destroy the Gospel? I believe the answer is simple—deceive the world in a religion or spirituality in the name of the Savior Jesus Christ—Christianity falsely so-called.

This is why I have referenced the term Christian Babylonianism several times. Because the plan to deceive the world for the cause of peace is so powerful and sinister, many who even believe they believe in the Jesus of the Bible can and will be deceived.

If the apostle John were alive today, his message would not be any different than it was two thousand years ago. Strongly consider his words and ask yourself whether you are following the call of the Good Shepherd, or have you been deceived by the voice of a false shepherd? If the latter, then come out of her!

> And I heard another voice from heaven, saying, Come out of her, my people, that ye be not partakers of her sins, and that ye receive not of her plagues. (Revelation 18:4)

24

A CALL TO ACTION FOR SHEPHERDS AND SHEEP

While the demise of Bible-believing Christianity seems unavoidable in light of the current trends, there *is* hope. Just as God promised there would never be another world-wide flood, He also promised He would "never leave" "nor forsake" the body of Christ (Hebrews 13:5). While the pattern of the past reveals many great periods in history where great apostasy, occurred, God has always raised up a remnant.

Yes, there is a wide way that leads to destruction, and many are those who find it. But on the other side, Jesus is the narrow way, and He will protect and preserve those who go down that narrow path, and God will always raise up a standard in the midst of the darkness.

As our times reflect a falling away from the faith and a darkness that seems utterly hopeless, the light of God's Word during this strong delusion will shine ever more brightly.

The task of every Bible-believing survivor is to shine the light of God's Word on those in the darkness. As Jesus said, "Let your light so shine before men, that they may see your good works, and glorify your Father which is in heaven" (Matthew 5: 16).

Or speaking of the light of God, consider what Jesus taught:

> No man, when he hath lighted a candle, putteth it in a secret place, neither under a bushel, but on a candlestick, that they which come in may see the light. The light of the body is the eye: therefore when thine eye is single, thy whole body also is full of light; but when thine eye is evil, thy body also is full of darkness. Take heed therefore that the light which is in thee be not darkness. If thy whole body therefore be full of light, having no part dark, the whole shall be full of light, as when the bright shining of a candle doth give thee light. (Luke 11:33-36)

Should not believers be witnesses of the grace and mercy of God despite the vicious attack happening during this time that the Word of God is being degraded and ridiculed? Yes, it is right to warn those who are deceived about the times in which we live, but while so doing, we must be aware that many are being seduced and deluded by the god of this world who has blinded their minds.

In all honesty, I would have preferred if this book did not have to be written. However, I was compelled to write it because I saw a great need for Christians to get their house in order. While I know others share my convictions and are still faithfully warning others, I believe it is necessary that like-minded brothers and sisters get together in some way to encourage one another. Pastors, ministries, publishers, men, women, and young people are faithfully doing their part. God has called them to warn the sheep in these perilous times in various ways.

A Like-Minded Message and a Common Identification

In order to establish a biblically sound common identification and a like-minded message that defines the ministry of a last-days watchman, we turn to the call of the prophet Ezekiel:

> Son of man, speak to the children of thy people, and say unto them, When I bring the sword upon a land, if the people

of the land take a man of their coasts, and set him for their watchman: If when he seeth the sword come upon the land, he blow the trumpet, and warn the people; Then whosoever heareth the sound of the trumpet, and taketh not warning; if the sword come, and take him away, his blood shall be upon his own head. He heard the sound of the trumpet, and took not warning; his blood shall be upon him. But he that taketh warning shall deliver his soul. But if the watchman see the sword come, and blow not the trumpet, and the people be not warned; if the sword come, and take any person from among them, he is taken away in his iniquity; but his blood will I require at the watchman's hand. (Ezekiel 33:2-6)

There is no alternative for believers. We have been called to be watchmen and watchwomen. We have been given the truth by God's grace, and we need to tell others. The Word of God is our plumb line. We must evaluate current trends underway in light of God's Word.

Whether we are talking about the controversy over origins, the New Age movement, experience-based Christianity, dogmas, traditions, the importance of Israel, Heaven, Hell, the ecumenical movement, or the coming one-world religion for peace, we must always search the Scriptures to find out what God has already revealed. In every case, we will find those who hold to the biblical view are in the minority while those who support man's view are in the majority. That's a heart-rending reality to accept, but that's just the way it is. And if you look back at biblical history, you will see that is the way it has always been. John, in writing his first epistle, alluded to this fact when he pointed out that the world at large has rejected the truth, and consequently, they will reject what *we* have to say too:

They are of the world: therefore speak they of the world, and the world heareth them. We are of God: he that knoweth God heareth us; he that is not of God heareth not us. Hereby know we the spirit of truth, and the spirit of error. (1 John 4:5-6)

So, if you are in a minority, take heart; you may be in the very place God wants you to be.

Satan's plan is to use man to attack the infallible Scriptures. If he can cause man to doubt God or reject what God has revealed in His Word, his work has been accomplished. We must always turn to the Scriptures as our final authority when it comes to standing for the truth and proclaiming the truth to others. And the Gospel must always be our gauge.

Perhaps a reminder from the Scriptures is what would be helpful at this point. The Psalmist wrote about our need to trust and believe in God and His Word in many verses:

> The fear of the LORD is the beginning of wisdom: a good understanding have all they that do his commandments: his praise endureth for ever. (Psalms 111:10)

> I have more understanding than all my teachers: for thy testimonies are my meditation. I understand more than the ancients, because I keep thy precepts. I have refrained my feet from every evil way, that I might keep thy word. I have not departed from thy judgments: for thou hast taught me. (Psalms 119: 99-102)

> Through thy precepts I get understanding: therefore I hate every false way. Thy word is a lamp unto my feet, and a light unto my path. (Psalms 119: 104-105)

> Let my cry come near before thee, O LORD: give me understanding according to thy word. (Psalms 119:169)

Paul also adds more direction in this regard in the letter he wrote to Timothy. I've quoted this Scripture already in this book, but it is so vital, it is worth quoting again:

> All scripture is given by inspiration of God, and is profitable for doctrine, for reproof, for correction, for

instruction in righteousness: That the man of God may
be perfect, thoroughly furnished unto all good works.
(2 Timothy 3:16-17)

Or writing to the church at Corinth, Paul makes it very clear
that believers have an advantage over those who are not born again:

But the natural man receiveth not the things of the Spirit
of God: for they are foolishness unto him: neither can he
know them, because they are spiritually discerned. But
he that is spiritual judgeth all things, yet he himself is
judged of no man. For who hath known the mind of the
Lord, that he may instruct him? But we have the mind
of Christ. (1 Corinthians 2: 14-16)

Of course, this does not mean that just because someone is a
believer and has the Spirit of God dwelling in him, he is guaranteed
to have complete understanding and knowledge. Very often man's
will and God's will go in opposite directions. The only way to know
God's will is to know God's Word and to trust Him that He will
always be faithful to His Word.

I will worship toward thy holy temple, and praise
thy name for thy lovingkindness and for thy truth:
for thou hast magnified thy word above all thy name.
(Psalm 138:2; emphasis added)

Our adversary is constantly interfering in the personal and the
corporate affairs of mankind. His agenda from the beginning has
been to deceive the world. This also means that even those who are
members of the Body of Christ are at risk of being deceived. Paul
wrote to the church at Ephesus:

For we wrestle not against flesh and blood, but against
principalities, against powers, against the rulers of the

darkness of this world, against spiritual wickedness in high places. (Ephesians 6:12)

In order to find common identification for pastors, church leaders, and all committed Christians coming from various church backgrounds and denominations, it would be important to lay out some groundwork. I believe that an end-times remnant God raises up would include those who are committed to both the offense and the defense at the same time.

As an example, I want to interject my personal experience from playing High School football. As I went to school in a small town in Saskatchewan where we were limited with the number of players to make up a team, some of the players had to play two ways—on the defense when the other team was on the offense and then switch to the offense when the other team was on the defense. This was the case for me. For three years, I played defensive right end as well as the position of offensive quarterback. Whether defense or offense, I was only one member of the team. We all had to work together with a common goal in mind—to win the game.

I see this as an example for what must be done now in the church. Gifted players are very capable of playing various positions on the team. However, the common goal should be to point the church and the unchurched to the Good Shepherd. We all have a common enemy, Satan, who hates what we are doing. As Paul challenged the church at Corinth:

> But if our gospel be hid, it is hid to them that are lost: In whom the god of this world hath blinded the minds of them which believe not, lest the light of the glorious gospel of Christ, who is the image of God, should shine unto them. For we preach not ourselves, but Christ Jesus the Lord; and ourselves your servants for Jesus' sake. For God, who commanded the light to shine out of darkness, hath shined in our hearts, to give the light

of the knowledge of the glory of God in the face of Jesus Christ. (2 Corinthians 4: 3-6)

It is apparent from these words that our first goal should be to reach those who are lost with the Gospel, which is the light that shines into the darkness. This is not about any person or any organization. This is about pointing people to Jesus Christ and His saving grace alone.

Second, as the defensive component, we must agree together to stand up against the teachings and ideas propagated by those who are knowingly or unknowingly deceiving others. We must direct them to the truth and tell them they are wrong in a spirit of love. Jude warned the church in his letter that summarized the problem they were facing. He stated:

> Beloved, when I gave all diligence to write unto you of the common salvation, it was needful for me to write unto you, and exhort you that ye should earnestly contend for the faith which was once delivered unto the saints. For there are certain men crept in unawares, who were before of old ordained to this condemnation, ungodly men, turning the grace of our God into lasciviousness, and denying the only Lord God, and our Lord Jesus Christ. (Jude 1:3-4)

Today, contending for the faith in the church as a requirement of Scripture has become a negative concept. Perhaps this has partially come about because some discernment or watchmen ministries have forgotten contending for the faith should also be associated with defining what is biblical faith and pointing those who have departed from the faith, back to the faith, in love. Remember the instructions Paul gave to Timothy about this very topic that "the servant of the Lord must not strive; but be gentle unto all men" being "patient" and instructing with "meekness" those who oppose them (see 2 Timothy 2: 24-26).

Recently, I read on a pastor's blog the term "hyper discernment" ministry for the first time. The pastor who was contributing to the blog used the term to single out those who were contending for the faith but in a negative way. The term was used in the context that discernment was harsh, hateful and without love.

May we proclaim the good news and contend for the faith in love, warning about the eternal consequences for not following the Good Shepherd.

Harvest Time

While this book is primarily focused on sheep and shepherds, the author of this book has quite a bit of experience with farming in general. And when it comes to the times in which we are living, there is not a lot of discussion about the return of the Savior Jesus. I see this period as harvest time in relation to sharing the Gospel. While apostasy is a sign of the soon return of Jesus, so is the fact that the Gospel will be proclaimed, and those who respond will be saved. This is also a time of decision where the decisions we make will have eternal rewards or consequences.

Sharing the Gospel amid this apostasy is an interesting challenge for Bible believers. While apostasy is on the increase, there is still opportunity to share the truth in the midst of an ever-increasing wave of deception. As the waves rise and more and more people reject the ark of salvation, the Gospel remains the gospel and never changes. The main variable that remains is how many will be left who will be faithful and share the Good News and how many who once were considered believers will show their true colors and deny that Jesus is the Son of God and join hands with the ecumenical movement.

This truly is harvest time and the workers are few.

> Say not ye, There are yet four months, and then cometh harvest? behold, I say unto you, Lift up your eyes, and look on the fields; for they are white already to harvest. (John 4:35)

EPILOGUE

WHAT CAN WE DO?

A Safe Shelter For the Sheep

Perhaps the most important task for any shepherd is to protect his sheep. Keeping an eye out for wandering sheep every moment of every day and night is nearly an impossible task. Sheep being sheep find ways of removing themselves from the rest of the flock. Sheep are a lot like people with strong wills and stubborn dispositions. When instructed to be obedient, they often do the very opposite. When instructed to eat, they may lie down and go to sleep or refuse to respond.

Most shepherds do not seek other humans for help to manage and protect their herds, but they often use highly trained sheep dogs to keep their flocks in line. But even with this precaution, when the sun sets and darkness comes, other requirements are needed to keep the wolves from devouring the sheep when the shepherd lays his head down to sleep. Thus, the sheepfold—a pen or an enclosure for sheep.

While we have warned about the many risks that exist because of false shepherds and their agendas as well as the presence of the dangerous wolves within Christianity, I would like to submit a few solutions to these problems. There are ways to seek and gather the scattered sheep and find ways to provide a safe zone so they can be protected and nourished.

We are living at a time when the church of Jesus Christ is facing a critical need for true pastors and leaders who are willing to gather the scattered sheep and give them biblical hope. Did not Jesus ask the question "when the Son of Man returns shall He find faith"? Certainly, this question from the Word of God should not to be taken lightly. Does it sound like true Christianity will be flourishing when Jesus returns, or will it be struggling with only a remnant remaining?

The Good Shepherd Calls
Website and Platform

On January 22, 2016, a round-table discussion and an open forum was held in southern California to discuss the problems outlined in this book.[1] These issues are cross-denominational and worldwide. So far, very little has been done to build a platform or forum where like-minded shepherds and sheep can gather and be encouraged or encourage one another.

On February 6, 2016, a 32-minute presentation was made at a conference in southern California summarizing the need for a platform for like-minded shepherds and sheep for these last days.[2]

These discussions have led to the birth of a new website, The Good Shepherd Calls: An Urgent Message for the Last-Days Church, and is an attempt to fulfill the vision to establish a platform for like-minded shepherds, church leaders, ministries, and sheep. The goal is to encourage one another and to focus on the "Good Shepherd," Jesus Christ, and His Word. We will follow Him and His Word and not the teachings of men who are inspired by other men who may not be following Jesus Christ.

Therefore, this website is not about following any man or any movement. The platform designed will deal with essentials of the Christian faith, sounding the warnings that need to be sounded, always with the Bible as our authority. We pray that God will lead us by His Holy Spirit so that this site can be used to contend for the faith while at the same time proclaiming the Gospel of Jesus Christ, according to the Scriptures.

A Vision in the Making

Ideas always have a beginning. For these ideas to develop and become successful in the secular world, there are generally three basic steps. First, someone or some group defines a problem or need that is not being addressed. Second, a product or service is developed that addresses that need. Third, the individual or group then tells others about the product or service by a process that is often called marketing.

While this is not a magic formula for success, this is often a hands-on, practical approach. In the case of establishing a platform that would unite Christians for a common cause (standing for truth) in these perilous times, there is a fourth and very important factor. Without this, all the efforts of man fail. Very simply, the ideas and plans must be directed and led by the Holy Spirit.

This is what I believe is happening. Through discussions with several friends and colleagues, some of whom are pastors of churches, it became very apparent that the time was right to do something. The falling away as described in this book is happening globally. Many who once contended for the faith now see this to be too divisive and have moved on. Others who once warned about the return of Jesus Christ, showing prophetic events were underway, now see this as too controversial and offensive to the ecumenical movement. Many who once taught that the Genesis record provided the foundation for the Gospel have shifted their view and now teach that Genesis is based on a Babylonian myth. Others who once saw events surrounding Israel as one of God's major indicators of the last days have now rejected or replaced Israel because they are too busy building the kingdom of God with Rome.

Keeping in mind the concept of being on the offense and the defense for the cause of the Gospel of Jesus Christ, a number of ideas have been proposed. While none of these suggestions are written in stone, they provide a foundation to build on. It is not our goal to follow any man or movement or have a common banner. The only banner will be the Lord Jesus Christ and His Word.

However, there will be various facets of the developing ministry for those who want to participate:

- A general statement of faith defining parameters, goals, and objectives will be created.

- The foundation will always be on the infallibility of the Scriptures and the finished work on the Cross.

- The fellowship will be broader than one denomination or group of churches.

- More round table discussions will be held and open to others by live steam.

- A web site will be developed for posting articles and equipping readers.

- An e-mail mailing list will be established for interested participants.

- Seminars and conferences with like-minded speakers and messages will be encouraged.

- Churches who desire to broadcast this message will host Internet radio programs.

- Social media will be used to get the message out.

- Feedback and input could be allowed, perhaps in the form of a blog or an online forum.

Action Not Reaction

Therefore, let us be led by the Holy Spirit. Let us find ways to counter the apostasy and proclaim the Gospel. While churches are becoming postmodern and scorning the Bible, there are those who remain loyal to Jesus Christ yet do not know where they can fellowship. While the Bible implores believers to continue to gather together in fellowship, it is hard to fellowship with those who have left the truth. Therefore, the alternative is to find ways to meet in small groups. If churches have closed their doors and locked Jesus Christ out, then find other ways to meet, either in houses or in fellowships led by a qualified teacher in the group or even an Internet pastor.

The best way to act is by using our feet. Why continue to attend a church that has gone south when you remain true to the Word. When churches go apostate, they usually have no idea they have strayed. They are under the strong delusion of Satan. About all you can do is let the pastor and the elders know that according to the Bible, they are misguided and leading the poor sheep over the cliff to a sad destruction.

While apostate churches may still grow in numbers, true Christianity was never determined based on a majority vote. Check out church history. It is better to love Jesus and be on the narrow path than to follow Satan on the wide road and headed to Hell.

My prayer is that when *The Good Shepherd Calls: An Urgent Warning to the Last Days Church* is published, the message contained in the book will be one of the ways to promote these goals.

We are living in troubled times; yet, one thing is for certain, God is still in control, and He is not left wondering what to do in this time of great apostasy. Our job is to follow Him as our Good Shepherd and to trust Him to be our provider and defender. Remember that throughout history, God has always had a remnant who follows Him—and He wants *you* to be among that remnant.

> And the Spirit and the bride say, Come . . . And whosoever will, let him take the water life freely. (Revelation 22:17)

A Shepherd With Courage

I n the 1960s, Bible-believing Christians in the Soviet Union were under terrible attack by the government. Churches that would not come under communistic authorities were shut down. While many pastors succumbed to this governmental pressure to become state-run churches, some did not. Pastor Georgi Vins was just in his thirties, but his own father years earlier had been arrested for resisting the governmental efforts to snuff out the Gospel in the Soviet Union and was sent to prison for his faith where he died. Georgi Vins was no stranger to persecution, and with the influence of a godly mother and the legacy of his father, Georgi was determined to remain faithful to God regardless of the price.

In 1965, a group of Baptist churches in the Soviet Union formed an alliance setting forth their declaration that they would continue teaching the Word of God and preaching the Gospel of Jesus Christ. They called the alliance the Council of Churches of Evangelical Christians and Baptists. Pastor Vins became its General Secretary. Still in his thirties, he was later arrested for his involvement in the underground church and was given a three-year sentence, leaving behind a wife and four children. Later, after his release, he was arrested again and given a ten-year sentence.

Pastor Vins, and many other Christian pastors during that period in the Soviet Union, showed great courage and fortitude in the midst of persecution and imprisonment.

Today, in the Western world, it is still legal to preach the Gospel and teach the Word of God. The price to stand for truth is not nearly as dear as it has been for countless martyrs of the past and for Bible believers in many countries presently. Will shepherds today follow the Good Shepherd and feed His sheep no matter the cost?[3]

Last-Days Watchmen

While all believers are called to be faithful servants for the Lord, I realize not every Christian is called to be a watchman. This is understandable. The body of Christ is made up of men, women, teens, and children with a variety of gifts and callings all important for the body of Christ to be healthy. The watchman or watchwoman is a person called by God to warn about the dangers of departing from the truth and being led astray.

This calling to warn those who are being misled is not without problems and difficulties. The watchman, even though his or her

Epilogue—What Can We Do?

voice may be biblical, is almost always considered by the majority to be too critical, especially today, when it is evident many Christian leaders are seeking after a Christianity that is more seeker friendly and purpose driven than God fearing and Spirit led. A person who attempts to exhort stray sheep back to the fold is considered negative, judgmental, and unloving. Why is this?

The answer is simple. When someone has departed from the Word of God, he is not always grateful to be told he has departed.

Almost every day I receive calls or e-mails from concerned Christians who are discovering that their role as watchmen or watchwomen is less and less appreciated by the leadership of their churches. Many of these concerns originate when pastors and church boards force congregations to sign "covenants" or "agreements" to ensure that all opposition to their plans be silenced before these plans are announced to the church.

History has revealed that not all plans promoted by man are God's plan for man—even though they may be promoted in His name. This is why it is so important to measure man's plans with God's Word.

I would encourage every committed believer in Jesus Christ to be on alert at the present time. If the Bible warns that deception will occur before the return of Christ, then deception *will* occur. As for me, I will continue to sound a spiritual alarm by documenting various ideas and trends sweeping the world in the name of Christ but actually from "another Christ."

We must ask ourselves, are we willing to do God's will and share the truth with those who are deceived—in love—no matter the cost? If we answer yes to that call, then we must trust Him that He will guide us, strengthen us, and use us.

ENDNOTES

Chapter 3: Following Men Instead of Following God

1. "A Beginner's Guide to Raising Sheep: http://www.sheep101. info/201/behavior.html.

Chapter 6: New Testament Warnings

1. Blue Letter Bible: https://www.blueletterbible.org/search/Dictionary/viewTopic.cfm?topic=IT0004227.

Chapter 7: More New Testament Warnings

1. Webster's Dictionary 1828—Online Edition: http://webstersdictionary1828.com/Dictionary/earnest.

Chapter 8: The Reformation and the Counter Reformation

1. History.com; The Reformation: http://www.history.com/topics/reformation.

2. Ibid.

3. Ibid.

4. Toward the end of his days, Luther became profoundly anti-Semitic, and the publishers of this book wish to dissociate themselves utterly from the views he expressed on the Jewish People during these final few years. As Perry, Peden, and Von Laue point out,

"Initially, Luther hoped to attract Jews to his vision of reformed Christianity. In *That Jesus Was Born a Jew* (1523), the young Luther expressed sympathy for Jewish sufferings and denounced persecution as a barrier to conversion. He declared, 'I hope that if one deals in a kindly way with the Jews and instructs them carefully from the Holy Scripture, many of them will become genuine Christians . . . We [Christians] are aliens and in-laws; they are blood relatives, cousins, and brothers of our Lord.'"

Based on this point, Luther went on to say: "if it were proper to boast of flesh and blood, the Jews belong more to Christ than we. I beg, therefore, my dear Papist, if you become tired of abusing me as a heretic, that you begin to revile me as a Jew."

Thanks in no small part to the appalling extent of Rome's past persecution of the Jews 'in the Name of Christ', the vast majority of Jews did not convert to Christianity, and this, combined with Rome's many false teachings about the Jews, prompted Luther toward his violent diatribes against them. It should also be borne in mind that he lived in a very anti-Semitic time, and in a very anti-Semitic part of the world. Tragically, centuries later, Adolph Hitler utilized the anti-Semitic sentiments of Luther to help justify to the Germany people his atrocities toward the Jewish People, which resulted in over six million Jewish deaths.

For further information on Luther's views of the Jews, read William Shirer's *The Rise and Fall of the Third Reich*.

5. http://www.history.com/topics/reformation, op. cit.

6. B. Kirkland D.D., *Calvinism: None Dare Call it Heresy* (Sarnia, ON: Local Church Ministries, www.fairhavensbaptist.com), p. 4.

7. Ibid.

8. Norman F. Douty, *The Death of Christ*, Rev. And Enlarged (Irving, TX: Williams & Watrous Pub. Co, 1978), p. 176.

9. http://www.history.com/topics/reformation, op., cit.

10. The Huguenot Society of America, "Huguenot History," http://huguenotsocietyofamerica.org/?page=Huguenot-History.

Chapter 9: When Christianity Becomes a Cult

1. Mike Oppenheimer, "How to Recognize if You are In a Cult" (Let Us Reason Ministries, http://www.letusreason.org/cults.htm).

2. Ibid.

3. Chris Lawson, *How to Know if You Are Being Spiritually Abused or Deceived—A Spiritual Abuse Questionnaire* (Eureka, MT: Lighthouse Trails Publishing, 2016); you can read the entire contents online at: http://www.lighthousetrailsresearch.com/blog/?p=21310.

4. You can read about Roger Oakland's years in the Calvary Chapel churches in his biography *Let There Be Light*, 2nd ed., Lighthouse Trails.

Chapter 10: The Good Shepherd—Our Creator

1. As told in *Let There Be Light* by Roger Oakland.

2. Lorenzago di Cadore, "Pope: Creation vs. Evolution Clash an 'Absurdity,'" (MSNBC News Services, July 25, 2007, http://www.physics.smu.edu/pseudo/PopeEvolution.html).

3. Ibid.

4. Taylor Wooford, "Pope Francis's Remarks on Evolution Are

Not That Controversial Among Roman Catholics" (Newsweek, October 30, 2014, http://www.newsweek.com/pope-franciss-remarks-evolution-are-not-controversial-among-roman-catholics-281115).

5. Kevin Harter, "Pastor's Protest District Policy: Letter Says Evolution, Bible Can Coexist" (Pioneer Press, December 17, 2004, http://web.archive.org/web/20050206192255/http://www.twincities.com/mld/pioneerpress/10435565.htm?1c).

6. Ibid.

7. Ibid.

8. Ibid.

Chapter 11: Evolution: Bringing an Idol Into the Sanctuary

1. See https://www.merriam-webster.com/dictionary/worship.

2. Former New Age follower Caryl Matrisciana has addressed this topic of "Christian Yoga" extensively in her documentary film, *Yoga Uncoiled* and in her biography, *Out of India* (available through www.lighthousetrails.com).

3. Breath prayer is when a single word or short phrase is chosen and then repeated in conjunction with the breath (focusing on breathing in and out while saying the word or phrase). This is classic contemplative mysticism.

4. To understand the dynamics of Yoga, read these two booklets, *Yoga and Christianity: Are They Compatible* by Chris Lawson and *Yoga: Exercise or Religion—Does it Matter?* by Ray Yungen.

5. Professor Subhas R. Tiwari, "Yoga renamed is Still Hindu (*Hinduism Today Magazine*, January/February/March 2006, https://www.hinduismtoday.com/modules/smartsection/item.php?itemid=1456).

6. "2016 Yoga in America Study Conducted by *Yoga Journal* and Yoga Alliance Reveals Growth and Benefits of the Practice" (http://www.prnewswire.com/news-releases/2016-yoga-in-america-study-conducted-by-yoga-journal-and-yoga-alliance-reveals-growth-and-benefits-of-the-practice-300203418.html).

Chapter 12: New Wine or Old Deception?

1. "The Church in the New Millennium" (*Charisma*, December 1999, Vol. 25, No. 5), front cover.

2. Marcia Ford, "The Blessing Spreads Worldwide" (*Charisma*, July 1997), p. 54.

3. Ibid., p. 55.

4. John Arnott, *The Father's Blessing* (Creation House, Orlando, FL, 1995), 58.

5. Benny Hinn, "Double Portion Anointing, Part #3" (Orlando Christian Center, n.d.), audiotape #A031791-3. This sermon was also aired on TBN April 7, 1991.

6. John Arnott, *The Father's Blessing*, op. cit., p. 59.

7. Paul Carden, "Toronto Blessing Stirs Worldwide Controversy" (*Christian Research Journal*, Winter 1995), p. 5.

8. Rodney Howard-Browne, *Manifesting the Holy Ghost* (R.H.B. E.A Publications, 1992), p. 16; read Warren B. Smith's booklet on Howard-Browne's laughing revival, *False Revival Coming: Holy Laughter or Strong Delusion*: http://www.lighthousetrailsresearch.com/blog/?p=16760.

9. Marcia Ford, "The Blessing Spreads Worldwide," op. cit., pp. 54-59.

10. John Arnott, *The Father's Blessing*, op. cit., p. 58.

11. Ibid.

12. Richard Riss, *The Latter Rain* (Honeycomb Visual Productions, Ontario, 1987).

13. Assemblies of God in the U.S.A., 23rd General Council Minutes (Seattle, WA, 1949), pp. 26-27.

14. *Charisma*, December 1996, p. 55.

15. Ibid., p. 60.

16. Rene DeLoriea, *Portal in Pensacola* (Shippensburg, PA: Destiny Images Publishers, 1997), back cover of book.

17. Ibid.

18. Ibid., p. 4.

19. Ibid. p. 5.

20. For a comprehensive look at the history and doctrines of the Latter Rain movement, refer to Roger Oakland's books *New Wine or Old Deception: A Biblical View of Experience Based Christianity* and *When New Wine Makes a Man Divine: True Revival or Last Days Deception.* Both books are currently out of print, but recirculated copies can be purchased through Amazon.

21. Bill Hamon, *Apostles Prophets and the Coming Moves of God: God's End-Time Plans for His Church and Planet Earth,* (Shippensburg, PA: Destiny Image Publishers, 1997), p. v.

22. C. Peter Wagner (editor), *The New Apostolic Churches* (Ventura, CA: Regal Books, 1998), p. 51, citing John Eckhardt.

23. Ibid., p. 47.

24. Bill Hamon, *Apostles Prophets and the Coming Moves of God*, op. cit., p. 279.

25. John Arnott, *The Father's Blessing*, op. cit., p. 61.

26. Read "They Call It "Bibliolatry" (Bible Worship)—But Could it Be a Contemplative Smoke Screen?" by the Editors at Lighthouse Trails,

27. Jim Fletcher, "Andy Stanley's Dangerous Path—Tells SBC Leaders 'Get the spotlight off the Bible'" (Lighthouse Trails blog, September 9, 2016, http://www.lighthousetrailsresearch.com/blog/?p=21418).

28. Albert James Dager, "Pensacola: Revival or Reveling?" (Media Spotlight, Special Report, 1997, http://www.mediaspotlight.org/pdfs/PENSACOLA.pdf), p. 18.

29. Ibid.

Chapter 13: A Second Pentecost?

1. E.S. Williams, "More About Gifts" (*The Pentecostal Testimony*, June 15, 1949), p. 8.

2. 23rd General Council Minutes, Assemblies of God in the USA, Seattle, 1949, pp. 26-27.

3. J. Preston Eby, *The Battle of Armageddon* (El Paso, TX: Kingdom Bible Studies, September 1976), p.p. 85-86; Kindle edition, location 1282.

4. Patti Gallagher Mansfield, *As By A New Pentecost: The Dramatic Beginning of the Catholic Charismatic Renewal* (Steubenville, OH: Franciscan University Press 1992).

5. Ibid., p. v.

6. Ibid., p. 5.

7. Ibid., p. ix.

8. Prayer of Pope John XIII, Humanae Salutis, Second Vatican Council, December 25, 1961. Cf. Walter M. Abbott, S.S., general editor, The Documents of Vatican II (The American Press, New York, 1966), pp. 709, 793.

9. Patti Gallagher Mansfield, *As By A New Pentecost,* op. cit., p. 6.

10. Ibid., p. 8.

11. Ibid.

12. Robert A. Larden, *Our Apostolic Heritage: An Official History of the Apostolic Church of Pentecost of Canada Incorporated* (Calgary, AB: Kyle Printing and Stationary,1971).

13. Ibid., p. 12.

14. Ibid., p. 14.

15. Ibid., p. 15.

16. Ibid., p. 16.

17. Clife Price, "A Revival Without Walls" (*Charisma*, November 1995), p. 54.

18. Daina Doucet, "What is God Doing in Toronto?" (*Charisma*, February 1995), p. 26.

19. J. Lee Grady, "Catholics and Protestants Join Forces" (*Charisma*, October 1995), p. 26.

20. Ibid., p. 28.

21. "Celebrate Jesus 2000," brochure, mailed from Christian Conference Office, 1235 University Blvd. Steubenville, OH 43952.

22. Ibid.

23. Ibid.

24. Ibid.

25. "Roman Catholic Doubletalk at Indianapolis '90" Foundation, July-August 1990, excerpts from talk by Father Tom Forrest to the Roman Catholic Saturday morning training session.

26. Alpha News, Holy Trinity Brompton, London, July-October, 1997, 1.

27. Ibid.

28. Ibid.

29. Ibid.

30. Ibid.

31. Ibid.

32. Erin Benzinger, "Alpha Course's Gumbel Invites Vineyard UK Founder Eleanor Mumford & Furtick, Hybels to Leadership Conference" (February 3, 2013, http://www.donotbesurprised.com/2013/02/alpha-courses-gumbel-invites-vineyard.html).

33. http://www.inplainsite.org/html/the_alpha_course.html.

34. Roger Oakland, "Alpha and the Pope, http://www.understandthetimes.org/commentary/c25.shtml, quoting Nicky Gumbel from "Alpha News," March-June 2004, p. 7.

35. "Nicky Gumbel Interview Transcript" (*The Guardian*, August 28, 2009, http://www.theguardian.com/commentisfree/belief/2009/aug/28/religion-christianity-alpha-gumbel-transcript).

36. Mary Danielsen and Chris Lawson, *The Alpha Course: An Evangelical Contradiction* (Eureka, MT: Lighthouse Trails, 2016, http://www.lighthousetrailsresearch.com/blog/?p=20704), used with permission from Lighthouse Trails.

37. Patti Gallagher Mansfield, *As By A New Pentecost*, op. cit., p. 35.

38. Ibid., p. 39.

39. Ibid.

40. Ibid., p. 41.

41. Ibid.

42.Ibid., p. 167.

43. Ibid., p. 171.

44. Ibid.

45. Don Stefano Gobbi, "To The Priests, Our Lady's Beloved Sons" (The National Headquarters of the Marian Movement of Priests in the United States of America, St. Francis, ME, 1998, online edition: http://www.heartofmaryarabic.com/wp-content/uploads/2015/04/The-Blue-Book.pdf).

46. Ibid., p. 1165.

47. Ibid., pp. 1165-1166.

48. Ibid.

49. Ibid., pp. 359-360.

50. Ibid., p. 359.

51. Chris Mitchell, "Spirit-Empowered Believers Praying for Second Pentecostal Outpouring" (Charisma, April 1, 2014, http://www.charismamag.com/spirit/revival/20088-spirit-empowered-believers-praying-for-second-pentecostal-outpouring).

Chapter 14: Another Spirit

1. "Vatican II: A Walk-Through—Decree on Ecumenism" (Holy Spirit Interactive, December 5, 2016, http://www.holyspiritinteractive.net/features/vatican2/15.asp).

2. Ibid.

3. "Rejecting Holy Spirit's work in Vatican II is 'foolish,' Pope says" (CNA/EWTN News, April 17, 2013, http://www.catholicnewsagency.com/news/rejecting-holy-spirits-work-in-vatican-ii-is-foolish-pope-says).

4. Christopher Wells, "Pope Greets Members of the Renewal of the Holy Spirit" (March 17, 2015, http://en.radiovaticana.va/news/2015/07/03/pope_greets_members_of_the_renewal_of_the_holy_spirit/1155920).

5. Rick Wiles, "Why Did Copeland, Robison Meet With Pope Francis?" (Charisma News, July 7, 2014, http://www.charismanews.com/opinion/44555-why-did-copeland-robison-meet-with-pope-francis), used with permission from TruNews.com.

6. https://www.youtube.com/watch?v=82X3nORuYBY.

7. Elise Harris, "In First Prayer Video, Pope Stresses Interfaith Unity:

'We are all children of God'" (*Catholic News Agency*, January 7, 2016, http://www.catholicnewsagency.com/news/in-first-video-message-pope-francis-stresses-unity-we-are-all-children-of-god-39381).

Chapter 15: Rick Warren's Dangerous Ecumenical Pathway to Rome

1. The full interview can be viewed by visiting: https://www.youtube.com/watch?v=no9Lvlt7m4s.

2. For more information on the Roman Catholic Church's New Evangelization Program, read Roger Oakland's book, *Another Jesus: The Eucharistic Christ and the New Evangelization* and his booklet, *The New Evangelization From Rome and Finding the True Jesus.*

3. You can see a transcript of this portion of the interview, Section 1, here: http://www.understandthetimes.org/commentary/transcripts/rwinterview1.shtml.

4. Ibid.

5. See *Faith Undone* (Roger Oakland), *A Time of Departing* (Ray Yungen), and *Deceived on Purpose* (Warren B. Smith) for documented information.

6. Gerald May, *The Awakened Heart* (New York, NY: Harper Collins, First Harper Collins Paperback Edition, 1993) p. 87, citing from *The Practice of the Presence of God* by Brother Lawrence, translated by John Delaney, Image Books, 1977, p. 34.

7. For numerous actual quotes by Teresa of Avila, read *Castles in the Sand* by Carolyn A. Greene (a Lighthouse Trails novel based on the life of Teresa of Avila and a modern-day college girl).

8. See http://www.lighthousetrailsresearch.com/johnofthecross.htm.

9. Transcript, section 1, op. cit.

10. Ibid.

11. Transcript, section 3: http://www.understandthetimes.org/audio%20commentary/transcripts/rwinterview3.shtml.

12. Ibid.

13. Ibid.

14. Rick Warren, PEW Forum, Key West, Florida, May 23, 2005, http://pewforum.org/events/index.php?EventID=80.

15. Transcript, section 4: http://www.understandthetimes.org/audio%20commentary/transcripts/rwinterview4.shtml.

16. Ibid.

17. Jean Vanier, *Essential Writings* (Orbis Books, 2008), p. 76.

18. Ibid.

19. Ibid.

20. Transcript, section 5: http://www.understandthetimes.org/audio%20 commentary/transcripts/rwinterview5.shtml.

21. Ibid.

22. Ibid.

23. Read the story of Mrs. Prest from *Foxe's Book of Martyrs* by John Foxe at: http://www.lighthousetrailsresearch.com/blog/?p=7606.

24. Transcript, section 5, op. cit.

25. http://en.wikipedia.org/wiki/Chaplet_of_Divine_Mercy.

26. "The Image of the Divine Mercy" (Diary, Saint Maria Faustina Kowalska, Divine Mercy in My Soul, 1987, Congregation of Marians of the Immaculate Conception, http://www.ewtn.com/devotionals/mercy/image.htm).

Chapter 16: The Kingdom of God on Earth Without a King

1. Pope Francis, "Pope's Mass: We're not Christian without the Church" (Rome Reports TV News Agency, May 5, 2015, http://www.romereports.com/2014/05/15/pope-s-mass-we-re-not-christian-without-the-church).

2. Ibid.

3. "Outside the Church There is No Salvation" (Catholicism.org, "an online journal edited by the Slaves of the Immaculate Heart of Mary," St. Benedict Center, NH, http://catholicism.org/category/outside-the-church-there-is-no-salvation).

4. Taken from "Kingdom-Now Theology" (Lighthouse Trails blog, March 6, 2007, http://www.lighthousetrailsresearch.com/blog/?p=3295).

5. Interview by Leif Hansen (The Bleeding Purple Podcast) with Brian McLaren, January 8th, 2006); Part 1: http://web.archive.org/web/20090103090514/http://bleedingpurplepodcast.blogspot.com/2006/01/brian-mclaren-interview-part-i.html; Part II: http://web.archive.org/web/20060127003305/http://bleedingpurplepodcast.blogspot.com).

6. Brian McLaren, *The Secret Message of Jesus* (Nashville, TN: Thomas Nelson, 2006), pp. 78-79.

7. Brian McLaren, *The Great Spiritual Migration* (New York, NY: Convergent Books, an imprint of the Crown Publishing Group, a division of Penguin Random House LLC, 2016), Kindle location 2768.

Chapter 17: Lying Signs and Wonders

1. John Wimber with Kevin Springer, *Power Evangelism* (Bloomington, MN: Chosen Books, 2014 edition), p. 142.

2. Ibid. p. 28.

3. Ibid. p. 190.

4. Jim Tetlow, *Messages From Heaven: A Biblical Exploration of the Apparitions of the Virgin Mary and Other Supernatural Activity in the End Times* (Fairport, NY: Eternal Productions, 2002), chapter 1; this book is sold and distributed by The Berean Call, Bend, Oregon: www.thebereancall.org.

5. Ibid., chapters 1, 4 and 12.

6. Sandra K. Chambers, "Pentecostal Evangelist Calls Christians to Expect the Unusual When Revival Hits" (*Charisma*, March 1999), p. 25.

7. Ibid.

8. Ibid.

9. Ibid., p. 26.

10. *Charisma*, July 1999, p. 70.

11. Ibid.

12. Ibid.

13. *This Time Is Our Time: The Messages of The Lady of All Nations,* (The Lady of All Nations Association, Amsterdam, 1999), p. 7.

14. Ibid., p. 2.

15. Ibid.

16. Third International Day of Prayer in Honor of the LADY OF ALL NATIONS (Family of Mary Coredemptrix, Civitella del Tronto, 1999), (III)—Issue #10.

17. Ibid., p. 4.

18. *This Time Is Our Time*, op. cit., p. 8.

19. Ibid.

20. Ibid., front cover.

21. Ibid., p. 3.

22. Ibid., p. 8.

23. See "Mary's Immaculate Conception" by Father William G. Most, https://www.ewtn.com/faith/teachings/marya2.htm.

24. "Apparitions of Our Lady and Eucharistic Miracles in Rome" (May 16, 2000. Messages given on June 21, 1997 and June 26, 1997, http://web.archive.org/web/20000303223238/http://www.geocities.com/Athens/Forum/6832/index.html).

25. Ibid., messages given on June 21, 1997 and June 26, 1997.

26. Don Stefano Gobbi, "To The Priests, Our Lady's Beloved Sons," op. cit., pp. 676,640.

27. Thomas W. Petrisko, *Call of the Ages* (Santa Barbara, CA:

Queenship Publishing, 1995), p. 17.

28. Peter Kreeft, *Ecumenical Jihad: Ecumenism and the Culture War* (San Francisco, CA: Ignatius,1996), p. 151.

29. Ibid., 145.

30. Ibid., 145-146.

31. Ibid., 159-160.

32. Ibid., 158.

33. Ken Boa, *Faith Has Its Reasons* (Downers Grove, IL: InterVarsity Press, 2005), p. 61.

34. Sharon E. Cheston (editor), Steve Muse (contributor) *Mary The Mother of All: Protestant Perspectives and Experiences of Medjugorje* (Chicago, IL: Loyola University Press, 1992), p. 57.

35. Benny Hinn with Steve Brock "This is Your Day" Television broadcast, March 29, 2000 from 700 Club Studios, Virginia Beach, VA.

Chapter 18: Israel, the Jews, and the Church

1. James O. Jackson, "More Than Remembrance" (*Time Magazine*, February 6, 1995,), p. 37.

2. Max Kutner, "Israel; What Happens When We Get There?" (*Newsweek,* February 13, 2016, http://www.newsweek.com/french-jews-israel-jobs-424729).

3. Daniel Greenfield, "The Left's Muslim Replacement Theology for Jews" (*FrontPage Magazine*, December 18, 2015, http://www.frontpagemag.com/fpm/261127/lefts-muslim-replacement-theology-jews-daniel-greenfield).

4. Ibid.

5. Tony Blair, "A Battle for Global Affairs" (Foreign Affairs, January/February 2007 issue, https://www.foreignaffairs.com/articles/2007-01-01/battle-global-values).

6. Ibid.

7. Mike Oppenheimer, *Israel: Replacing What God Has Not* (Eureka, MT: Lighthouse Trails, 2013, can be read at: http://www.lighthousetrailsresearch.com/blog/?p=11341), p. 8.

Chapter 19: How to Build a Church

1. "Peter Drucker's Life and Legacy" (Drucker Institute, http://druckerinst.dreamhosters.com/peter-druckers-life-and-legacy).

2. See "Eye-Witness Account: Global Peace Forum at Saddleback with Rick Warren and Tony Blair Raises Serious Questions About Global

Peace Plan" by Roger Oakland (http://www.lighthousetrailsresearch.com/blog/?p=6022).

Chapter 20: How to Know When the Emerging Church Emerges in Your Church

1. For a detailed expose of the emerging church, read Roger's 2007 book *Faith Undone: The Emerging Church—A New Reformation or an End-Time Deception.*

2. Lighthouse Trails Research Project has numerous articles, books, and booklets that deal with these three books. Their author Warren B. Smith has written extensively on The Purpose Driven movement as well as *Jesus Calling* and *The Shack.*

3. Read Ray Yungen's book *A Time of Departing,* an excellent overview of the contemplative prayer movement and how it has entered the evangelical church. It discusses many of these mystics.

4. Some colleges say that they only teach the "good" Spiritual Formation, but we contend that the term itself is so integrated into the Catholic contemplative mystical prayer movement that if colleges teach Spiritual Formation, they will be either directly or indirectly pointing their students to the mystics.

Chapter 21: The Unification of Christianity Under the Pope

1. Stoyan Zaimov, "Pope Francis Asks Protestants for Forgiveness for Catholic Mistakes" (*The Christian Post,* January 27, 2016, http://www.christianpost.com/news/pope-francis-asks-protestants-forgiveness-catholic-mistakes-156052).

2. Lisa Cannon Green, "From Antichrist to Brother in Christ: How Protestant Pastors View the Pope" (*Christianity Today,* September 25, 2015, http://www.christianitytoday.com/gleanings/2015/september/antichrist-brother-christ-protestant-pastors-pope-francis.html).

3. Laurie Goodstein, "Pope Francis, Catholics, and Lutherans Will Recall Reformation" (*New York Times,* January 25, 2016, http://www.nytimes.com/2016/01/26/world/europe/pope-francis-catholics-and-lutherans-will-recall-reformation.html?_r=0).

4. Ibid

5. Ann Schneible, "Church Unity is Found in Christ, Eucharist, Pope Francis Tells Bishops" (*Catholic News Agency,* March 6, 2015, http://www.catholicnewsagency.com/news/church-unity-is-found-in-christ-eucharist-pope-francis-tells-bishops-24156/ 3/6/2015).

6. Ruth Gledhill, "Lutherans Receive Holy Communion at the Vatican Despite Ban on Intercommunion" (*Christian Today*, January 22, 2016, http://www.christiantoday.com/article/lutherans.receive.holy.communion.at.the.vatican.despite.ban.on.intercommunion/77425.htm).

7. George T. Dennis, "1054 The East-West Schism" (*Christianity Today*, Christian History, Issue 28: 100 Most Important Events in Church History, http://www.christianitytoday.com/ch/1990/issue28/2820.html).

8. Laurie Ieraci, "Pope, Orthodox Patriarch Express Commitment for Unity" (*National Catholic Reporter,* June 19, 2015, http://ncronline.org/blogs/francis-chronicles/pope-orthodox-patriarch-express-commitment-unity).

9. Dr. Jeff Mirus, "Evangelization Deformed or Delayed: A Danger of the Quest for Religious Unity " (*Catholic Culture*, January 27, 2016, http://www.catholicculture.org/commentary/otc.cfm?id=1358).

10. Ibid.

11. Heather Clark, "'Together 2016' Organizer Meets With 'Pope Francis' to Unite Christians, Catholics on National Mall" (*Christian News Network*, June 10, 2016, http://christiannews.net/2016/06/10/together-2016-organizer-meets-with-pope-francis-to-unite-christians-catholics-on-national-mall).

12. Brandon Showalter, "Together 2016: Pope Francis Urges Millennials to 'Find the One Who Can Give You an Answer to Your Restlessness'" (*Christian Post*, July 16, 2016, http://www.christianpost.com/news/together-2016-pope-francis-urges-millennials-to-find-the-one-who-can-give-you-an-answer-to-your-restlessness-166598).

13. In *A Time of Departing*, Ray Yungen explains: In Richard Foster's book *Streams of Living Water,* Foster emanates his hoped-for vision of an "all-inclusive community" that he feels God is forming today. He sees this as "a great, new gathering of the people of God." On the surface, this might sound noble and sanctifying, but a deeper examination will expose elements that line up more with occultist Alice Bailey's vision than with Jesus Christ's. Foster prophesies: "I see a Catholic monk from the hills of Kentucky standing alongside a Baptist evangelist from the streets of Los Angeles and together offering up a sacrifice of praise. I see a people." The only place in "the hills of Kentucky" where Catholic monks live is the Gethsemane Abbey, a Trappist monastery (the home of Thomas Merton). (p. 139, *A Time of Departing*, 2nd ed., Lighthouse Trails).

14. "Evangelicals & Catholics Together: The Christian Mission in the

Third Millennium" (http://www.leaderu.com/ftissues/ft9405/articles/mission.html).

15. Visit these links for documentation on Rick Warren's "new reformation": 1) http://www.lighthousetrailsresearch.com/rw2ndreformation.htm; 2) http://www.lighthousetrailsresearch.com/blog/?p=8948.

16. Read "Is Beth Moore's "Spiritual Awakening" Taking the Evangelical Church Toward Rome?" at http://www.lighthousetrailsresearch.com/blog/?p=15914.

17. Read "Evangelical Church Takes Another Big Step Toward Rome—This Time? Franklin Graham" at http://www.lighthousetrailsresearch.com/blog/?p=15966.

18. See: http://thegathering2016.com/about.

19. See: https://www.facebook.com/bpraysutton. (Scroll to February 2, 2016).

20. Donald Philip Veitch, "Caesaropapist-Reconstructionist Ray Sutton on the Resurgence of the Reformed Episcopal Church" (Reformed Prayerbook Churchmanship, July 8, 2013, https://www.facebook.com/notes/reformed-prayerbook-churchmanship/caesaropapist-reconstructionist-ray-sutton-on-the-resurgence-of-the-reformed-epi/48648435143099).

Chapter 22: Christian Babylonianism Unites All Religions

1. Emma Green, "The Pope Pleads to the UN: The Planet Is Ours to Save" (*The Atlantic*, September 25, 2015, http://www.theatlantic.com/international/archive/2015/09/pope-francis-united-nations/407347).

2. Daniel Burke, "Pope Francis: 'Revolution' Needed to Combat Climate Change" (*CNN*, June 18, 2005, http://www.cnn.com/2015/06/18/world/pope-francis-climate-technology-encyclical).

3. Lorenzago Di Cadore, "Pope: Creation vs. Evolution Clash an 'Absurdity'" (*NBC News*, July 25, 2007, http://www.nbcnews.com/id/19956961/ns/world_news-europe/t/pope-creation-vs-evolution-clash-absurdity/#.VqoWShHPauU).

4. John L. Allen Jr., "Pope Francis Makes Surprise Visit to Buddhist Temple" (*Crux*, January 14, 2015, http://www.cruxnow.com/church/2015/01/14/pope-francis-makes-surprise-visit-to-buddhist-temple).

5. "Pope: Muslims Are Brothers" (News Max, November 30, 2015, http://www.newsmax.com/Newsfront/pope-christians-muslims-brothers/2015/11/30/id/703875).

6. Ibid.

7. Ibid.

8. Elise Harris, "In First Prayer Video, Pope Stresses Interfaith Unity: 'We Are All Children of God'" (*Catholic News Agency*, January 7, 2016, http://www.catholicnewsagency.com/news/in-first-video-message-pope-francis-stresses-unity-we-are-all-children-of-god-39381/?utm_source=newsletter&utm_medium=email&utm_campaign=email).

9. "Six new Beatitudes proposed by Pope Francis" (*Catholic News Service*, November 1, 2016, http://www.catholicherald.co.uk/news/2016/11/01/six-new-beatitudes-proposed).

10. Ibid.

11. *Catechism of the Catholic Church* (New York, NY: Doubleday, 1995), p. 228. Taken from Warren B. Smith's booklet *Be Still and Know That You Are Not God* (Eureka, MT: Lighthouse Trails Publishing, 2015), pp. 10-11.

12. Ibid., p. 129.

Epilogue

1. You can view that discussion at: 1)https://www.youtube.com/watch?v=BLsH5DlBQy0;2)https://www.youtube.com/watch?v=eUUZqyIrRts.

2. You can view that discussion at: https://www.youtube.com/watch?v=7eHhXaA-Ulw.

3. You can read more about the courage and faith of Georgi Vins in *The Gospel of Bonds* by Lighthouse Trails.

Index

Index

THE GOOD SHEPHERD CALLS

WEBSITE AND FORUM

AN URGENT MESSAGE
TO THE LAST-DAYS CHURCH

www.goodshepherdcalls.org

Internet Church
Recommended Churches
Like-Minded Ministries
Media & Music
and much more . . .

BRYCE HOMES INTERNATIONAL

ROGER OAKLAND WITH BRYCE HOME ORPHANS IN MYANMAR

Bryce Homes International was founded by Understand The Times in 2002 as a program to assist Christian widows and orphans around the world. The program is in memory of Bryce Oakland, son of Bryce Homes founder Roger Oakland and his wife Myrna, who passed away in 2002.

The program has expanded over the years to include Myanmar, Kenya, the Philippines, South Africa, Haiti, Mexico, the USA, and India. Presently, there are over 500 children in 80 homes.

Through donations, Bryce Homes International is able to provide housing, monthly food support, education, latrines, clothing, and certain medical needs to these families. In addition, Bryce Homes is developing a pilot program in Kenya in which Bryce widows are able to begin their own cottage business that gives them the means to sustain themselves so that they may become self-sufficient, allowing other widows to enter the program.

While Bryce Homes International helps to meet the physical and educational needs of these widows and children, their spiritual needs are also addressed. The children as well as the widows are taught the Word of God and are encouraged in their personal walks with the Lord by local pastors who have been mentored by Bryce Homes International.

BRYCE HOMES
INTERNATIONAL

Serving the needs of
Christian widows and orphans
around the world.
www.understandthetimes.org

BRYCE HOMES INTERNATIONAL
P.O. BOX 27239
SANTA ANA, CA 92799
(800) 689-1888

P.O. BOX 1160
ESTON, SK, SOL 1AO
CANADA
(306) 962-3672

UNDERSTAND THE TIMES INTERNATIONAL
AN INTERNATIONAL MISSIONARY OUTREACH DEDICATED TO EVANGELIZING
THE LOST BY SHARING THE GOSPEL ACCORDING TO THE SCRIPTURES

The ministry of Understand The Times (UTT) was founded by Roger Oakland in 1990.

The goal of UTT is to work with like-minded ministries, to reach as many people as possible as effectively as possible with the Gospel of Jesus Christ. Roger Oakland's calling is to proclaim that the Scriptures are the key to understanding the past, the present, and the future. His gifting is to make difficult subjects understandable. His desire is to strengthen the faith of believers, and challenge those who do not believe to consider the Bible as God's infallible Word.

Following the formation of Understand The Times (non-profit organization in both Canada and the USA) doors opened for Roger to travel internationally and share the Gospel world-wide. He has ministered in over 70 different countries and has been to Russia and other republics of the former Soviet Union 37 times since 1990.

His books, lecture DVDs, and radio commentaries have been translated into many different languages. The Understand The Times website is an exhaustive database of news articles, special reports, YouTube videos, radio interviews, and much more. You can visit that site at www.understandthetimes.org.

Understand The Times is an independent non-profit organization in Canada and the United States. Understand The Times is not affiliated or dependent upon any other organization or denomination. Understand The Times is accountable to a board of directors in the United States and Canada and accountable, first of all, to Jesus Christ and His Word.

P.O. BOX 27239
SANTA ANA, CA 92799
(800) 689-1888

P.O. BOX 1160
ESTON, SK, SOL 1AO
CANADA
(306) 962-3672

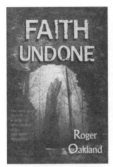

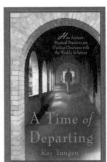

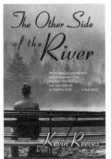

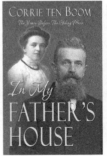

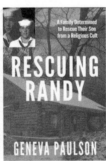

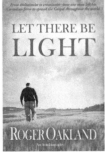

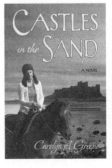